"The earth is the Lord's, and the fullness thereof; the world, and they that dwell therein."

Psalms 24:1

ACKNOWLEDGEMENTS

This book is really a team effort. Behind the scenes were literally dozens of individuals and organizations who gave generously of their time and advice in order to bring these experiences to their publishing fruition.

The National Tourist Office of each country that I visited did invaluable advance research for me. Fortified with this material, I called upon well over 100 individual tourist agencies throughout my trip. In every instance I received the gracious and patient service which is available to every visitor. These people are wonderfully knowledgeable. They converse in many languages and have thousands of valuable facts and schedules at their fingertips. I found these offices in almost every large village or small town.

I am also indebted to Iberia, Pan America, Lufthansa, and Alitalia Airlines and Air France for consideration in arranging flights to Europe.

BOOK DESIGN: Janice Lindstrom
ILLUSTRATIONS: Janice Lindstrom
MAPS: Jane McWhorter, Susan Reiber
COPY EDITOR: Virginia Rowe

Library of Congress #78-51115
ISBN 0-912944-48-X
Copyright 1978, Berkshire Traveller Press

Printed in the United States of America by Studley Press, Dalton, Massachusetts

European Edition

COUNTRY INNS and BACK ROADS

Revised and Enlarged

(Including some castles, pensions, country houses, chateaux, farmhouses, shooting lodges, chalets, villas and small hotels.)

By THE BERKSHIRE TRAVELLER
Norman T. Simpson

THE BERKSHIRE TRAVELLER PRESS
Stockbridge, Massachusetts, 01262

On Revising and Enlarging

Don't misunderstand me. I love my work. I enjoy traveling, new experiences, and new people. I also take pleasure in sharing my experiences in this book. However, when I undertook the enlarging and revising of the first volume of *Country Inns and Back Roads, Europe,* which was published in 1976, little did I anticipate some of the interesting problems involved.

With the assistance of Virginia Rowe, the copy editor, letters asking about changes were written to every lodging in the nine countries included in that first version. There was a gratifying response from inns, small hotels, manor houses, pensions, and castles with news of an unprecedented influx of visitors as a result of our book—along with a raft of changes in rates and telephone numbers. However, there were still many to be heard from, and feeling that perhaps language was a barrier, we had our letter translated into the necessary languages and, voila!— we got answers—but in seven different languages!

Meanwhile, I was off on my 1977 travels, making four more trips to Europe—the Canary Islands, Italy, France, and Germany —replete with cameras, tape recorders, tapes, and tentative itineraries.

Since each and every fact in the book must be checked and double-checked, I would return home weighed down with maps, brochures, travel folders, color negatives, and cassette tapes full of my recorded adventures. (Any reports about a bearded gentleman who wanders through Europe, talking continuously into a tape recorder held close to his mouth, are not apocryphal—it's me!) All these mutterings, observations, and interviews filled up both sides of fifty cassettes which were transferred from tape to typewriter by my invaluable secretary, Maureen Barquinero, and ultimately, along with the gleanings from all those brochures and travel folders, to the printed pages reposing between these covers.

But I am getting ahead of my story—there was still the painstaking checking to be done—spellings of lodgings and towns, correct addresses, new rates, telephone numbers, and all other pertinent facts. The copy editor was assiduous in making this information as accurate as humanly possible. Our decision to include simple directions led to hours of poring over road maps tracing and retracing my travels, checking route numbers, and searching for obscure towns. At this point, it occurred to me that the road maps I had carefully collected in Europe might not be easily available in North America, so we have included a special section in the back of the book from which the reader may order guides and maps directly from us if they cannot be had at the local bookstore.

As much as it hurt, I realized that with the addition of new countries, of necessity, the first version would have to be shortened. Although accounts of my visits to specific inns have remained much the same, some of the "side pieces" had to go. Ruthlessly removed was my trip from the fjord to the mountain-top in Norway. On the cutting room floor were my adventures in walking about Amsterdam. But the most unkind cut of all, the love of my life—Rosarillo, the dancer in the nightclub in Granada—had to go.

And thus, the day approached finally when the book would be delivered to the Studley Press in Dalton, Massachusetts. Then came word that one of my favorite restaurants in Holland had burned to the ground. It was too late to remove it from the book, so with regret, this tragedy was noted in an added paragraph. Word arrived from Denmark with the news that another inn was no longer in business. Even as this is being written (the last writing to go to press), other changes are arriving almost daily.

And now an apology. The special diacritical marks in certain foreign languages are very helpful in providing a key to the pronunciation of sounds that are not found in English; for example, the umlaut in German and Swedish, the various circles and slashes in Norwegian and Danish, as well as the accent in French and Italian, change the sound of the words completely. I am sorry that the typeface used in setting this book does not provide any of these diacritical marks.

Rates

The rates quoted in this book are meant as guidelines only, and there is a certain inconsistency because translating changes frequently left us a little confused. Basically, they are the cost of one night's lodging for two people. Most of the time they are quoted in the money of the country involved; however, in some cases, it was necessary to give the 1978 cost in American dollars. Please bear in mind that the rates given are designed only to give the reader a general idea; the fluctuation of the American dollar in the European money markets is such that there could be a difference of as much as ten to twenty percent.

Renting a Car for Europe

All of the airlines mentioned in this book have Fly-Drive excursions in which the auto rental can be part of the package.

However, a great many people traveling in Europe find it more convenient to make separate automobile arrangements. Mine were made through Auto-Europe. I found that I could pick up a car in one country and leave it in another. Arrangements must be made before departing the United States, and there are automobiles available in every one of the countries covered in this volume. The toll-free Auto-Europe number in New York is 800-223-5740. From New York State, call collect 212-535-4000. I found it a very satisfying service. There are others as well.

Incidentally, a Eurailpass can be purchased only in the United States.

Making Arrangements

I heartily recommend the services of a travel agent for unraveling the tremendously intricate special air fares that seem to be undergoing constant change these days. A travel agent can be very useful also in simplifying the myriad details of travel by making reservations for most of the places in this book — although individual inns may be contacted directly by the traveler. There is no additional cost for their services.

A Final Word

Most Americans who travel independently in Europe travel by twos, but four compatible people can have a wonderful time together and help share the expenses in the process. The Europeans are great travelers themselves — I found Germans and Austrians visiting in Italy and Spain, and many English people in the Scandinavian countries.

This book is really based on nonstructured European travel. It is probably wise to plan the first two nights' accommodations and perhaps the last two, but in-between, feel free to move about with maps, guides, and a light heart, expecting the best. You will find it. I do not speak any foreign languages, although I rapidly learned to communicate wherever I went.

Norman T. Simpson

CONTENTS

ENGLAND

LAKE COUNTRY

• Sharrow Bay

• Grasmere
• Windermere

• YORK

• MANCHESTER

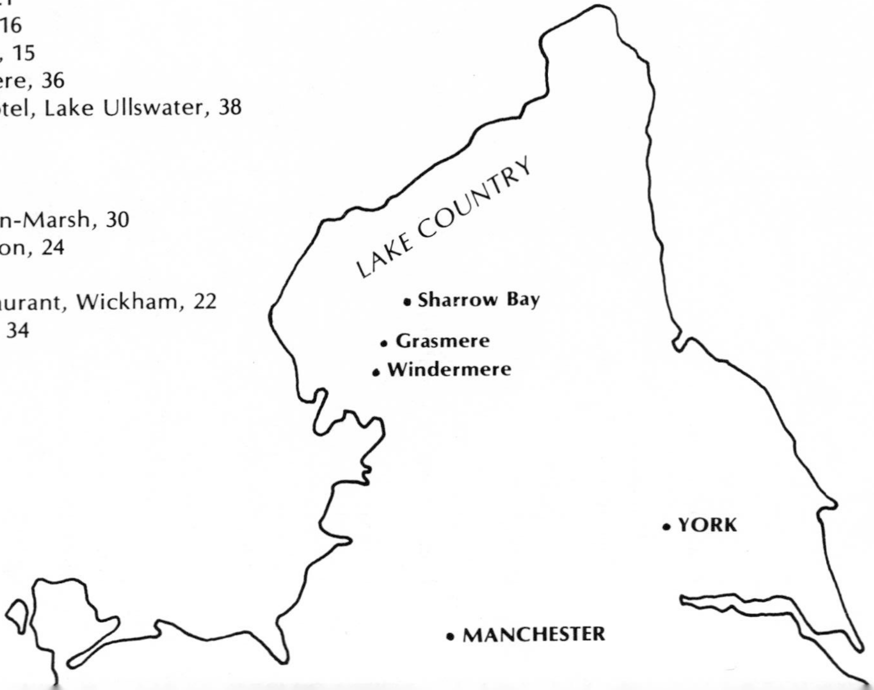

TRAVEL SUGGESTIONS FOR ENGLAND

How to Get There

Pan American and British Overseas Airways provide excellent service to London.

Country Inns in England

Although I have come to think of the word "inn" in America as having a broad enough connotation to describe certain kinds of personal accommodations, I have discovered that in England it has a more specific meaning. It is a type of pub, and has a definite legal meaning usually in reference to the class of liquor-dispensing license it holds. As a result, most of the English accommodations mentioned in this book are hotels, whereas the same places might well be called inns if they were relocated in the United States.

In my search for country inn hospitality in the British Isles there were a great many times when I felt very much at home for there are, indeed, quite a few owner-operated and family-managed inns found in a rather wide variety.

These accommodations run from stately manor houses and country hotels to smaller, more intimate lodgings perhaps converted from former country houses. There are also the traditional small hotels which are sometimes known as inns themselves.

Dining in England, Scotland, and Ireland

Basically, menus in England, Ireland, and Scotland fall into three categories. The first is pub food which is generally salads and meats such as sausages, cold cuts, meat pies, etc. The next basic classification is hearty country food such as the ever-present English roast beef and Yorkshire pudding, various cuts of lamb, veal, poultry, ham, etc., served with vegetables and usually with a "starter" course that in the States we call appetizers. Actually, with a few exceptions, this is the kind of food that is served in a great many country inns in America.

The third category is those places specializing in French menus with a great deal of emphasis on what is almost, but sometimes not quite, gourmet cooking in a great many instances. Here the continental interest was at its peak and there were many French chefs working in kitchens everywhere.

There are local food specialties for various parts of England, Scotland, and Ireland. Most of the time they are easily recognizable on the menu. In some instances where the food itself has been a real adventure I have tried to share my experiences by reporting menu specialties.

Driving Tips

The principal, obvious difference between motoring in America and the British Isles is that in the British Isles they drive on the left-hand side of the road!

However, this should not alarm anyone since it is very easy to make the adjustment. For one thing the rented cars all place the driver on the right so that he is next to the center line, just as in America. I'd suggest an automatic rather than a stick shift automobile, since if there is any adjustment, it is in telling your left hand to do the shifting.

Of course it is necessary to be alert. Be sure to mentally prepare in advance for the traffic circles or round-abouts, as they are known. Always enter to the left and remember the traffic already in the circle has the right-of-way.

I found British Isles drivers to be most polite and considerate. I think they are adjusted to the idea that a great many visitors are not used to driving on the left since this is the only country in Europe where it is the rule. See special section on Scotland.

11

My Itinerary in England

I started in London and drove south and east through Sussex to the channel port of Rye. I then skirted the southern part of England turning north to Bath and then on to the Cotswolds and the lake district. To obtain road maps, see section in back of the book on "Maps and Guides."

Car Rentals

See section near front of book on "Renting a Car for Europe."

DUKES HOTEL, St. James's Place, London

Staying at Dukes Hotel is probably the closest thing to staying at a private London club. It is the essence of restrained elegance, but the atmosphere is very friendly and accommodating. There is a Cockney concierge in attendance who has an excellent memory and a sharp wit.

Dukes is to the left on St. James's Place, about 200 yards after turning off St. James's Street. It is one of the few remaining streets enjoying romantic gas lighting in London. The hotel is a combination of two buildings placed at right angles to each other and hidden in a cul-de-sac. Because of the confined street area, a man is always available to whisk cars off to a parking garage.

Mr. Peter Proquitte, the ebullient manager, showed me through the hotel and the adjacent group of suites available for longer stays.

"We're really rather modest here," he said. "The staff likes to keep a low profile and allow the guests to enjoy themselves quietly.

"We do have baskets of fruit for each arriving guest and they tell us that it is much appreciated. The *London Times* is left at each door every morning. Our dining room is small and although it is open for breakfast, most of our guests prefer to enjoy breakfast in their rooms. Reservations are always necessary for dinner. Our houseguests most generally fill the dining room."

All of the rooms are named after historic dukes and decorated in a ducal style. These are on the medium to small side because each one has been remodeled to include a private bath and w.c. Many of them have an interesting view of London rooftops.

One guest described Dukes Hotel in the guest book as "the smallest castle in England."

I have a feeling that Beau Brummel, the arbiter of London fashion who lived at 39 St. James's Place, would thoroughly approve of Dukes today.

DUKES HOTEL, St. James's Place, London SWI. Telephone: 01-491-4840. A modest 46-room hotel plus some apartments and suites near Buckingham Palace and other London attractions. Breakfast, lunch, and dinner served daily. Rates: from 30 pounds.

STAFFORD HOTEL, St. James's Place, London

St. James's Place is one of London's well-kept secrets. It is on a dead-end street two blocks long with a right-angle turn. St. James's Place has its very own history. Oscar Wilde lived and wrote here for quite a time and I noticed one of the polished brass plates had the name of Sir Francis Chichester. The street has buildings which date to 1695.

I was having tea in the lounge of the Stafford Hotel on St. James's Place. Other guests in the hotel were beginning to drop in after a day of touring and shopping and I nodded to some people that I had met in the elevator and they promised to tell me about an exceptional restaurant they had visited at noon. Still another woman from Scotland with whom I had enjoyed a short chat at breakfast gave me a sprightly "hello." The tea appeared almost instantly and since I was having a late dinner I ordered some small cakes as well.

The public rooms at the Stafford are large and comfortable and the atmosphere is similar to that of an English club. The building is most interesting. In the late 19th century it did indeed house various London clubs and in 1902 it combined with the adjacent house and formed one building. Later it added still another building and became the Stafford Hotel after the former Stafford Club. During World War II it was a club for Canadian and American overseas officers.

STAFFORD HOTEL, St. James's Place, London, SW1A 1NJ; Tel. 01-493-0111. A 70-room hotel with all the amenities located in the fashionable Mayfair district of London within walking distance of many of the sights. Breakfast, lunch, and dinner served daily. Rates: From 29 pounds for a double room.

BROWN'S HOTEL, Albermarle St., London

In a city of institutions, Brown's Hotel is a true London institution. I realized this when I was presented with a 32-page color brochure that chronicles the hotel's history, ownership, expansion and distinguished visitors.

I arrived at 10 P.M. just for a "look," but was taken in tow by a very pleasant assistant manager who showed me all of the famous private dining rooms and suites including the Roosevelt (named for America's T.R.), Kipling, Niagara and Graham Bell. All of these have their very own significance.

We looked at a half-dozen lodging rooms which were individually furnished and seemed very pleasant.

My "look" turned into about two and a half hours, ending with a relaxing chat in one of the lounges with one of the regular Brown's patrons who "never stays anywhere else when in London."

Brown's is just off the Mall in downtown London. Time and schedules did not permit me to either lodge or dine there, however, I was glad to make its acquaintance.

BROWN'S HOTEL, Albermarle St., London, England W1A 4SW. Telephone: 01-493 6020. A famous, smaller hotel conveniently located in the heart of London. Rates: 29-48 pounds.

GRAVETYE MANOR, East Grinstead, Sussex

Contentment was indeed upon me. I had just finished a splendid lunch at Gravetye Manor and was seated on the edge of the formal gardens watching David, the head gardener, attend to the myriad flowers and plants.

Gravetye is an Elizabethan manor house built about ten years after the defeat of the Spanish Armada. According to the records, Roger Infield built it for his bride, Katherine Compton. Their initials, "R" and "K", are carved over the entrance to the formal gardens. To add to the romantic note, the likenesses of Roger and Katherine are carved in oak over the fireplace in the master bedroom.

However, Gravetye has had many changes of ownership and fortune. At one time it was used as a smugglers' hideout and part of what is called Smuggler's Lane is still to be seen on the grounds.

The Gravetye's most notable owner, William Robinson, had a worldwide reputation as one of the greatest gardeners of all time. He bought the Manor and the one thousand acres on which it stands in 1884. It was his home until he died, well into his nineties, in 1935. It was here that he realized many of his ideas for the creation of the English natural "garden style" which is now admired and copied all over the world.

Robinson's simple good taste included improvements in the manor. He paneled the interior of the house with wood from the estate and enriched the rooms with chimney pieces and fireplace furnishings kept entirely in the mode.

Today there are basically two types of accommodations among the 15 rooms. One group is done in the grand manner. Some of these rooms have canopied beds and walls that are intricately paneled. The master bedroom is a classic. The furniture is "manorial" to say the least.

The other type of room is a bit smaller and has a more modest demeanor. However, they enjoy many of the same views of gardens and countryside.

Guests enjoy trout fishing on the three-acre lake which I explored and fly fishing instruction courses are arranged as well.

Walking in the gardens and the nearby forest is one of the most popular amusements although there are golf and horseback riding nearby. There are many beautiful country houses and gardens to be seen and the Glyndebourne Opera is also within a driving distance, as well as Brighton with its race courses and seashore activities.

Unlike many of the English manor houses of the 16th, 17th and 18th centuries, Gravetye is probably entering into its most useful and exciting period because it is available for all to enjoy.

RELAIS CHATEAU 218, THE GRAVETYE MANOR, East Grinstead, Sussex. Telephone: Sharpethorne (STD 0342) 810567. A beautiful manor house, approximately 30 mi. from London. Breakfast, lunch, and dinner served daily. 15 lodging rooms. Rates: 15-20 pounds.

KENNEL HOLT HOTEL, Cranbrook, Kent

I was driving on Route 262 between Goudhurst and Cranbrook when I saw a little sign that said "Kennel Holt Hotel." I followed the road back into the woods and around a curve and there next to a pond was a trim English country house. I knew that I was going to like it.

Geoffrey Fletcher walked through the beautifully trimmed boxwood hedge and called out, "The Berkshire Traveller, I presume." (He gave it the British pronunciation.)

He is a very easy man to like, a former RAF test pilot and most enthusiastic about his rather small inn. He introduced me to his wife Audrey, who looked cool and trim in a blue frock. I was surprised to learn that she was also the cook. Dinner would be served in less than an hour and she looked as though she had been at a garden party all afternoon. "Oh, she is quite well-organized," explained Geoff.

We all repaired to a sort of family room-cum-office and talked about country inns in general and Kennel Holt in particular.

"It is a way of life for us," she explained. "There are only seven rooms but it is our home. Our guests are like part of our family. We do things as a family. For example, all of our guests sit down for dinner at the same time—7:30 p.m. This means that the vegetables we serve are always crisp and fresh—incidentally, they are right from our garden. The roast is always just right because it hasn't been held on the back of the stove for later diners."

We were joined at this point by the Fletchers' son, Ian, and his wife, Françoise, so the party was getting bigger.

Audrey excused herself to go into the kitchen. Ian and Françoise took a late afternoon walk, and Geoffrey took me on a brief tour of the inn. I continued to be impressed with its light and airy feeling. It is a small Elizabethan Manor House with five acres of landscaped grounds, a croquet lawn, a natural pool and many walks.

On the ground floor there were many exposed beams and wood panels set off by very beautiful white walls. There were containers of fresh flowers everywhere. There were two lounges both with fireplaces and one of them with a TV set.

Bedrooms, which come in various sizes, were very homey with their own particular feeling. Because this house sits back considerably from the road, views from the bedroom windows were of either woods or fields. Geoff told me that parts of the house date back to the late 15th century.

I mentioned the flowers to him and he said that both the vegetable and the flower gardens were part of the joys of living in the country. There were dozens of varieties of flowers. I recognized violets, fuchsias, camellias, roses, and petunias.

Although he was rather modest, I was tremendously impressed with the vegetable garden where a great deal of continual work has been done. It supplies the kitchen with beautiful fresh vegetables such as acorn squash, zucchini, beans, onions, turnips, raspberries, apples, and a half dozen more. These are canned for out-of-season use.

Audrey's kitchen was as neat and orderly as Audrey herself. The aromas were tempting beyond belief.

A lovely place, the Kennel Holt Hotel in Cranbrook.

KENNEL HOLT COUNTRY HOUSE HOTEL, Cranbrook, Kent. Telephone: Cranbrook 2032. A 7-room inn offering dinner, bed and breakfast, in the Kentish countryside. Pets at proprietor's discretion. Golf, fishing, garden tours, horseback riding, swimming, squash and bird-watching all on the grounds or nearby. Rates: 12 pounds.

MERMAID INN, Rye, Sussex

"Good night, Norman, I will see you at breakfast. Will 8:30 be suitable?" That was Michael Gregory speaking, owner and innkeeper of the Mermaid Inn in Rye. We had spent a most congenial evening in the dining room with a dinner of good English roast beef and Yorkshire pudding, and then in the lounge over second cups of coffee.

Naturally most of the talk centered around the Mermaid. "How old is it, Michael?" I asked. "Do you really know?"

"Well, we think it was rebuilt in 1420 after the French had burned the town in 1377 on one of their frequent raids. Local legend says that the inn was visited by Queen Elizabeth I when she visited Rye in 1573.

"The inn has seen and made its own episodes in history," he pointed out. "During the Reformation many priests were sheltered here during their flight to France."

He took me upstairs to point out the initials "JHS" in one of their bedrooms. "This was the symbol of the escaping clerics," he said. Then he showed me the secret staircase which was probably used many times as members of the clergy slipped away from their oppressors. In the huge Back Lounge of the inn I saw the "Priest's Hole." "Just take a look up the chimney," he said. "That's another hiding place. A bit warmish, but quite safe.

"The history of the inn has always reflected the history of the town. Perhaps the most exciting period was during the times when smugglers' gangs were the bully boys of Rye. One group called the Hawkhurst Gang didn't do our reputation any good at all. They sat about in the windows of the inn cursing and carousing with their loaded pistols on the tables, and no magistrate would interfere with them.

"In February, 1735, a smuggler named Thomas More who was out on bail went to the Mermaid and dragged the bailiff from his room and into the street by his heels taking the bail bondsman's warrants with him. The bailiff was taken to a ship in the harbor but eventually rescued by the captain of another ship. I could go on at great length about famous people who visited here," Michael said, "and, of course, the ghosts."

Jan Lindstrom's drawing of the inn taken from my photograph shows the Elizabethan half timbers and entrance arch. The entrance hall reflects the motif of the entire building. The walls are faced with oak paneling and the timbered ceiling is supported by a kingpost. In a way, four centuries just fall away.

Michael and I said good night and I walked up the staircase past "Dr. Syn's Lounge," which is another whole piece of Mermaid tradition.

I fell asleep quickly but in the middle of the night I awakened hearing whispers in the hall and a clicking sound like the cocking of an ancient pistol. Footsteps went down the passageway and stairs and then it was quiet. When I asked Michael about it the next morning he just smiled.

MERMAID INN, Rye, Sussex, England. Telephone: 3065 (STD 079 73). One of England's oldest inns still being kept in the ancient tradition. 30 rooms, 24 with private baths. Located on the English Channel adjacent to other famous ports. All manner of entertainment and sports are available nearby. Breakfast, lunch and dinner served daily. Rates: From 9½ pounds.

Rye at Dawn

Michael Gregory told me that Rye was fascinating at sunrise, and an early morning walk over hill and dale and into the town, with all its fascinating little shops, proved him to be altogether correct. The old houses and the flowers lining the cobbled streets; the church at the top of the hill with its ancient churchyard graves; Battings Tower, built in 1250, and redolent of English history; and that place on the hill where stood (until a bombing in 1940) the garden house of Henry James, who had lived there from 1898 to 1916, were all part of a magical sunrise walk through Rye.

THE CROWN INN, Chiddingfold, Surrey

Oh, we were a merry group all right, comprised of Jean Hynes, the postmistress of Bosham; Angus Lamont, the resident proprietor of the Crown, two other couples on a holiday, and myself. It began when Jean, Angus and I were enjoying a "get-acquainted" lunch at the Crown, and what with one thing and another, a conversation with the four people at the next table became a party.

Angus and I excused ourselves to do a tour of this snug little inn which dates back to somewhere around 1285!

"Yes," said Angus, "we are one of the oldest inns in England. It was originally built as a rest home for Cistercian monks on their pilgrimage from Winchester, the ancient capital of England, to the shrine of Thomas Becket at Canterbury. In 1383 it became an inn. In 1552 Edward VI, the boy king, camped with his retinue on the village green and went on a journey to London."

We passed through the lobby and Angus pointed out the telephone booth enclosed in an antique sedan chair. "We have a lot of fun with that," he said.

We stepped into the main dining room where a restoration of old paneling and antique furniture creates a warm atmosphere. Some of the glass in the windows is really quite old according to Angus. This section of Surrey was one of the glass-making centers. The decorated windows are examples of Chid-dingfold stained glass.

The Bistro is the oldest part of the inn with a great Ingle-nook fireplace, genuine oak beams, and beautiful Linenfold paneling.

Angus also explained that every night during the summer, weather permitting, barbecue fires are lit in the Courtyard. "We supply the food, and our guests do their own cooking,"

There are four bedrooms at the Crown. One of them is called the Elizabeth Room and has a four-poster canopy bed with intricate ornamental carvings on the headboard. This section could be from 500 to 700 years old.

In all four rooms a continental breakfast is put into a refri-gerator the night before, and then the guests can put it into a little oven and have breakfast when they like in the morning. This is the first time I have seen this arrangement and Angus tells me that it is most convenient. Breakfast may be eaten in the bedroom or taken down onto the front terrace or court-yard. Wouldn't Edward VI have enjoyed this!

CROWN INN, Chiddingfold, Surrey, England. Telephone: Wormley 2255. An ancient 4-room inn within an hour's drive of London and the south coast. Near Chichester, Brighton, Guilford, Bosham, Goodward and Arundel Castle. Restaurant open from Wednesday to Sunday for luncheon and dinner. Bistro and pub open daily. Rates: 20 pounds for two (includes breakfast).

THE OLD HOUSE HOTEL AND RESTAURANT, Wickham

"This is a duck's nest coal-burning hearth," Annie Skip-with was showing me the lodging rooms at the Old House in Wickham. We were in a most attractive second floor bedroom where the stately windows overlooked the other Georgian townhouses on the hollow square in the center of the town.

Everything about this inn was delightful. The young inn-keepers, Richard and Annie, were full of joie-de-vivre. They are a most handsome couple. Richard is a debonair Englishman and Annie is a delightful French girl.

Each of the 10 lodging rooms is totally different. The fur-niture was refinished by Richard. The upstairs hall has some engaging prints originally done by a man named Gould, and

curtains have been found whose patterns match the prints. There are several small things that make it seem very much like a private house. For example, there is a little cabinet in one corner of the hallway downstairs which is filled with carved pieces and china.

In the back of the house which was part of an old barn, the bedrooms have exposed beams, beautiful flowered wall-paper in tones of blue and green, and curtains to match. There was one double bedroom with dozens of books. In fact, there are books in every bedroom on the nightstand.

There are porcelain door knobs on the paneled doorways and all of the floors in this house of many levels are shining clean and well varnished.

On the first floor there is a series of small lounges all showing Richard and Annie's interest in prints. One room has some excellent sailing prints and also a collection of different size keg taps mounted.

The restaurant is part of the old converted barn and has exposed beams with a big window that overlooks the garden in the rear. This is an excellent breakfast room.

The menu is made up of French provincial dishes. For lunch that day I had a dish with green peppers, tomatoes, onions, garlic cooked in spices and herbs and then topped with a whisked egg white which, when put in the oven, turns into a four-inch meringue. It was just right. Other main courses were pot roasted chicken and escalloped veal and sirloin served with tomatoes and garlic sauce and topped with olives.

In discussing the inn clientele with Richard, he said that for the most part people stayed for one night although many men staying here while traveling on business during the week very frequently returned with their wives and families for a weekend holiday. "They like our little garden in the rear and our countryside is appealing."

THE OLD HOUSE HOTEL AND RESTAURANT, Wickham, Hants, England PO 17 5JG. Telephone: Wickham 833049. A 10-room in-town hotel on a Georgian square in the south of England. Breakfast, lunch and dinner served daily. Specializing in French provincial cooking. Rates: 14 pounds.

CHEWTON GLEN HOTEL, New Milton, Hampshire

Sunday in England dawned bright and clear and the sky was a most delicate blue. In the distance I could hear the persuasive sound of the bells of the village church summoning the faithful to its portals.

The Chewton Glen swimming pool, which I could see from my bedroom, was clear, clean and beckoning. I donned my trunks, wrapped myself in a terrycloth robe and made my way as quietly as possible down the broad staircase out to the terrace and down the steps into the water.

Even so, I was not the first one in. A mother and her 10-

year-old son had already had the honor of the first dip. "Oh, we've been walking the glen," she said. "And putting the cup markers in the holes on the putting green. Do you play croquet? They have an excellent course here!"

I asked her how her children were enjoying themselves in this quiet country house atmosphere.

"Beautifully," she said in that marvelous way English people have with that word. "Actually we have been here before and we are now getting the hang of the best way to visit the New Forest. Have you been there yet?"

"Only on the edge," I replied. "Oh, you really ought to go into the middle," broke in her son. "There are deer and ponies and even wild pigs," he said. "I think it is very keen there. We take a picnic in and walk all day. Besides, we can go over to Bucklers Hard and watch the yachts."

Chewton Glen is elegant without being stuffy. It is really made up of the projected ideas of Martin and Sally Skan, an attractive English couple fond of the good things of life, who saw in this country house great possibilities for a comfortable, lively, holiday accommodation.

The restoration, decoration and extension are all in keeping with the considerable history of the manor and there are many interesting touches including impressive collections of Spy and Max Beerbohm prints, old photographs and many original paintings.

There are quite a few spacious lounges and salons, many with a view of the croquet area, the swimming pool, tennis courts and the sweeping glen from which the house gets its name. The lodging rooms in the main house are large and luxurious with many 20th century conveniences.

Because Chewton Glen is also a member of Relais de Campagne, the accent is on service and the menu is French. I enjoyed a most delicious dinner there with Martin and Sally and the dining room is a congenial place with a great rib roast of prime beef on a wheeled cart proceeding from table to table. Other items on the menu that evening were calves' kidney served with diced bacon, mushrooms and croutons, breast of chicken on a bed of fresh spinach coated with a light cheddar cheese sauce, and a poached fillet of salmon garnished with creamed mushrooms and served in a Bernaise sauce.

RELAIS CHATEAU 219, CHEWTON GLEN HOTEL, New Milton, Hampshire. BH256Q5. Telephone: Highcliffe (04252) 5341. A luxurious resort hotel on the steps of the New Forest with several holiday amenities. Rates: from 40 pounds for two (includes breakfast).

North to Bath

Now, after skirting the New Forest, the way led north to Bath. This city is one of the most beautiful in England and I would dearly like to have been able to stay for several days. But on this first trip I would have to devote my time to finding inn accommodations rather than extensive sightseeing.

And sights there are indeed in Bath. A great deal of the architecture owes its origin to the fact that in the 18th century it was a focal point for many people who came to Bath to "take the waters," at the famous Roman baths.

The Georgian style for which the city is renowned, dominates the design, and the graceful town houses and public buildings make Bath a delightful experience. The baths are still in existence attracting a continuous stream of visitors.

There are also many famous castels and country houses nearby as well as several typical English villages.

On the outskirts of Bath is an astonishing link with North America. It is an American museum, the only one in England, which has a most gratifying collection of early American furniture and artifacts all very attractively displayed. I could have lingered there all day and even longer, and recommend it as one of the sights of Bath not to be missed.

THE PRIORY HOTEL, Bath, Wiltshire

Thea Dupays was serving tea in the main drawing room at the Priory Hotel in Bath. What a welcome respite it was to be in this quiet and restful room overlooking the spacious lawn and fine Cedar of Lebanon trees, numerous flower beds, and at the bottom of the garden, a swimming pool. The Priory is deceptively unobtrusive. It sits back from the street behind a high stone wall with many trees. At first glance it doesn't look like a hotel. The building is of grayish Bath stone in Georgian Gothic style. The quietness reminded me of a country house rather than a small hotel in a sizeable English city.

The first floor has two dining rooms, one overlooking an

open courtyard, a terrace and a lily pond. The other is more formal with Georgian furniture and period paintings. Scattered throughout the dining rooms and the drawing rooms were original oils and watercolors which indicated the Dupays' great interest in the arts. These created a most pleasant atmosphere. Many of the paintings were done by Thea.

There are 15 individually decorated and furnished bedrooms, all with private bathrooms and w.c.'s, color television and telephones.

John Dupays proved to be a most interesting revelation. It was hard for me to realize that this modest, studious appearing man, formerly a schoolteacher, was the chef at the Priory, which is also a member of the Relais de Campagne. He professed to being an amateur, but after looking at the menu, which he prepares himself and includes such interesting choices as rum steak and kidneys, veal Marengo, Suliman's lamb, tarragon chicken, oxtail with grapes, duck Albigeoise, roast grouse, sole St. Germain, and Navaran of lamb, I was certain of his professional status. The homemade desserts included cheesecake and blackberry and apple pies.

The Priory is a most elegant experience.

RELAIS CHATEAU 216, THE PRIORY HOTEL, Weston Rd., Bath, Wiltshire, BA1 2XT. Telephone: Bath 21887. An unobtrusive in-town hotel in one of England's most elegant cities. All recreational amenities within a short distance. 1 mi. from center of Bath. Rates: 16-22 pounds (includes Continental breakfast).

THE MANOR HOUSE HOTEL, Castle Combe, Wiltshire

Oliver Clegg, the owner of the Manor House Hotel, had given me directions to the village of Castle Combe which were perfect to the letter.

Driving through a little valley I suddenly found myself proceeding over an old stone bridge and into the center of the village. At the Market Cross which still survives after many centuries, the buildings are a beautiful beige color which seems to be characteristic of the region. The reddish roof tiles, narrow streets, old signs, and the air of antiquity all combine to make it one of the unusual travel experiences in the British Isles. Many people that I have met since returning to the states ask me if I have visited Castle Combe.

It is fitting that such an unusually attractive village should also have country inn style accommodations at a stately manor house. The Manor House Hotel is down at the end of a village lane which opens out into a great parkland with beautiful trees, a river, much open space and high hills.

Oliver Clegg was a most cordial gentleman. I had undoubtedly arrived at an inopportune moment for him but he insisted that I would be most welcome at the midday meal with the other members of his family. "Then we will look the place over," he said.

Lunch was great fun for me, because it gave me the opportunity to meet more English people. They couldn't have been more gracious.

Oliver told me a few things about the building while I was enjoying a fine cut of roast beef.

"The manor of Castle Combe existed before the Norman conquest," he said. "However, both the original manor and the castle were destroyed, and only a portion of the subsequent Manor house built in the 14th century still remains. The present building is mostly from the 16th, 17th, and 18th centuries — apart from our own additions in the 20th.

"We've done a lot of work here modernizing it to what might be called luxury standards, although we have tried to keep everything in the Manor House theme. That Italian frieze in the main lounge commemorates the Shakespearean character of Sir John Falstaff and it may well be that Shakespeare got his inspiration from the lord of the Manor of that period, one Sir John Fastolf.

"While we were reconstructing some of the old cottages and the coach houses in the new garden wing, we found some most interesting things. These include quite a few open fireplaces, beamed ceilings and even the remains of a circular staircase. We've now put them all together into an area that has 20 bedrooms with private baths. You passed them on the way in but probably didn't realize it."

After lunch Oliver and I took a leisurely tour of the Manor House and the really impressive adjacent gardens which have many sequestered walks, stone statues, secluded corners and some unusual trees. There are many, many roses.

I left the Manor House at Castle Combe with a great deal of reluctance. It is an ideal place to remain several days and enjoy the unusual atmosphere of Bath and the surrounding countryside.

THE MANOR HOUSE HOTEL, Castle Combe, Wiltshire. Telephone: Castle Combe 0249 782206. A manor house hotel in an old country home. Modernized lodging rooms. Beautiful gardens, all the countryside amenities and recreation available. 12 mi. from Bath and 2 hrs. from London. Rates: 14.70 pounds (includes breakfast).

The Cotswolds

The Cotswolds is a most unusual collection of villages, back roads, lakes, manor houses, high rolling hills, stone-walled fields, green valleys, clear streams, and unexpected distant views from far across the Severn River to the mountains of Wales.

29

There are wonderful names such as the Swells, the Slaughters, Bourton-on-the-Water, Northleach, Burford, and Chipping Campden. It is possible to walk through miles of this part of England, and there are many reference works to be purchased which enable the traveler to enjoy these Cotswold walks.

In addition to the two towns that I visited in the Cotswolds, where I found three country inn accommodations, the Cotswolds also includes Shakespeare's Stratford-upon-Avon with its famous theatres. Nearby are great historic houses such as Sulgrave Manor, the ancestral home of George Washington's family, whose crest contained in a stained window there became the basis for our stars and stripes.

MANOR HOUSE HOTEL, Moreton-in-Marsh, Gloucestershire

The Manor House Hotel is an informal village inn run by John and Cecile Blanchard who are very much in evidence. John is a man with an excellent sense of humor and a great deal of innkeeping experience.

The house is from three to five hundred years old and new additions have been made with great care to match the different colors and textures of the original mellowed yellow stove blocks.

As in the Mermaid Inn in Rye, there is also a priest's hiding hole, a secret passage, and a bedroom reputed to be haunted.

The bedrooms in the old buildings are furnished in the traditional style but with modern services.

The English people all love gardens, and the garden at this inn is really exceptional. The buildings of the inn and long high walls keep the noise of the outside world from intruding into its tranquility. There are many varieties of flowers including many roses, and a considerable number of happy songbirds. The old church in Moreton-in-Marsh is off one corner of the garden and the ancient font which was used in the church is now the center of a quiet reflecting pool.

I sat for some time on a sunny morning in the rear of this garden looking back toward the old building with its characteristic casement windows and old chimney pots. There was the buzzing of bees and an occasional butterfly darting from flower to flower. I used this quiet moment to read about the Cotswolds.

On the previous evening I arrived just in the nick of time for the cold buffet which had cold lamb chops, delicious roast beef with creamy horseradish sauce and many kinds of salads. The full breakfast was excellent and is served in the room if the guest so desires.

MANOR HOUSE HOTEL, Moreton-in-Marsh, Gloucestershire, England GL560LJ. Telephone: Moreton-in-March 50501. An informal village inn in the middle of the beautiful Cotswold country. Approximately 80 mi. from London. Centrally located for visits to Stratford-upon-Avon and other Cotswold centers of interest. Rates: 25.50 pounds.

DORMY HOUSE, Broadway, Worcestershire

The Dormy House is a 17th century farmhouse with a marvelous view of the surrounding countryside. It is bounded on three sides by the Broadway Golf Course with its spacious fairways.

In almost every part of the house I found mellowed old stone, exposed beams, wood paneling and large windows. The sitting room has a raised hearth of huge stones and a fender big enough for sitting. It was similar to the one at the Lincklaen House in Cazenovia, New York.

I understand that the entire inn underwent a complete renovation in 1971 in which all of the lodging rooms were provided with private baths and w.c.'s. Modernization did not affect the high ceilings and the collection of attractive

antique furniture which includes very handsome wardrobes in almost every one of the 20 bedrooms.

The proximity of Stratford-upon-Avon and the influence of the Royal Shakespeare Theatre probably accounts for the fact that there are a great many line drawings on the walls of these bedrooms showing actors and actresses in various period costumes.

Naturally, golf dominates the sporting activities for guests at the Dormy House, and almost everyone who comes to the inn for a holiday spends some time on the adjacent course.

The end of this story took place at the Boulders Inn in Lake Waramaug, Connecticut, where one of the guests happened to overhear a conversation I was having about my trip to the Cotswolds and said, "Oh, excuse me for interrupting, but if you went to the Cotswolds I do hope that you stopped at the Dormy House. We have been going there for many, many years and it's one of our favorite places in England!"

DORMY HOUSE HOTEL AND RESTAURANT, Willersey Hill, Broadway, Worcestershire, England. Telephone: Broadway 2241. A sophisticated farmhouse high on a Cotswold hill, approximately 1½ mi. from the center of Broadway. Rates: 18 pounds.

LYGON ARMS, Broadway, Worcestershire

Guests at the Lygon Arms are presented with a brochure which offers a brief history of the inn since 1535. I mention this to emphasize just how much history has taken place in this inn over the centuries.

Peter Wilson, who was my host on a tour of this rather grand inn, had some interesting stories of famous historical personages, like Oliver Cromwell, who have stayed here — all of which can be found in the brochure, which makes fascinating bedside reading. The Lygon Arms, according to Peter, was probably a manor house originally, but was known as the White Hart Inn for several centuries, and the brochure notes that in one of the four-foot-thick walls "there is a fireplace that appears to be 14th century work, and one of the mullioned windows ... had dates from 1586 to 1640 cut in it." Among other interesting features of this famous old inn are the carved Elizabethan fireplace, an unusual 17th century plaster-enriched ceiling and frieze (believed to have been done by traveling artisans, as there are other similar ceilings in manor houses in that area), and the 17th century oak panelling and spiral staircase.

Today, the Lygon Arms is a large, country hotel with many luxury features. The atmosphere, particularly in the front part of the inn is definitely old world. Low ceilings, lots of well-polished wood beams and panels, old fireplaces and antique wooden chairs and tables are a thrust backward in time. Every room has an individual color scheme and fine antique furniture, which is one of the finest collections of old English furniture in England, I am told.

To accommodate the many visitors to Broadway and the Cotswolds, new wings have been added including lodging rooms that have modern furniture and decorations. I am happy to say I found reading books in every room.

When I was there in the height of the season in August, the main street of Broadway on which the inn is located was a very busy place. Therefore the garden area including some very natural fields and orchards to the rear was most welcome. There was also a good tennis court in this area as well.

RELAIS CHATEAU 212 LYGON ARMS, Broadway, Worcestershire, WR127DU. Telephone: Broadway (038-681) 2255. One of England's best-known old inns located in one of England's best-known villages. Rates: from 16.20 to 18.20 pounds per person per night (includes early morning tea and newspaper).

On To The Lake District

After leaving the Cotswolds I drove straight north through the midlands and arrived on the edge of the Lake District. It was a complete change of scenery. This was a land of fat cattle grazing in green meadows and stone walls which seemed almost like paths themselves over the hills.

After a few miles the road dropped down into a valley which contained the small city of Kendall. I didn't expect such a sizeable town to be at the end of such a narrow road. It was a pretty little place with lots of flowers in front of houses, each of which had its own low stone wall.

The road out of Kendall to Windermere led up and along the top of the ridge and I now entered the Lake District National Park. Windermere was about 7½ miles distant.

The terrain in the lake country is criss-crossed by footpaths up over the hills (called fells) and into the distance. I resolved to come back here sometime in the future and spend three or four days just roaming.

The road dropped into Windermere from the ridge and I had my first look at an English lake. Here I was, on the last section of my English journey, in the land of the great lake poets headed by no less than William Wordsworth. With great anticipation I began looking for my first stop, the Miller Howe in Windermere.

THE MILLER HOWE, Windermere

At the Miller Howe each arriving guest is presented with a small booklet specially inscribed with his name that contains a diamond mine of information to enhance a three-day stay (the minimum according to the tariff sheet) at this unusual lake country inn.

Here's a partial list of its contents: a rather complete description of each of the four meals served including early morning tea (I learned to really appreciate this); the full breakfast; boxed lunches (very important for all-day excursions and tours); and dinner which is, at least, the *piece de resistance.*

There follows in various order a list of additional attractions in the Lake District including cinema, public gardens, art galleries, libraries (very important for the guest who wishes to be well-informed about the area), all the outdoor recreational facilities, a group of guided walks (the principal activity in the lake country), other nearby establishments in the British Isles,

and a generous dollop of interesting Lake District statistics about mountain heights and lake dimensions. The booklet concludes with space to keep a diary!

The author of the booklet and the innkeeper at the Miller Howe are one and the same, Mr. John Tovey, a man who has a reputation for being one of *les enfants terribles* of the English innkeeping business. He is a first-rate pastry chef, an excellent public relations man, an organizer, a deft conversationalist, innovator, extrovert, and a really nice guy.

I mention all of these things because it is very difficult to imagine the Miller Howe without his guiding presence. It is obvious that he had some pretty unusual ideas and I think a lot of them are most advantageous for the guest. For example, each guest room is filled to overflowing with magazines and books. Incidentally, as far as I could see, every one had a view of the magnificent lake and the hills beyond. I imagine it took some physical planning to arrange this particular feature.

The Miller Howe is not out of the mold. For one thing, it has a Modified American Plan which includes the four meals I mentioned plus the boxed lunch. Everybody is invited to be at dinner at 8 o'clock and it is served at 8:30 p.m. It is a set five-course meal using lots of local produce. The night I was there the main course was local veal with no less than eight vegetables on my plate. The fish course was a very light sole. The dinner is basically English-oriented with an emphasis on country dishes. This can be a welcome change from French menus.

The furnishings and decor are all extremely attractive and the service, which is mostly by young men wearing brown suits, is quick and friendly.

The view from the front of the house including the dining rooms and the four lounges as well as the lodging rooms is tremendous. There is a meadow leading down to the lakeshore where there was a colt cavorting when I awakened almost at first light.

"John Tovey," I said, "has done it again."

MILLER HOWE, Windermere, English Lakes. Telephone: (096 62) 2536. A 14-room inn on the shores of Windermere Lake. Rates: 17-25 pounds (includes dinner and breakfast).

THE WHITE MOSS HOUSE, Grasmere

Arthur and Jean Butterworth are wonderfully English. However, their little inn would be equally appropriate in Massachusetts, Virginia, or Nova Scotia. It is the essence of personal country inn hospitality.

John Tovey directed me to them and I am forever grateful. For some years Jean was a teacher of home economy and Arthur was an accountant, and now they keep this lovely little stone inn with five rooms just like a home. Some of the rooms have their own baths, others share.

There is a terrace overlooking the lake with lovely flowers and well-trimmed hedges. As soon as I walked through the

front door I had a marvelous feeling of being at home. In fact, it was like being in a friend's house.

Arthur and Jean seated me at a table in a big bay window and we all had a cup of tea and talked about the Lake District, and keeping a country inn, and how much fun it is to meet new people all the time.

The living rooms, dining rooms and lodging rooms all have Jean's marvelously feminine touch with fresh flowers, gay curtains and bedspreads. I was delighted to see many books in the bedrooms, especially books on the Lake District. "We try to have them because we realize that many of our guests stop for only a few days, and they would like to have information about this area readily available."

"It takes most people at least a day to wind down, but then they like to know more about the entire region," remarked Arthur.

"The best way to enjoy the lake country is to get out and walk in the hills. It makes all the difference," he said, "in getting the feel of the place.

"As far as walking is concerned, I think that our English lake country is quite unique because it is possible to walk over most all of the hills and not get lost. They are not heavily forested as are your hills in New England."

I looked over the dinner menu when I paid them a visit and Jean explained that the tomato and chive soup was home-made as was the cheese and fresh herb paté with homemade date walnut bread. The main dish that night was chicken served with new potatoes, garden peas, cauliflower amandine, and squash (which is called "marrow" in England) baked with butter.

Desserts included black currant wholemeal shortcake and chocolate roulade with mint cream. There were English cheeses with White Moss oat biscuits. Dinner is served at 7:30 every night.

The White Moss looked like great fun. I would like to go back next time for at least three days.

WHITE MOSS HOUSE, Rydal Water, Grasmere, English Lakes LA22 9SE. Telephone: Grasmere (096-65) 295. A 5-room informal Lake District inn, part of which was originally owned by William Wordsworth. Rates: From 15 pounds per person. Room, break-fast, and dinner. (Boxed lunch is extra.)

SHARROW BAY COUNTRY HOUSE HOTEL, Lake Ullswater

Sharrow Bay is situated on the extreme edge of Ullswater and the waves come right up to the walls of the inn and the terrace. The view from the main lounge received an award a few years ago for being the best in Great Britain. Fortunately there is a large window with comfortable love seats on either side and I would imagine that these are some of the most coveted seats in the inn.

Sharrow Bay is owned and managed by two men whose interests seem to have blended beautifully. Francis Coulson does all of the cooking and is devoted to making everything as nearly perfect as possible.

His partner, Brian Sack, handles the myriad details that are connected with the rooms and "the front of the house." This has been going on for more than 20 years and as far as I can see the real beneficiaries from this partnership are the Sharrow Bay guests.

The main house sits among 12 acres of gardens and woodlands and there is a half mile of lakeshore for all the guests to enjoy.

In addition to the 12 rooms in the main house there are other accommodations including a converted farmhouse about one mile up the lake with another beautiful view where long-staying guests can enjoy peace and solitude.

As Francis Coulson explained to me, "Sharrow Bay was built in 1840 and up until 1949 was a private house. The style of the building is unusual for this area and some of our guests remarked that it has a continental flavor that you might expect to find in Italy or Switzerland."

There are two comfortable lounges and two dining rooms. One in which I dined was L-shaped and almost every table had a gorgeous view of the lake. There were round tables set with attractive chairs.

Up on the second floor are lodging rooms, each of which has its own name. Each was filled with such interesting things as an occasional chaise lounge, antique desks, chests, much porcelain, and many prints and reproductions from as far back as Watteau. It has a real country house atmosphere, radiating comfort and warmth.

I enjoyed an unusual lunch here because I was very much impressed with the wide selection of "starters" as they are known. I decided on three starters and a dessert. Sharrow Bay is especially well known for its soups and there are several very original varieties including a carrot and orange cream soup and a French peasant vegetable soup among others. I had the puree of carrots and oranges which is the supreme specialty of the house. It was delicious. The next starter was an avocado mousse with dressed prawns, also very tasty. I wound up with the chicken livers served in a small dish in a pastry shell.

What did I miss out on? The roast loin of English lamb Doria cooked on a bed of cucumbers and shallots and served with a red currant and orange sauce; roast sirloin of Scotch

beef served with Yorkshire pudding and horseradish cream sauce, and a choux pastry with a filling of partridge, duck, chicken and herbs and served with bacon. It took all my resolve to resist ordering that third offering.

I had one of the house specialties for dessert—sticky toffee sponge cake served with cream.

Now I knew why everytime I said, "Sharrow Bay," someone else would sigh and say, "Ah, yes."

RELAIS CHATEAU 211 SHARROW BAY COUNTRY HOUSE HOTEL, Lake Ullswater, Penrith Cunbria CA 10 2LZ. Telephone: Pooley Bridge 301. A 29-room country inn with lodgings in the main house annex and nearby cottages. Located in the English lake country, 295 miles from London. Adjacent to all of the lake country recreational amenities. Closed from end of November through January. Rates: 40 pounds (includes room, breakfast and dinner).

Floating through England

What they call the "Heart of England" is the magical country between Stratford-upon-Avon, Shakespeare's town, and Worcester, to the west.

This spring and summer it will be possible to enjoy luxury boat cruises through this country, which includes the Vale of Evesham, Tewkesbury, where Richard III won a famous battle, and Bidford, which Shakespeare called "drunken." Nowadays, it's only a lovely country town.

Twin boats, specially built, will cruise the Severn and Avon rivers, starting either in Stratford or, at the western end, in Worcester. It's six days each way.

The pace is leisurely, the Avon is a small peaceful rambling river, the banks overhung with willow, much unchanged since the Bard's own time. The route passes through the famous Cotswold Country.

On the Severn, south of Worcester, there are great castles and cathedrals, and at Worcester a famous porcelain factory.

The boats travel together, and a chauffeured minibus goes along to carry the travelers on excursions to interesting places along the way.

For sailing dates from either Worcester or Stratford, and booklet, write Floating Through Europe, 501 Madison Avenue, New York City, N.Y. 10022.

Plans for the Future

In 1980, I expect to publish a full, separate book on my inn-going adventures in England, Ireland (North and South), Wales, and Scotland. With this in mind, I will spend much of 1979 in those countries, visiting new inns and getting reacquainted with innkeepers who are already in this book.

Upon publication in 1977 of the first edition of this book, I received many letters from enthusiastic readers recommending *additional inns and small hotels, and I hope the generosity of my readers will continue, as all such suggestions will be of tremendous assistance in preparing the larger, separate book on the British Isles and Ireland.*

SCOTLAND

John O'Groats

Nairn
Inverness

Old Meldrum

ABERDEEN

Ballater

GRAMPIAN

Contin

Loch Ness

WESTER ROSS

Torridon
Shieldaig

Isle of Skye

Sligachan

ENGLAND

EDINBURGH•

PERTH•

Uphall•

GLASGOW•

Loch Lomond

Strachur•

•Oban

Isle of Mull

Tobermory•

INNS and LOCATION
Tullich Lodge, Ballater, 59
Coul House, Contin, 53
Culloden House, Inverness, 54
Sligachan Hotel, Isle of Skye, 49
Sconser Lodge Hotel, Isle of Skye, 50
Newton Hotel, Nairn, 55
Meldrum House, Old Meldrum, 57
Tigh An Eilean Hotel, Shieldaig, 51
The Creggan's Inn, Strachur, 45
Western Isles Hotel, Tobermory, 47
Loch Torridon Hotel, Torridon, 52
Houstoun House Hotel, Uphall, 60

TRAVEL SUGGESTIONS FOR SCOTLAND

How to Get There

British Overseas Airways supplies direct service from the United States to Prestwick, although many travelers fly Pan Am to London and use a rented car to tour both England and Scotland.

Country Inns in Scotland

Inns in Scotland cover a wide spectrum, ranging from traditional inns to resort hotels, from hunting lodges to manor houses and castles, and I have presented a sampling of each. For extended touring, the Michelin Red Guide lists further accommodations.

In July and August it is impossible to readily find accommodations without advance bookings; quite a few Scottish innkeepers will hold a telephone reservation only until 5 o'clock.

Reservations can be made by mail (a deposit helps) or by telephone.

Driving Tips

Motoring in the Scottish Highlands is fascinating. Much of the time I was traveling paved, well-maintained roads wide enough to accommodate only one car; however, there are "turn outs" every 75 to 100 yards, and the courtesy of the road determines which car going in either direction will pull over and wait for the other to pass. Sheep and cattle on the road have the right-of-way. The roads in the Highlands are so curvy and twisty that when I took a moment to glance at a loch or a glen I frequently found myself confronted by an implacable bovine animal.

The entire experience, from the broad expanse of the tremendous scenery to the minutiae of individual plants, flowers, trees, rocks, houses, animals, and clouds make it splendid backroading country. Along with the ruggedness there is a certain gentleness, because everything but the craggy mountains is covered with green grass and heather.

My Itinerary in Scotland

I drove north from the English Lake district around Glasgow and up the west side with visits to the Isles of Mull and Skye. In the Highlands I turned east to Inverness, and on into the Grampian Region near Aberdeen, swinging back to the center of Scotland and returning to Uphall near Edinburgh.

To obtain Scotland road maps, see the section at the back of the book.

The Creggan's Inn was my first overnight stop north of England. I had driven around the Glasgow traffic flow, and then headed north on A-82 next to Loch Lomond to Tarbirt where I picked up A-83 westward among the crags of the western Highlands. I stopped for just a moment at a small Scots village called "Rest and Be Thankful."

Here I had turned south on A-815 following the eastern shores of Loch Fyne a few miles to Strachur.

THE CREGGAN'S INN, Strachur, Argyllshire

I was having breakfast at The Creggan's Inn at Strachur. It was one of those somewhat rare, totally cloudless Scots Highlands mornings, with Loch Fyne gleaming in the newly risen sun. A light breeze rippled the blue waters.

This was a placid contrast to my arrival on the night before in the late twilight. Then there had been great rolling clouds occasionally opening long enough to allow a shaft of golden

sunlight to brilliantly light the loch or the little town of Inverar-
ay on the opposite shore.

Mrs. Laura Huggins, the manager of the inn, and Sir Fitzroy
Maclean, the owner, joined me at dinner and the three of us,
encouraged by generous cuts of roast beef and Yorkshire
pudding, talked well into the evening.

Sir Fitzroy is a fine figure of a man with a most varied
background. During World War II he was Winston Churchill's
personal liaison with Marshal Tito of Yugoslavia, and he still
remains very close friends with Tito today. Later he served in
Churchill's cabinet and was a member of Parliament for many
years as well. In America he is well known as an author, with
three books on the Balkans to his credit.

A great deal of our conversation that evening dealt with
Lady Maclean who was in Yugoslavia during my visit. She is
the author of a cookbook and supervises the inn menu. Mrs.
Huggins told me that a great deal of the inn's atmosphere
reflects Lady Maclean's ideas.

The dining room is very gay with colorful flowered wallpaper, pleasant country furniture and the view of the loch.
The lodging rooms are pleasant and well furnished.

A waitress arrived at my table with a plate of Loch Fyne
kippers which I am told had been not only caught locally but
also smoked on the shores of the loch. They were unusual and
delicious.

"Did you know that Mary, Queen of Scots, landed right here on her way to the Highlands?" This was the young waitress who was eager to share some of her Scottish enthusiasm with me. "That was over 400 years ago," she said.

Looking out across the Loch Fyne to the prospect of hills and water, I couldn't help but think that perhaps Mary had left this beautiful part of western Scotland, as I would, with a great deal of regret.

THE CREGGAN'S INN, Strachur, Argyllshire, Scotland PA27 8BX. Telephone: Strachur 279. A 27-room homelike Scottish inn on one of the lochs of the western Highlands. Walks and excursions by land and water available as well as deer stalking, fishing, boating, swimming, wildlife watching and pony trek-king. A private woodland walk is at the disposal of guests. Approximately 1¼ hours from Glasgow. Rates: 15-19 pounds (includes breakfast).

The Isle of Mull

I can enthusiastically recommend the Isle of Mull for a no-less-than-three-day holiday for anyone who is interested in unspoiled natural beauty, history, walking, fishing, golf, sailing, painting, photography, botany, geology, or sea life.

The neighboring Island of Iona is rife with the historical antecedents of western Christianity since 563 A.D., when St. Columba landed there and from which he later sent his missionaries throughout Western Europe carrying the message of hope and establishing the roots of Christianity.

A guidebook for Mull and Iona can be obtained by sending $1 to: The Western Isles Hotel, Tobermory, Isle of Mull.

WESTERN ISLES HOTEL, Tobermory, Isle of Mull

What a beautiful, glorious, fantastic day this had been! I was wandering through the golf course at Tobermory on the Isle of Mull with Derek McAdam, who is not only the propri-etor of the links but the innkeeper of the Western Isles Hotel.

We reached the highest point and turned to look back over the Bay of Tobermory. Although their geographical lo-cations are quite disparate I was immediately reminded of looking up the bay on the north side of St. Thomas in the Virgin Islands. There were green islands, white fluffy clouds, blue

skies and even bluer sea waters. I was on one of Scotland's Western Isles at a very comfortable hotel run by a most energetic and enthusiastic young Scotsman and his wife.

The Western Isles Hotel has a truly commanding view of the Bay of Tobermory. The aspect from the sunporch is magnificent with sailboats scudding with the breeze and the more sedate fishing boats following in their wake. Tea on the terrace is delightful as I discovered. The drawing shows its location high on the cliffs overlooking the town.

It's a hotel of Victorian vintage built back in the days when whole families repaired to Tobermory for weeks at a time. Over the years there has been much necessary remodeling and renovation, but the original facade has been preserved.

When I asked about the food, Derek replied, "Well, we of course like to serve traditional Scottish dishes. We have fresh fish and Scottish beef and lamb along with locally grown vegetables. Our menu also has several continental dishes as well. We don't use powders or synthetic foods."

When I inquired about what his guests did besides gaze in rapture out over the Bay of Tobermory, he replied, "This nine-hole golf course is free to our guests and there is fishing and boating on the lochs, tennis, pony trekking, sailing, hill climbing, deer stalking and cruises to the nearby islands by the dozens. We have the Highland Games in July, yacht racing and summer theatre. Our guests never complain of being bored."

Of that I am most certain.

THE WESTERN ISLES HOTEL, Tobermory, Isle of Mull, Scotland. Telephone: Tobermory 2012. A four-story Victorian hotel overlooking the Bay of Tobermory on one of Scotland's classic Western Isles. Mull is reached from Oban by ferry to Craignure eight times daily, five times on Sunday. Another ferry runs from Lochaline to Fishnish sixteen times a day. Rates: 12-14 pounds.

The Isle of Skye

Like the Isle of Mull, the Isle of Skye is being "discovered," so the interested traveler should make plans to visit as soon as possible while both of them are relatively unspoiled. Since July and August are quite crowded, June and September would be my choices. October and May could be interesting, although a bit brisk at times.

Skye is much larger than Mull. Its crags and peaks attract walkers and mountain climbers from all over the world.

Skye is chock full of history, recreation, legends, Highland games, hiking competitions, an agricultural show, Hunt Ball, a Gathering Ball and other Highland activities. If a visit is planned at the height of the season, the best thing to do is to send $1.50 to the Tourist Information Bureau at Portree, Isle of Skye. They will mail an application blank and do the booking.

SLIGACHAN HOTEL, Isle of Skye

The Sligachan Hotel was built in 1820 and enlarged in 1930. It is a little on the austere side. Actually, I think that almost anything else would be out of place in such a rugged country. The main lounge has some tinted prints of the moors, hills and mountains of the vicinity. I really didn't see anybody because the hearty tourists and travelers who had spent the day walking in the hills and climbing the crags had all gone to bed.

My room was clean and the bed was comfortable. The

bath was most welcome and I was asleep as soon as I hit the pillow.

In the morning I was up very early and the chambermaid rescued me with a big pot of hot chocolate and some delicious biscuits, which held my hunger until breakfast time.

SLIGACHAN HOTEL, Isle of Skye, Scotland. Telephone: Sliga-chan 204. The Isle of Skye is reached by taking the car-ferry from Mallaig to Armadale or the car-ferry from Kyle-Of-Loch-alsh. I understand these do not operate on Sundays. Rates: 10.50 pounds (includes breakfast).

SCONSER LODGE HOTEL, Isle of Skye

I had left the Hotel Sligachan and was driving toward the Isle of Lochalsh ferry when I noticed a very imposing 3 story stone house next to the shores of the loch. A small sign said it was the Sconser Lodge Hotel so I pulled into the parking lot and found Mrs. Fione Campbell in the kitchen poaching eggs, making toast, frying bacon and keeping her eye on some fish.

The Sconser Lodge Hotel is a former shooting lodge. It has seven bedrooms and everything is very warm and home-like. There is a very good atmosphere about the place. The guests were having breakfast, already prepared for the day in their walking and climbing clothes. They all looked very fit and were talking about what beautiful weather they had enjoyed previously for walking in the hills and the moors.

Mrs. Campbell and I had a very nice chat over a cup of tea, and I was delighted that I had taken the time to stop in and see the Sconser Lodge Hotel. It balances perfectly with the Isle of Skye.

SCONSER LODGE HOTEL, Isle of Skye, Scotland. This atmospheric former shooting lodge is located approximately 30 minutes from the town of Broadford. Rates: 12 pounds.

TIGH AN EILEAN HOTEL, Shieldaig

The Highland villages on the shores of the lochs and firths are a bonny sight indeed. Shieldaig is just such a village. It stretches out around the shores of Loch Torridon and is a little larger than a hamlet but smaller than a town. I paid a very brief visit to this hotel on the water's edge because it looked neat and clean and quite busy during the height of the season. The day that I was there there was a sign on the door that indicated that one single room was available. One of the young ladies of the household gave me a brief tour and everything looked ship-shape. She told me all the meals are homecooked.

There are interesting walks in the vicinity of Shieldaig as well as many challenges for the climber. The scenery is magnificent; sea fishing is available on the loch.

TIGH AN EILEAN HOTEL, Shieldaig, Ross-shire, Scotland; Tel. Shieldaig 251. A small, clean owner-operated hotel about an hour north of Kyle of Lochalsh on Rte. 896. Rates: 21 pounds for two (includes dinner and breakfast).

Wester Ross

After crossing from the Isle of Skye to the mainland, I came into that part of the western Highlands known as Wester Ross. Here are the massive crags, majestic mountains, tranquil lochs and high, awesome moors. There are occasional sweeping views of the sea and mountains that rise to more than 3000 feet. There are deep ravines and gorges, gentle brooks and slashing waterfalls. The whole coastline of mountains, lochs, and bays has views that are beyond words. Here and there I saw waterside beaches with golden sands, clear green waters and a background of wonderfully sculptured hills. Many of the names found along the coast were from Viking days.

The influence of the gulf stream brings to Wester Ross a mildness of climate unexpected in a region which is as far north as Hudson Bay. Wherever there is shelter from the salt-laden west winds, many exotic varieties of plants and trees grow readily.

LOCH TORRIDON HOTEL, Torridon

This elegant country house hotel was built over 100 years ago by the first Earl of Lovelace. It has 56 acres of woodland with a view of both Loch Torridon and the heights of Ben Damph.

I introduced myself to Mr. Ian Campbell, the manager, who most graciously provided me with a lengthy tour of the mansion, filling me in on a little of the history. We talked in the library, a room overlooking the lakeshore, where I saw beef cattle and sheep grazing on the meadows. The furniture in all of the public rooms was massive and manor-like. We went up the broad staircase and there was an oil painting of a Highland warrior wearing a green velvet coat with twelve silver buttons. There were large rooms and large hallways at this country house. Many rooms had quite a few windows overlooking Loch Torridon and most of them had their own bathrooms.

Outdoor activities for the guests here are on the resort-

oriented side. They include croquet, a nine-hole putting green and a private pier with water skiing and fishing. As in all of Scotland, there is walking or climbing.

As Ian showed me through the main hallway, I noticed that there were inscriptions on the walls just below the ceiling commemorating Queen Victoria's diamond jubilee.

I enjoyed a very good bowl of potato and onion soup for lunch, skipped the main course and had apple pie served with hot custard sauce. The menu was a mixture of Scottish and French specialties.

LOCH TORRIDON HOTEL, Torridon, Wester Ross, Scotland. Telephone: Torridon 242. A manor house hotel located on Rte. 896 in the western Scottish Highlands. Approximately 7 mi. from village of Shieldaig. Open year-round. Rates: from 13.40 pounds.

I can't say enough for the hearty, enduring souls in the tourist offices all over the British Isles and Europe for the patient, excellent advice they dispense, sometimes under harrowing conditions with difficult tourists and many communications problems. Ella Fleming at the tourist office in Tarvie was most helpful in orienting me to the western Highlands. She directed me to the Coul House and other places I might have missed.

COUL HOUSE, Contin, Ross-shire
What had been a rather rocky road from Route 832 (the main West Coast road), was now a smooth-surfaced, short drive north to the Coul House, a modest mansion house with an imposing main entrance.

Inside, I followed the sound of piano music to a main salon where a young man was fervently playing Rachmaninoff.

I rang the bell for service, and soon made the acquaintance of the owner.

He was most considerate and pleasant and showed me through his hotel, which I was pleased to find because it was a good central location for Highland touring. It is about 40 miles southeast of Ullapool and about 20 miles from Inverness. It is well within driving distance of the very north of Scotland, including the village of John O'Groats.

I stayed long enough to see most everything and enjoy a

53

cup of tea. I would have stayed overnight except for other commitments.

COUL HOUSE, Contin, Ross-shire, Scotland. Telephone: Strathpeffer 487. A 20-room modest country house centered in the Scottish Highlands. Excellent fishing nearby. Rates: 5.90 pounds (includes breakfast).

CULLODEN HOUSE, Inverness

"Bonnie Prince Charlie did not sleep in this house but he did stay in a Renaissance castle on this site which burned down and on whose ruins this house was built in 1772."

Kenneth MacLennan, the resident owner of Culloden House was giving me some lessons in Scottish history over a hearty dinner in the sedate dining room.

"The Battle of Culloden was fought in 1746," he continued. "The Rebellion against the Hanoverian English kings had gained impetus, and Prince Charles Edward Stuart—Bonnie Prince Charlie—had gathered five thousand Highlanders to fight the forces of the Duke at Cumberland. He stayed in the old castle the night before the battle. The next day the Scots were defeated. The prince disappeared into the Highlands and although some of his followers tried to rally the cause, the great moment was lost.

"I came into the picture in 1974 when I purchased the property and began restoring it to what we hope somewhat resembles its late 18th and early 19th century 'Adamesque' style.

"We are listed by the Scottish Development Department as a building of 'special architectural and historic interest.'"

I should explain that all during Kenneth's discourse, which was more lengthy than I have reported, I was enjoying an excellent meal that included many traditional Scottish dishes. The service was by beautifully trained young Scottish lads and lassies, very polite and considerate without being obsequious. When I mentioned this to Kenneth his face lit up with pleasure. "Oh," he said. "A true Scot is alert, bright and anxious to help —but never subservient."

Searching for one word to describe Culloden House today I think it would be "luxurious." Everything adds up to a grand way of living. There is much period replica furniture and deco-

ration. There are beautifully decorated high ceilings with ornamental moldings, ornamental door handles, handsome huge bedrooms with clock radios and color TV's if desired. The bathrooms are a symphony of consideration.

As I was saying good-by to Kenneth and the staff the next morning, he accompanied me to the parking area, and as I was leaving made one final remark. "Norman, we have set some very high goals for luxury hospitality here at Culloden House. We've still got many to achieve. We know that we are more expensive than the average country house hotel, but we offer many things that I think are worth it."

CULLODEN HOUSE, Inverness, Scotland. Telephone: Culloden Moor 561. An unabashedly expensive country house accommodation, just a few miles from Inverness and the site of the famous Culloden battlefield. Limousines to and from Inverness airport and railway station if required. Fishing, golf nearby. Visits to many famous sites including Loch Ness (home of the legendary monster). Well within driving distance of the western Highlands. Rates: from 35-150 pounds (includes breakfast).

NEWTON HOUSE HOTEL, Nairn

Driving along A-96 from Inverness to Aberdeen, I almost missed the modest entry to the Newton House Hotel. It was on the left side of the main road. I turned into a long curving country road with large trees arched overhead. At the end facing the Moray Firth, I found a country house in a setting of broad lawns, gardens, and mellowed old stone walls. The sweep of the lawns to the firth side was something most beautiful.

Characteristic of the many that I had visited thus far in the British Isles, the lounges, libraries and hallways had high ceilings, large windows, and impressive elegant period furniture. Many of the bedrooms were quite large with views of either forest or firth.

Golf is one of the principal recreations of the guests and Mrs. Isobel Ian, the manager, enthusiastically explained that there are a great number of courses in the Grampian section of Scotland. There is a 9-hole golf course immediately adjacent to the hotel. "Nairn Course, just a few minutes away, is one of the finest seaside courses in Scotland," she said. "It is a full 18-hole championship layout."

The house sits on thirty-five acres of quiet grounds and the view across the firth is to the hills of Ross and Cromarty. The architecture is Georgian and Scottish baronial and there is an entirely different formal entrance at the opposite end of the castle.

Nairn and the Moray Firth Coast, according to Mrs. Ian, has one of the finest sunshine records and are in the area of the lowest rainfall in Scotland. "Our guests love the bracing air and the clarity of the atmosphere," she said. "I think we have an ideal holiday climate."

As I left this inn I noticed a blue flag of Scotland flying valiantly in the breeze from its battlements. Bonnie Prince Charlie's forces may have lost the day at nearby Culloden, but the spirit of Scotland was never diminished.

NEWTON HOUSE HOTEL, Nairn, Scotland. Telephone: 066-75-3144. A 34-room manor house inn on the edge of Scotland's Grampian Region. Many golf courses nearby as well as ample opportunities for all types of recreation. Rates: from 20 pounds.

Scotland's Grampian Region

I found that Scotland had many different faces to display. One of the most beautiful is the country to the east of Inverness which takes its name from the dominating mountain range which runs almost to the east coast. There are beautiful salmon and trout rivers and on the eastern and northern sides there are fishing villages and harbors. Its center comprises some of the best farmland in the world.

It is still a part of the Highlands and has many high hills and moors (called muirs by the Scots). It is, however, a more gentle land than the western Highlands.

One of the best ways to travel in Scotland is to use roads with either 3 or 4 numbers on them, rather than the 1 or 2 digit roads. The former are the real back roads and it is possible to pick out routes that go to the same place but on much less traveled ways.

MELDRUM HOUSE, Old Meldrum

The drive from the shores of Moray Firth through a corner of the Grampian section of Scotland had taken me through Fochabers, Keith and Huntly. In the village of Old Meldrum I received directions to Meldrum House, and on the approach stopped to take a few photographs of the arched entrance to the castle grounds.

The road curved through the forests and then the glowering outlines of Meldrum Castle came into view. It looked stern and stout—built no doubt to resist invasion.

I walked into the reception area which was at the moment, being guarded by a sleepy dog who thumped his tail on the rug in greeting. A small sign instructed me to ring the bell for service. I did so.

I started walking around looking at the oil paintings on the oaken paneled walls and suddenly I realized I was being confronted by a full-size tiger that seemed to be emerging from the underbrush. I actually took a step backward.

"Oh, you needn't worry, it's not alive. I shot it in India myself, a few years ago. Good afternoon, I'm Robin Duff. You must be Norman Simpson."

And thus began a most interesting overnight visit at a Scottish castle that included an excellent dinner cooked by the 32nd Laird of Meldrum.

"It is a matter of necessity," explained Robin. "This castle has been in my family for 750 years, and since the economics of this age make any castle somewhat impractical, I decided to make it into a hotel. It is still my house, however, and I regard it just as anyone would his home.

We began a very pleasant tour of Meldrum Castle, with a short stop in the kitchen while Robin checked the roast. "I do the cooking—mostly because I have very definite ideas about how good food should taste," he stated. "I tried other chefs, but in the long run, I preferred my own cooking."

We walked through the long high hallways, the inner walls of which have dozens of prints and portraits of the inhabitants of Meldrum Castle from centuries past.

"That portrait," he said, indicating a very imposing and handsome gentleman in full Highland regimentals, "is one of my ancestors who was commander-in-chief in India during the late '90s. I, myself, was there for many years."

We looked at a number of bedrooms which had a wide variety of furnishings. Some have private baths and all had very large windows overlooking the extensive lawns and fields adjacent to the castle.

Dinner that evening was excellent, and I also got into an enjoyable conversation with some people at the next table who were from nearby Aberdeen. They enthusiastically supplied me with a great deal of information about the Grampian Region.

MELDRUM HOUSE, Old Meldrum, Scotland. Telephone: Old Meldrum 294. An ancient Scottish castle converted into a hotel *located about 15 mi. from Aberdeen. All of the recreational facilities of the Grampian Region nearby. Rates: 13.50 pounds per person per night with private bath and breakfast.*

TULLICH LODGE, Ballater

It was lunchtime at Tullich Lodge. We were all sitting on bar stools around tiny tables or on the seats in the bay window. Neil Bannister and Hector McDonald, the proprietors kept bringing in platters of good things to eat and by the time we had finished the cheese soup many of us were on a first name basis. The inn sits above the Aberdeen Road about a mile east of the village of

Ballater on five acres of woodland. It has an excellent view of the Highlands and the River Dee.

What remains in my mind about Tullich is a really outstanding resident lounge located on the second floor. As soon as I stepped inside I was tempted to sit down in front of the windows and pick up one of the many magazines and spend the afternoon reading and relaxing and looking at the view. There is even a piano in one corner.

On the first floor there is a large glass Victorian telephone booth which is elegance personified. The dining room is richly paneled with spacious bay windows again with an impressive view.

Among the specialties frequently on the menu are steak and kidney pie with a suet crust, fresh vegetables from the garden, roast beef, baked whole lemon sole served with new potatoes, leg of lamb cooked in honey and herbs, and salmon from the River Dee nearby.

There are many opportunities for excursions through this section of Scotland and many castles and gardens to visit, including the grounds of Balmoral Castle which are open to the public when the Royal Family is not in residence.

Highland games are also very popular and held in several locations during the summer. There's a summer season of Scottish theatre, music, and dance at nearby Braemar during August and September. There are also five golf courses within 20 minutes of Tullich Lodge.

TULLICH LODGE, Ballater, Aberdeenshire, AB 3 5SB, Scotland. Telephone: 033-82 406. A 10-room (all with private bath or shower rooms) country house accommodation in a most beautiful section of Scotland. Closed January, February, and March. Golf, fishing, shooting, stalking, skiing including chair lift, and walking all available nearby. Rates: 15 pounds (includes breakfast).

HOUSTOUN HOUSE, Uphall

Houstoun House is just a few minutes from Edinburgh's new air terminal and enjoys the distinction of being a restful place to stay but still convenient to one of Scotland's great cities. It is also just a few miles from the direct route north into the eastern Highlands and the Grampian Region.

It is owned and operated by Mr. and Mrs. Keith Knight and Keith, himself, supervises the kitchen. He is a former architect and has put this ancient house into excellent shape. I found the service friendly without being pretentious.

The stone steps lead to a group of traditionally furnished

rooms in the main house and there are also more modern additional rooms.

I remained here overnight, prior to catching an Aer Lingus flight to Dublin. Dinner was comprised of chicken curry soup, hot chicken liver mousse, sirloin steak garnished with cheese and tomato sauce, and a fresh raspberry tart.

One of the unusual things about Houstoun House is the rather extensive formal garden. There are many, many handsome boxwood hedges which act as dividers for a wide variety of flowers which eventually find their way into the hotel's rather sophisticated lodging and public rooms.

HOUSTOUN HOUSE, Uphall, Scotland. Telephone: Broxburn 85 3831. A former manor house that has been modernized into an excellent conventional hotel accommodation approximately 20 minutes from Edinburgh. Rates: 17 pounds (includes breakfast).

KILDARE
CARLOW
TIPPERARY
WICKLOW
WATERFORD
CORK

IRELAND

DUBLIN •

Straffan •

• Naas

Blessington •

Roundwood •
Rathnew •
Wicklow •

Port Laoise •

Carlow •

Arklow •

Shannon

Bagenalstown •

• Cashel

Cahir •

• Mitchelstown

Dungarvan •

• Mallow

Waterford •

• Cork

• Shanagarry
• Ballycotton

INNS and LOCATION
Lorum Old Rectory, Bagenalstown, Carlow, 69
Ballyana, Ballycotton, Gork, 72
Beechmont Farm, Mallow, Cork, 74
Longueville House, Mallow, Cork, 73
Ballymaloe House, Shanagarry, Cork, 70
Barberstown Castle, Straffan, Kildare, 79
Chez Hans, Cashel, Tipperary, 77
Knock-Saint-Lour House, Cashel, Tipperary, 75
Longfield House, Cashel, Tipperary, 76
The Downshire House, Blessington, Wicklow, 78
Hunter's Hotel, Rathnew, Wicklow, 66
The Roundwood Inn, Roundwood, Wicklow, 67
Knockrobbin House, Wicklow, Wicklow, 68

TRAVEL SUGGESTIONS FOR IRELAND

How to Get There

Aer Lingus provides excellent service from the U.S. to Ireland from New York, Boston, Chicago, and Montreal.

Country Inns in Ireland

Basically I found two kinds of accommodations in Ireland. The first type is converted country houses, mansions, and castles which are similar to those I saw in England and Scotland. However, the service is much simpler and the menus are frequently not continental but English oriented.

These somewhat luxurious country mansions and castles are really resort-inns. Most of them have rooms with private baths and serve an elaborate meal. In most cases I found them owner-operated and comfortably informal. There are usually quite a number of recreational facilities on the grounds, and since they are located in resort areas, there are plenty of additional sports and recreational activities nearby.

The second type of accommodation is the farm and country houses. The main difference between the two, as far as I under-stand it, is that the farmhouse actually has land that is being used for farming. In both instances the traveler is in a private home.

Those that I saw had five or six rooms and resembled the American farmhouse with the individuality and creativeness of the owners expressed in terms of bright curtains, multi-colored sheets, flowered wallpaper, and very comfortable living rooms where the guests and family gather to watch TV or talk. In all cases cleanliness is very important. I understand that the Irish Tourist Board checks into the farm and country houses several times a year to make certain that high standards are being maintained.

The food is generally right off the farm at all farm accommodations that I visited, and this is one of the main points of pride. Meals are very informal and everyone sits around a big table, very often with the family.

Incidentally, all of these offer bed and breakfast. Partial or full board is also obtainable for a longer period of time.

Reservations

The best way to make reservations at Irish inns is to write or telephone directly. To assure your reservations send a deposit.

Car Rentals

Many of the Aer Lingus "Fly-Drive" programs include an automobile. For travelers not on a package plan, see section in front of this book on "Renting a Car for Europe."

Driving Tips

Sooner or later anyone traveling in the Irish countryside has to get directions from one village to another. Irish signposts are in two languages. Most of the time one of them is English. The main problem is that the signs only direct the traveler from one village to the next and very seldom to villages beyond. I found that when the village I was looking for was not on my map I had to stop and ask directions. These directions were given in that wonderfully charming, polite, melodious manner and always ended up with the assurance that "you can't miss it." Well, "miss it" I did—quite a few times in spite of some of the most intricate detail that accompanied each direction.

The most frequent direction is, "straight on." One of the problems is that "straight on" usually led to another four-way crossroads and it was necessary to go through the whole process again.

As in Scotland and England driving is on the left hand side of the road. I found very few traffic tie-ups even in the larger cities.

Maps and Guides

As an added convenience the Michelin Road Map for Great Britain and Ireland is available to our readers. Please refer to the section in the back of the book marked "Maps and Guides" for ordering information.

My Itinerary in Ireland

I started visiting inns and hotels on the east side of Ireland in county Wicklow, working my way south as far as Cork and then back up the center of southern Ireland returning once again to Dublin.

HUNTER'S HOTEL, Rathnew, County Wicklow

"This hotel has been in my family for four generations: it's a way of life for us." Mrs. Maureen Gelletlie, the owner of Hunter's Hotel, and I were having a mid-morning cup of tea in the gardens.

The garden, dear to the hearts of Irish people, has sloping lawns, pebbled walks, rustic seats and flowering shrubs alongside a small river, the Vartry, which flows through one end. A strange phenomenon was the presence of tropical palm trees here and there.

"I guess we have always been known for our good food," Mrs. Gelletlie continued. "Many people come just for our salmon and sea trout. We have vegetables and fruits from our own gardens. Many people come for afternoon tea for which we make our own cakes and scones; we really are famous for

our strawberry jam. The garden always has quite a few people in the late afternoon."

Earlier at breakfast, I had talked to a man from northern Ireland and his wife from Yorkshire about their holiday in Wicklow and they told me that this hotel is especially nice for people with children. There were, so they told me, many things for people with families to enjoy in the vicinity. Their plans included touring and walking in the Wicklow Mountains and a visit to the beaches which are located a short distance away.

Rooms at Hunter's Hotel are quite similar to those of many country inns that I have visited in the United States. Some rooms have their own w.c.'s; others share one on the corridor.

A visitor to Hunter's Hotel in 1815 wrote in the visitor's book, "This superior family hotel has long been celebrated for the beauty of its situation and the excellence of its internal arrangement." Another more recent visitor wrote, "Pleasantly furnished with plenty of bathrooms, hot water and smiling Irish faces that provide good service."

It looks as if Hunter's Hotel has successfully spanned the centuries.

HUNTER'S HOTEL, Rathnew, County Wicklow, Ireland. Telephone: Wicklow 4160. A 19-room country inn just south of Dublin. Touring, hiking, golf, tennis, fishing and horse riding and beaches nearby. Close to the famed Mount Usher Gardens. Lunch and dinner served daily. Rates: 13 pounds.

THE ROUNDWOOD INN, Roundwood, County Wicklow

It was my first evening in Ireland and after an overcast day in County Wicklow the sun burst out of the clouds and the entire atmosphere was changing. I was on my way across the Wicklow mountains from Rathnew to Roundwood, complete with careful directions from Hunter's Hotel.

True to the mark, I was now in sight of this lovely village where lights were winking at me in the late Irish twilight. I turned up the village street and immediately recognized a gleaming half-timbered white building that was the Roundwood Inn.

My host, a most ebullient man, was the owner, Florian

Binsack, who was most anxious that I catch the true spirit of the place.

The Roundwood Inn is over 350 years old and has had a long list of owners and innkeepers. Florian has exercised a great deal of imagination and verve in restoring the interior using exposed beams, clever wall hangings and old furniture to the best advantage.

The inn's dining patrons may enjoy the Resident's Lounge which is a very handsome room most conducive to good conversation and pleasant moments. However, I was quite taken with the public bar where the local people were gathered in jolly conversation and a rousing game of darts. Florian was very proud of this section of the inn for he felt that it made a significant contribution to the cohesiveness of the community.

The menu at the Roundwood Inn neatly walks a middle path between Continental service and cuisine, and Irish offerings. One of the specialties of the inn is Wicklow lamb served in every conceivable manner.

The Roundwood Inn, which incidentally has no rooms, is really good fun and is an excellent way to start an Irish excursion. It is on the main Dublin-Glendalough road, just 24 miles from Dublin in the Wicklow Mountains.

THE ROUNDWOOD INN, Roundwood, County Wicklow, Ireland. Telephone: Dublin 818107. A jolly country restaurant near Dublin with a surprisingly large menu. Open for lunch and dinner every day except Tuesday. No lodgings.

KNOCKROBBIN HOUSE, Wicklow

This was my first visit to a residential farmhouse. There was a modest sign saying, "Knockrobbin House" on the Dublin-Wicklow Road, so I turned in and had a very pleasant surprise.

I found a rather elegant country house in a secluded parkland with the main entrance through some graceful arches. Inside Mrs. Bittel was good enough to show me through a great deal of the house which at the time had a number of guests from France. There were six very attractive rooms with fine views of the mountains and the sea.

This particular place is a little more sophisticated than most farmhouses, since it also maintains a public restaurant.

The menu had quite a few English and continental dishes. Mr. and Mrs. Bittel are German and I noticed some German specialties as well.

I was glad that I had followed the tree-lined avenue off the main road. Knockrobbin House looked like a very good place to spend part of an Irish holiday.

KNOCKROBBIN HOUSE, Wicklow, County Wicklow, Ireland. Telephone: Wicklow 0404/2344. A 6-room residential farmhouse, all rooms with bath, 1 mi. from Wicklow and 30 mi. from Dublin. Lunch and dinner also served to travelers. All of County Wicklow's recreational facilities are available, including bathing, boating, fishing, walking, riding. Rates: 8 pounds (includes breakfast).

LORUM OLD RECTORY, Bagenalstown, County Carlow

I liked Lorum Old Rectory and Mrs. Betty Young immediately. She's a wonderful lady and like many other of my new Irish friends, a great conversationalist. She explained that her husband was a bank manager and that they both enjoyed running this 125-year-old cut-stone farmhouse in the country. I met her strapping young son who had just come off the fields.

All of the rooms in the Old Rectory are pleasant and homey —not luxurious but very clean and comfortable. One of the first things that attracted me about this place was the fact that there are books everywhere.

I've had a letter from Mrs. Young since I returned from

Ireland and she says in part: "I'm happy that you hope to list me in your book of Irish country inns. I don't know whether I mentioned it to you or not, but we are rather special for our food and the presentation of the same. Practically everything is homemade. I hope you come back next year and that you will be able to stay longer."

Mrs. Young, I assure you that I am looking forward to returning to the Lorum Old Rectory again in the future.

LORUM OLD RECTORY, Bagenalstown, County Carlow, Ireland. Telephone: 0503-25282. A friendly farm guest house in the Barrow Valley midway between Bagenalstown and Borris. Fishing and swimming in river; walking, climbing and golf nearby. Homestyle farm cooking and accommodations. Rates: 5 pounds.

After leaving Mrs. Young's in Bagenalstown, I followed the main road south through Thomastown and into Waterford which is the home of the famous Irish Waterford crystal. From there the main road heads south-westward with frequent glimpses of the Irish coast passing through Dungarvan and Youghal. At Ladysbridge I began another "cat and mouse" game of directions to try and find Shanagarry, which is the town closest to Ballymaloe. It is quite beyond my limited description to explain how I arrived, but it took at least four stops.

BALLYMALOE HOUSE, Shanagarry, County Cork

The Ballymaloe House is one of Ireland's manor house accommodations. The house is part of an old Geraldine Castle which has been rebuilt and modernized through the centuries, one portion dating back to the 14th century. It is in the middle of a 400-acre farm on the Cork-Ballycotton Road about 2 miles from the coast of southern Ireland.

The dining room is open to the public from Tuesday through Saturday and is reserved for house guests only at the other times. It is known as the Yeats Room and contains a number of paintings by Jack B. Yeats, brother of the famous Irish poet.

Fifteen of the 20 bedrooms are in the main house and there are other lodging facilities in a 16th century gate house

and other farm outbuildings.

My room was located on the front overlooking a very pleasant terrace and some beautiful fields and meadows which stretched out to some low hills a few miles away. I understand that this particular part of Ireland is not developed as a tourist area as yet. The coastal area is just a few minutes away.

Shortly before dinner I met some other house guests in one of the living rooms who were on holiday from Dublin. It was then that I realized that there were a great many children in residence and discovered that it was a long weekend. My new acquaintances had two children and explained that they had been in Ballymaloe several times because there is horse-back riding which, along with the golf, tennis and swimming, is free. "We Irish are great lovers of horses," one of them explained. "Our children get a chance to ride here as much as they wish."

After dinner I took a short walk in the gathering darkness, strolling on the country lanes between the fields of ripening wheat. The lights of Ballymaloe gleamed softly and occasionally I could hear the delighted cries of some young people who were being allowed to stay up a little longer because it was a special occasion.

BALLYMALOE HOUSE, Shanagarry, County Cork, Ireland. Telephone: Midleton 62531. A 20-room manor house accommodation approximately 20 mi. east of Cork. Most resort facilities located on the grounds with sea fishing and hunting and beach activities nearby. Rates: 10 pounds.

BALLYANA, Ballycotton, County Cork

This farm guest house is located a few miles from Shanagarry just outside of the village of Ballycotton.

Just as in the case of the Lorum Old Rectory, Ballyana is a working farm with 92 dairy cows and a good steady crop of sugar beets. There are stone buildings that look as if they could be there for 1000 years and the entry is through a wrought-iron arched gate leading to a very pleasant garden.

I arrived at breakfast time and was shown through the house while the other guests were enjoying the morning meal. The parlors had very homey furniture with paintings on the wall and also many pictures of the Roberts family. There was a chess board in one corner.

On the second floor there are some handsome bedrooms, some overlooking the garden in the rear and some of them with a view of the sea. There are two w.c.'s and one bathroom for the five bedrooms.

Ballyana provides bed and breakfast. Mrs. Roberts is pleased to recommend places for lunch and evening meals nearby.

There are many kinds of recreational possibilities in the area including golf, fishing, swimming, beaches, boating and horseback riding. Ballyana is a very quiet place—a real Irish farmhouse where I could feel quite at home.

BALLYANA, Ballycotton, County Cork, Ireland. Telephone: (021) 62731. A large attractive old farmhouse in pleasant surroundings close to the sea, sandy beaches and cliff walks. Dinner not served. Rates: 6 pounds.

LONGUEVILLE HOUSE, Mallow, County Cork

It was at Longueville House that I had my most intriguing contact with Irish history. Michael O'Callaghan, the resident owner of this handsome Georgian manor house, and his wife, Jane, entertained me royally with a high tea that included some simply fabulous homemade ginger cookies.

The house overlooks one of the most beautiful river valleys in Ireland, the Blackwater Valley. The central portion was built about 1720 on a 500-acre wooded estate which was then the property of an ancestor of Michael O'Callaghan. As Michael said, "Since then, Longueville has had a checkered history." Now it has been considerably enlarged and is an excellent country house surrounded by an area particularly rich in scenery.

The size of the building took my breath away. The entrance is through a stately arch, and the first thing I noticed approaching the front entrance was a tremendous brass lock on the door. The center hallway and reception area are most elegant as are the library, living room, smaller parlors and dining rooms. The impressive main staircase rises to the full height of the house on both sides and repeats from the second to the third floor. One of the most unusual areas is a glass conservatory which is left over from the Victorian days and contains many tropical plants, trees and flowers. All the lodging rooms that I saw were comfortable, large and very tastefully furnished.

Over tea I asked Michael about the outdoor sports and recreation in the area. He replied, "Well, athletic salmon abound in the river which runs across the southern boundary of our estate. There is also trout fishing as well. We are just a few miles from the south coast where there is good sea fishing and shore angling. There are 18 golf courses in the county including one at Mallow which is free to our guests. We have horses and ponies available for trekking nearby.

"There are many castles in this section of Ireland that are open to the public, and quite a lot of history was made in this vicinity. For example, the oak trees that you see out the win-

dow were planted in the formation of the English and the French battle lines at Waterloo," he said.

Although I had only tea at Longueville, I learned that Jane O'Callaghan was in fact a Cordon-Bleu trained chef and supervises all of the food. She has received several awards for her cuisine.

LONGUEVILLE HOUSE, Mallow, County Cork, Ireland. Telephone: 27156. A luxurious manor house inn just a few miles from Cork in southern Ireland. All recreational amenities available on grounds or nearby. Rates: 10 pounds.

BEECHMOUNT FARM, Mallow, County Cork

I followed Mrs. Myra Fitzpatrick up the stairs of the 17th century stone farmhouse to the second floor where I found five bedrooms all furnished in bright colors and all very neat and clean. The second floor view included the fields and the meadows and I was happy to see a reading lamp with each bed and many books. The countryside also offers a splendid view of the Boggerogh mountains.

Once again, this was a working farm with several dairy cows. Mrs. Fitzpatrick is most conscientious and obviously makes an effort to make her guests feel as comfortable as possible.

I asked her about the meals and she said that the menu offered things such as homemade soup, roast stuffed turkey, mashed potatoes with cream, white turnips and cauliflower. "For dinner tonight I am making a banana surprise." Other things served on the evening menus included ham and cabbage, roast beef, Irish stew, roast pork and applesauce. "Most everything comes from the farm here," she said.

Beechmount Farm was an excellent example of an Irish farmhouse accommodation. Incidentally, Mrs. Fitzpatrick said that there was a constant stream of visitors from all the countries in Europe who stay with her. "A sort of United Nations," said she.

BEECHMOUNT FARM, Mallow, County Cork, Ireland. Telephone: (022) 21764. A 17th century Georgian-style farmhouse on 187 acres with much recreation nearby. Home cooking. Rates: 7 pounds (includes breakfast and dinner).

KNOCK-SAINT-LOUR HOUSE, Cashel, County Tipperary

I was sitting in Mrs. O'Brien's kitchen enjoying a cup of tea and watching her prepare the evening meal. "Tonight it is ham and chicken," she said, "and we'll have roast pork tomorrow night."

Mrs. O'Brien loves flowers. The house is surrounded on three sides by a truly intricate rock garden that was a rainbow of colors. "My mother tends the flowers outside," she said, "and I do the arranging on the inside. It keeps both of us very busy but we love it."

Color is found throughout the house. Each bedroom is pastel-hued with harmonizing sheets and pillowcases and curtains. Knock-Saint-Lour House is a farmhouse and almost everything served is home grown. "I do a lot of freezing in the summer and early fall," she explained, "so that we have our own produce through most of the year."

I noticed a donkey grazing in a nearby field. "Oh, that's for the children. They love it."

She pointed out that there was a good view of the famous Rock of Cashel through one of the kitchen windows. "Everyone wants to visit there."

KNOCK-SAINT-LOUR HOUSE, Cashel, County Tipperary, Ireland. Telephone: 062-61172. A 6-bedroom farmhouse just a mile and a half from Cashel. Golfing, tennis, horse riding and pony trekking available nearby. Rates: 8 pounds per person.

LONGFIELD HOUSE, Cashel, County Tipperary

Longfield is an Irish country house cum castle. It was built in 1770 with six-foot-thick walls but a symmetrical Georgian grace that belies its defensive mood. The towering center section has been likened to a huge lantern. The interior still reflects the grace and good taste that were characteristic of the house when it was owned during the mid-19th century by Charles Bianconi, a man of acute business and artistic vision.

Today's spirit of Longfield is personified by Kevin and

Christa Byrne, the innkeepers. These young people are graduates of Trinity College in Dublin and they have enthusiastically made this lovely manor house their way of life.

On the evening that I was there it was wonderfully comfortable in the main living room with a low fire and huge mirror over the mantlepiece. There were great high chests in the corners and a beautiful piano.

Guests were talking to each other in French and German, and handsome Kevin with a red beard and beautiful Christa with blonde hair were most graciously mixing with their guests.

At a given signal from Christa, who all of this time was supervising what was going on in the kitchen, we all crossed through the entrance area with its two granite pillars topped with two Roman busts through to the red dining room with its large circular table and great heroic-sized oils on the walls. There were three bay windows looking out over the beautiful Irish countryside.

With Kevin at one end of the table and Christa at the other, dinner was a huge success. We had starters of fresh fruit which was served with extremely good fresh bread that had been soaked in garlic butter and herbs. The main course was chicken baked with parmesan cheese and bread crumbs. Dessert was a delicious variation of a chocolate mousse.

I was fortunate enough to sit next to Christa and much of our conversation dealt with Longfield and with the activities for the guests. "There are many ruins of castles, towers, mills and houses in this area," she said, "and one of the more renowned features is the Rock of Cashel which rises 300 feet above the plains.

"Our guests have the freedom of our 60 acres for woodland walks. There is a mile of fishing on the River Suir and there are bicycle rides, fishing, boating, tennis, golfing and rambling."

LONGFIELD HOUSE, Cashel, County Tipperary, Ireland. Telephone: Goold's Cross 63. A 10-room manor house about 20 min. away from center of Cashel. This house is entrusted to the care of the Irish Georgian Society. Many recreational facilities available on grounds or in nearby area. Rates: 17.50 pounds.

CHEZ HANS, Cashel, County Tipperary

Florian Binsack of the Roundwood Inn first told me about Chez Hans. "It is," he said, "a must for you. It's one of the most unusual restaurants in the British Isles."

First of all, I must explain that I did not have the opportunity to dine there but I did pay a late evening visit just for the pleasure of meeting Hans and seeing this truly unique restaurant.

Unique—of that there is no doubt. In Europe and America I have visited inns and restaurants in castles, caves, libraries, bookstores, barns, ships, railroad cars, but to my knowledge this was the first time I visited an inn in a church.

Rock of Cashel

Hans was quick to state that the edifice had never been consecrated as a church. It was built in 1854 and was used for many years as a community hall. My recollection is that he has had the restaurant here for about 10 years.

The interior is ecclesiastical in tone without being overwhelming. Gothic arches and heavy stone highlight the decor. An additional room in the same mode was added a few years ago.

"This place represented to me something that I have always wanted, and we are constantly trying to improve it," he said. "We listen carefully to our patrons who come from all over the world."

Some main dishes featured are sole, lobsters and lamb. He said that the pastries were very popular.

CHEZ HANS, Cashel County Tipperary. Telephone: 062 61177. A restaurant located in a stone chapel just at the foot of the towering Rock of Cashel. Open for lunch and dinner except Mondays. Reservations essential. No lodgings.

THE DOWNSHIRE HOUSE, Blessington, County Wicklow

The Downshire House is only 18 miles from Dublin but it has a very "countrified" atmosphere and the advantage of being near the main road to Wicklow, Wexford, Waterford, Cork and Limerick and on the edge of the Blessington Lakes, some 600 feet above sea level. Some guests that I spoke to were using it as an alternative to staying in Dublin because they preferred the feeling of being in the country.

The oldest part of the house is a Georgian mansion built about 1800 and converted to a hotel with additional buildings in 1959. It is on the main street of the village of Blessington and is the center of the community social activity.

The rooms are on the American motel side. In the rear of the house there is a children's play area, as well as a small garden and a hard surface tennis court.

Actually the Downshire is well located for dashes into the Wicklow Mountains or to the beaches, while still having the convenience of being close to Dublin. There is quite a bit of fishing nearby in both rivers and lakes. I understand the hotel owns a private lake about 3 miles away with rainbow and brown trout for fly fishing. It also owns two sailboats which may be sailed by the guests on Lake Blessington.

I enjoyed a good lunch there and a long talk with Mr. Billy Flynn, the manager.

THE DOWNSHIRE HOUSE, Blessington, County Wicklow. Telephone: Naas 045/65199. A 25-room (all with private bath/ shower) village hotel. Located 18 mi. from Dublin. Many recreational amenities available nearby. Rates: 9-14 pounds.

BARBERSTOWN CASTLE, Straffan, County Kildare

What a way to wind up a tour to Ireland—in a castle with all the trappings.

The oldest part was built in 1172 and a portion of it with walls four feet thick still stands. An Elizabethan wing was added in 1594 and an Edwardian wing in 1830.

The castle passed through many hands and then was confiscated during the Cromwellian era. Barberstown became the property of Sir Richard Talbot, Lord Lieutenant of Ireland in 1689, and his two-year tenancy was abruptly halted when he was removed from office.

There is a persistent legend to the effect that a man is said to be interred between the top of the main stair and the roof of the tower. His family, having held the castle by a lease which would expire when he was put underground, determined to delay relinquishing their hold by keeping him always

"above the earth." Just how successful that maneuver was I never found out.

The castle is situated just 15 miles from Dublin in the heart of Ireland's horse country. Here in the countryside of County Kildare Irish horses have been bred to be sold all over the world. There are several famous race courses all within a 30-minute drive of the castle.

On the ground floor there is a dining room decorated in the Norman style with armor of the period. The first floor has a lounge which has an excellent view of the plains and meadows of Kildare. The two wings have 15 bedrooms, some with quite luxurious bathrooms.

During my short stay I talked with four people from the Boston vicinity who were traveling for three weeks in Ireland. In addition to providing me with some excellent references they also stated that Barberstown Castle was one of their most enjoyable stops.

Straffan, the village in which the castle is located, is only an hour from Dublin Airport under even the most trying of traffic conditions.

Barberstown Castle is a fine example of how private capital can preserve the Ireland of the past, blending it with the

Ireland of present and future. The O'Mahony Family all seemed to be working very hard to make a go of it. I wish success to them and to all of the inventive, hopeful keepers of inns in castles and mansion houses everywhere.

BARBERSTOWN CASTLE, Straffan, County Kildare, Ireland. Telephone: 288206. A restored castle just 15 mi. to the south of Dublin on the edge of the Wicklow Hill country. Convenient to the cultural advantages of Dublin and the recreational offerings of the countryside. Rates: 20 pounds (double with bath—includes breakfast).

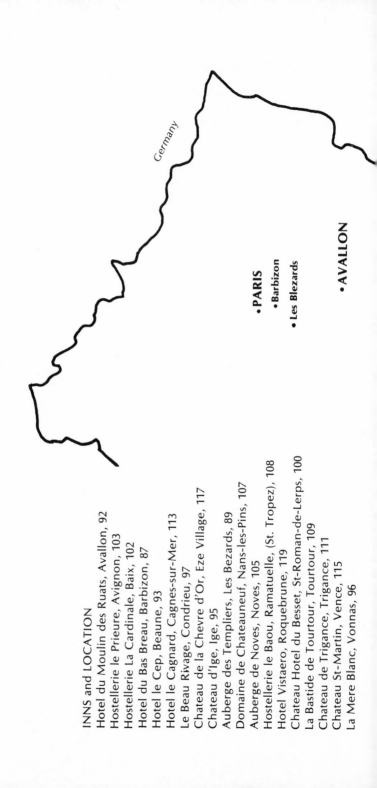

EASTERN FRANCE

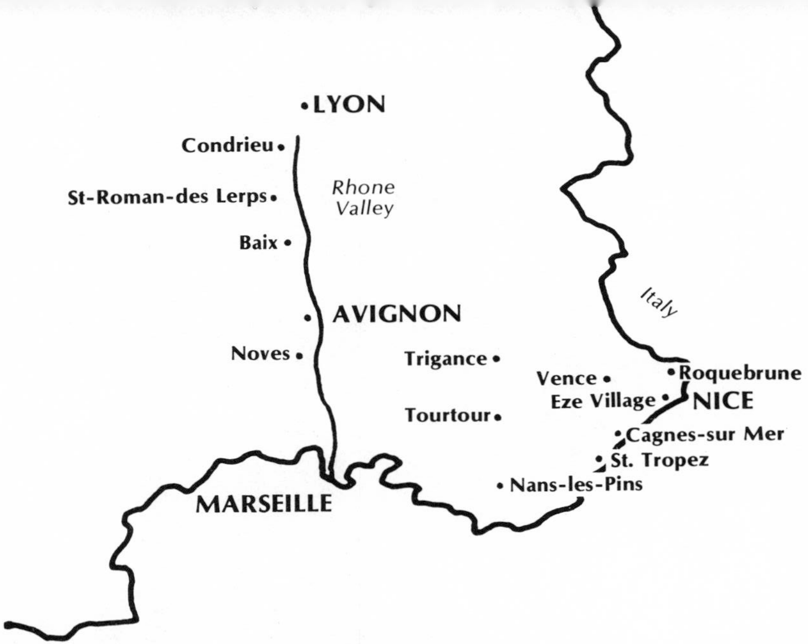

LYON

Condrieu

St-Roman-des-Lerps

Baix

Rhone Valley

AVIGNON

Noves

Trigance

Tourtour

MARSEILLE

Nans-les-Pins

Vence

Eze Village

Roquebrune

NICE

Cagnes-sur Mer

St. Tropez

Italy

TRAVEL SUGGESTIONS FOR FRANCE

How to Get There

Air France provides excellent service from many principal U.S. cities. A Eurailpass is good in France.

Country Inns in France

The country inns I visited in France were located in ancient castles, chateaux, country houses, priories, and steep-walled villages. There is a long tradition of personal innkeeping in France, and in most cases the proprietors themselves make their guests feel very much at home.

Reservations

Almost all the hotels and inns in France and Italy that I have included belong to the highly prestigious Relais de Campagne Chateaux-Hotels, an organization dedicated to the highest innkeeping standards. After you have chosen a few Relais Chateaux in France, Italy and even England and Denmark, you or your travel agent should contact the Relais de Campagne Chateaux-Hotels, 17 Place Vendome, 75001 Paris, France (Tel. 261-5650; Telex RCH Paris 220319F) to determine the availability of the rooms you require. These reservations are not confirmed until a deposit has been sent directly to each Relais Chateaux.

I would suggest that you rely on the real professionals — your travel agency; their services will not cost you any more. In most Relais Chateaux, breakfast is additional and in some cases the service charge is added. Prices shown are for two people for one night.

Dining in France

I am not a gourmet in any sense of the word, and I don't consider myself an expert on food. Furthermore, my perusal of guides to French cuisine with the star ratings made me quite apprehensive about displaying my ignorance to French waiters and headwaiters. To top it all off, I really don't know anything about wines, except that it is red wine for meat and white wine for fish. However in all of the restaurants, brasseries, auberges, snack bars, bistros, and cafes I visited, I was treated with courtesy and consideration. I was surprised at how quickly I picked up "menu French."

In the French restaurants there are usually three fixed-price (prix fixe) menus. The higher the price, the wider the choice of the main dishes.

The a la carte menu has several advantages; for one thing, it is possible to skip a course or two and concentrate on something special. I quickly learned that only ordering soup (potage), bread (pain), salads, desserts, or cheese would not evoke any raised eyebrows or disdainful glances. There are over 400 different varieties of cheese in France, made from goat's, cow's, and ewe's milk. Sometimes they are served from a large tray and the diner can make a choice.

I encourage anyone going to France to put aside their preconceived notions about French cuisine and service. It is a delightful education and if approached with an open mind and a carefree heart can be a delightful experience. Enjoy.

Car Rentals

Air France has many Fly-Drive Flexi-Plans that include automobiles. Travelers for whom France is part of a Continent-wide itinerary should see the section near the front of this book, "Renting a Car for Europe."

Driving Tips

Let's begin with Paris. Paris, like all of the principal cities of Europe and America, has lots of traffic . . . but it is not as bad as I expected. While driving my rented car, I discovered that the drivers on the whole were quite courteous and the problem looks a lot worse than it is.

The Beltway around Paris is called the Periphique. There are roads leading from it in all directions. The best thing to do is to look for main highways (Autoroutes) that lead to principal cities such as Orleans, Chartres, or Lyon. Study the Michelin map in advance, and instead of looking for route signs, exit the Periphique at roads leading to the main city on your itinerary.

The Michelin Green Guide has all the information needed about the road signs.

My Itinerary in France

My travels in France started in Paris and after dipping slightly to the southwest on the edge of the chateau country, I traveled south through Avallon, Lyon, and Avignon to Provence and the Riviera. To obtain Michelin road maps and guides for France see the section in the back of this book marked "Maps and Guides."

Chez des Amis

One of the most unique ways of enjoying at least part of a trip to France is the opportunity to be a houseguest in a French home. This can be arranged through Chez des Amis, (the house of friends), 139 W. 87th St., New York, New York 10024 (212-787-0221). Arrangements are made for travelers to be received as paying guests in French homes and there is an opportunity to see France through the eyes of the people who know it best and love it profoundly.

Notes on Paris

The Air France 747 took me out of New York and into the outskirts of Paris after a very pleasant overnight trip. The in-flight dinner provided an interesting preview of French cuisine. After a very short wait for luggage, Air France provided buses to take its passengers into the center of the city. It is a very nice way to be welcomed to France.

I took a Cityrama Bus Tour which provides an excellent overview of the city. With this orientation I was ready to make the most of my few hours. It's really quite easy to get around in

Paris and I would encourage anybody to use the Metro (subway) as frequently as possible. In some of the principal Metro stations there is an electronic map which includes a graphic demonstration of how to reach all of the principal attractions. Push a button for the Eiffel Tower or the Louvre, for example, and the map will show you the Metro lines to take.

The city is divided into sections called Arrondissements and everything is geared around knowing about the locations of these sections. There are tours everywhere and all types of guidebooks. One of them which I found useful is called, "Paris and its Outlying Regions," which was available for two francs.

I would suggest a consultation with your travel agent about hotel reservations in the city; however, once there, do not hesitate to change hotels for a longer stay. You can choose one in the Arrondissement you prefer.

Paris is great fun. In future editions I will have more to say about hotels and restaurants, but at this time my main interest was in getting out into the country and visiting as many inns as possible.

HOTELLERIE du BAS-BREAU, Barbizon

I was having my first dinner in a French country inn, and to make it even more exciting, I was having my first genuine French soufflé. It's golden crust rose from the traditional white soufflé dish, proclaiming with a magnificent Gallic insouciance that it was, indeed, master of all it surveyed. For one breathless moment I was allowed to dwell on this model of perfection. Such style! Such grace! Such nobility! Such a divine fragrance!

The last, alas, was to be its undoing—I could wait no longer And even while administering the *coup de grace*, I realized that this *chef d'oeuvre* had withheld its crowning achievement to the very last moment. Closing my eyes to savor that first heavenly morsel, my senses thrilled to the indescribable taste of—praline soufflé!! I lost all touch with time and space . . . I was, indeed, on Olympus and this was ambrosia of the gods.

"You are, perhaps, enjoying your soufflé?" It was Jean-Pierre Fava, the innkeeper of du Bas-Breau who stood beside my table with a twinkle in his eye. For a moment I could only nod vigorously, and then I regained my voice. "It is unlike anything I have ever tasted," I said.

"You are very kind," he replied. "And I am happy to say we

receive many compliments for our praline soufflé."

One hundred and fifty years ago this inn on the edge of the Barbizon Forest carried on its sign board the name of its proprietor, M. Siron, and its best-known guest was Robert Louis Stevenson. The name was changed in 1867 to Hotel de l'Exposition because it was being used as an exhibition hall for the Barbizon painters including Corot, Rousseau, and Millet, all of whom painted in the forest. It became du Bas-Breau in 1937 when M. and Mme. Fava arrived, and in 50 years its tradition, elegance, comfort, and gastronomy have become well-known. Jean-Pierre the present innkeeper is continuing the ideals of his parents.

The entrance of the inn is through the arch of a building into a small courtyard with cobblestones and two big pots of geraniums and ivy. There are flowers everywhere, even in little flowerpots on the roof. An ancient French lamp hangs from this arch and a stairway leads up to some lodging rooms with window boxes full of flowers.

The next entrance is into the main reception hall and bar, where petit déjeuner is served each morning. Through the windows I could see the dining courtyard and other buildings containing more lodging rooms. In the evening, the scene is lit with discreet lanterns, and the tables are occupied with happy diners.

All of the bedrooms have triple sheets, handsome bedspreads, and show pillows; many of them overlook a terrace, and others provide a generous glimpse of the gardens of the village. During my visit, the fruit trees and lilacs were in vivid blossom.

One of the most prestigious visitors to the inn in recent years was Emperor Hirohito of Japan. The dining room has been named in honor of his visit. Other guests include Winston Churchill and his daughter Sarah, Art Linkletter, the Shah of Iran, and Princess Grace of Monaco, whose entire family were guests.

As Jean-Pierre said, "Our guests enjoy walking in the Fontainebleau Forest, driving through the countryside, and spending hours in the local shops."

I will also add that I am sure they enjoy the praline souffles."

RELAIS CHATEAU 7, HOTELLERIE du BAS-BREAU, 77630 Barbizon; Tel. (1) 066.40.05. A 19-room exceptionally comfortable inn with first class service on the edge of the Fontainebleau Forest approximately 1½ hrs. south of Paris. Breakfast, lunch, dinner. Closed from Nov. 20 to Dec. 29. Rates: 250-300 Fr. M. and Mme. Fava, Innkeepers.

Directions: Michelin sect. map 61. Follow Autoroute A6 marked Lyon to Fontainebleau. Use exit (Sortie) for Barbizon.

AUBERGE des TEMPLIERS, Les Bezards

Following Jean-Pierre Fava's directions, I left du Bas-Breau and Barbizon, and within a pleasant hour-and-a-half drive I pulled up at the great gates of the Auberge des Templiers. This is on the road southwest to the chateaux country.

I stepped through a heavy front door into the reception area and found a two-story room with a very impressive tapestry on the far wall. I moved into still another vaulted room with a replica of a Crusader's cross over the massive mantle.

An extremely attractive French woman with short blonde hair, wearing a very chic striped grey and charcoal pantsuit introduced herself: "I am Francoise Depee. Welcome to our modest little place."

She apologized for the temporary absence of her husband and introduced me to her husband's mother who, along with his father, started the Auberge about thirty-two years ago. Francoise said that Madame Depee had been the cook for thirty years.

She and I set out on a short tour of the many buildings and grounds, walking across the garden, past the swimming pool and the barbecue lunch area. The tennis courts were just beyond. There were many trees and attractively landscaped lawns. We looked at several lodging rooms and I found them beautifully furnished. "We are just a short, pleasant drive from Paris, so many of our Parisian guests come and stay for a few days at a time," she said. "There is much to be seen and done all within an automobiling distance."

At lunch the headwaiter, Stewart Cunningham of Edinburgh, Scotland, who had been at the Auberge since 1969, explained that this particular region of France sent many knights to the Crusades, and that this building at one time must have been an abbey and a meeting place for the men-at-arms who set off on the great adventure. The word "Templiers" actually refers to a certain order of Crusaders. I found many references to this historical event throughout southern France.

As it all turned out, Francoise's husband, a very handsome man, returned in time to join all of us on the terrace for a late afternoon cup of tea. It was from him that I learned (Francoise was too modest to tell me) that she had been a cover girl. "Yes," he said, "Francoise's picture was on the cover of many French magazines."

A beautiful inn, a congenial innkeeping family, tranquillity and graciousness. I found these at Auberge des Templiers. It was like an American country inn with a French accent.

RELAIS CHATEAU 12, AUBERGE des TEMPLIERS, 45290 Les Bezards; Tel. (38) 31.80.01. A 25-room exceptionally comfortable inn with first class service located in a chateau 135 km. south of Paris. Breakfast, lunch, dinner. This is a resort accommodation with a swimming pool, two tennis courts, horseback riding, and golf nearby. Closed Jan. 15 to Feb. 15. Rates: 160-260 Fr. M. and Mme. Depee, Innkeepers.

Directions: Michelin sect. map 65. Exit A6 at Dordives. Follow N7 south to Les Bezards. If continuing into chateaux country (south-

west), I advise Michelin 64, 68, and 72. (My line of direction in this book is almost due south.)

French Villages

I fell in love with the French villages . . . the old stone houses sometimes covered with stucco of all colors, depending upon local soil . . . the trees which had been there for centuries shading the squares and their outdoor tables and chairs . . . the churches, the small shops, and the ever-present fountain in the center of each village.

After a first trip to France, everyone has a favorite village and it is great fun to go back and see if it has changed. Basically, of course, it never does. In the spring and fall, many villages are innundated with flowers . . . flowers in windows, in front yards, and in the square. Lucky indeed the traveler who arrives in the village on market day or even better when there is a carnival or a festival. It is a wonderful opportunity to see the villagers in a holiday mood.

HOSTELLERIE MOULIN des RUATS, Vallee du Cousin, Avallon

Sometimes now, I can close my eyes and return in my mind to the boardwalk which extends from the garden of this little inn out over the river Cousin, and the rippling, bubbling, gurgling water as it rushes under the bridge, tempts me to dip my hand into its chilly depths. Overhead, the blue skies of Avallon form a natural cyclorama which is visible through the lacy patterns of the trees now in half-leaf. Songbirds are busy building their nests, stopping long enough to lend encouragement to each other with chirps and an occasional few bars of melody. The tables on the riverside terrace are set in gleaming napery and guests in twosomes are sitting a little closer to each other.

I well remember the day of my visit. After leaving Templiers, I relished a very leisurely drive across the Burgundian country-side with its fields, gentle slopes, and villages framed with vine-yards. In the steeper sections there were narrow valleys where brooks, filled to the banks from recent rains, fought their way among blocks of granite en route to the sea. They joined the more sedate rivers lined with poplar and hawthorn trees flowing through ancient villages.

One of these is the village of Vezelay with its proud cathedral rising at the top of the mountain. In a waning afternoon sun it imparted an uplifting serenity.

In such a setting it was little wonder that my rather shy, English-speaking hostess explained that many visitors came to this little inn in the valley for one night and remained for two or three. It is about 170 kilometers south of Orly Airport outside of Paris. It might well be a first night in France for many American visitors.

I saw quite a few of the lodging rooms, all of which appeared very comfortable, and lingered for a few moments in the lounge which had an old-fashioned country fireplace which, in this season, was filled with fresh flowers instead of a crackling fire. The main dining room is decorated with yellow tablecloths, brass chandeliers, brown paneling and heavy beams. A row of windows on each side overlooks the brook on the right and the forest on the left.

All French inns have menu specialties and in the Moulin des Ruats it is chicken fondue, as well as freshly caught trout from the Cousin River. Fittingly enough, a third is escargots Burgundy. Other menu items that caught my eye were chicken in wine, special house crepes, and coffee-flavored soufflé ice cream.

All of these worldly things seem quite temporal when I remember the eternal sounds of the forest and the brook.

RELAIS CHATEAU 9, HOSTELLERIE du MOULIN des RUATS, Vallee du Cousin, 89200 Avallon; Tel. (86) 34.07.14. A 21-room, small, comfortable but simple country hotel 200 km. south of Paris. Breakfast, lunch, dinner. Fishing, horseback riding and tennis nearby. Closed Nov. 2 to Mar. 5. Rates: 85-160 Fr. M. and Mme. Bertier, Innkeepers.

Directions: Michelin sect. map 65. From Paris take Autoroute du Soleil (A6) to Avallon exit. Inquire for Rte. D957 to Vallee du Cousin. (Takes a bit of patience.)

HOTEL LE CEP, Beaune

"We've been traveling all over France with our two children, ages 6 and 9, and this is one of the best experiences we have ever had." It was time for petit déjeuner (breakfast) at Hotel Le Cep. I looked again to see whether or not the mother of the two active children seated opposite me in the tiny dining room was kidding, but I could see that she definitely was not. "You know, the owner of this place, M. Falci, is so nice. He apparently loves children and when we arrived he seemed to take them right in tow."

Hotel Le Cep is located in the heart of the town of Beaune and I learned from Mme. Mary Hibiki, the manager, that it is one of the richest wine towns in France. "People come from everywhere," she said, "to sample the Burgundy wines at Beaune and many of them return to the hotel year after year."

Le Cep is an interesting experience in more ways than one. Although a formal dinner is not served, guests are invited to take "pot luck," which might be a hearty country soup (which I enjoyed), lots of fresh bread, a small order of veal, a very good salad, and a toothsome piece of cake.

Other people in the very small low-arched dining room were reading at the table, or carrying on a conversation with the young waiter. It was quite informal . . . different from the savoir faire that I found at other places. I got out my copy of the *Paris Herald Tribune* and caught up on things in the USA.

The rooms in Le Cep are each decorated in the style of a different century of French architecture. Mine was in Louis XV. This was very carefully done by Monsieur Falci, himself, who has been a collector of antiques for many years.

According to a private joke, M. Falci had too many visitors in his home one night about 13 years ago, and then and there he decided to open a hotel.

The previous evening, after dinner, I joined my American friends who felt perfectly safe in leaving their children in their room, and we walked around this beautiful old town. Upon our return from this 11 p.m. walk, I had a short conversation with Monsieur Falci. I could feel his warmth, enthusiasm, and humor. He summarized the spirit of Le Cep very well: He refers to it as a "home with room service."

RELAIS CHATEAU 44, HOTEL LE CEP, 21200 Beaune; Tel. (80) 22.35.48. A 20-room in-town comfortable but simple hotel in the Burgundy wine district, 37 km. south of Dijon. Beaune is an extremely interesting and prosperous town with a great deal of emphasis on the surrounding vineyards. The hotel has an impromptu dinner each evening except Sunday. Closed Dec. 1 to Feb. 1. Rates: 65-165 Fr. A. Falci, Innkeeper.

Directions: Michelin sect. map 65. Follow one-way road circling

*the inside of the city about ¾ of the way around. Look for hotel
sign on left. There is an exit at Beaune from Autoroute A6.*

CHATEAU d'IGE, Ige

"We are," said Monsieur Jadot, "very quiet." I was visiting
my first ancient chateau hotel and I liked it immediately. This was
enhanced by the smiling M. Jadot, who was the very personifi-
cation of innkeeping joviality. It was obvious that he, too, was
much attached to this 13th-century fortified home in the Burgundian countryside which seemed so far away from the
demands of the 20th century.

First, we walked around the outside of the chateau where
the massive walls are overgrown with a green cloak of ivy. In
the gardens a deep pool has been created by the waters of the
brook which was shared by playful ducks and unusually large
trout. "The trout are too large for the ducks," said M. Jadot. There
was a little outdoor dining terrace, which he explained was used
for dinner in the warm weather. His German shepherd, Puff,
walked ahead of us. Overhead the sky was blue, the spring birds
were singing, and some of the flowers were in bloom. It was, to
say the least, idyllic. In one corner of the garden there was a
tower with a most pleasant apartment. "Very popular with
honeymooners," he said. The bedroom window on the top floor
had a beautiful view of the village and the valley.

Inside the main building were several apartments, many of them also in the towers, reached by well-worn stone steps twisting around a center pole. Bedrooms were varied in size and looked comfortable.

This chateau had many, many old tapestries which relieved the rough texture of the grey-yellow stone walls. The furniture in the living and dining rooms was massive in style, and appropriate to the scale of the rooms.

Throughout my entire tour, Monsieur Jadot was smiling and laughing. We found several words in French and English which we shared in common.

Dinner is served only to houseguests and there is a choice of five main dishes. "We have a very good chef," he promised.

Chateau d'Ige was small by comparison to other castles I was to visit, but it had an undeniable warmth. I am sure its quiet atmosphere brings joy and happiness to many guests.

RELAIS CHATEAU 46, d'IGE, 71960 Ige; Tel. (85) 33.33.99. A 9-room, very comfortable 13th century fortified chateau enhanced with modern conveniences. Approximately 80 kms. north of Lyon. Breakfast and dinner served to houseguests only. Romantic countryside, golf, horseback riding, and sailing nearby. Closed Nov. 5 to Feb. 1. Rates: 100-175 Fr. H. Jadot, Innkeeper.

Directions: Michelin sect. maps 69, 73. Exit A6 at Macon Nord and from Macon follow road marked Charolles. A few km. out of Macon turn right at the village of Vineuse (D85). Follow road to Ige and inquire for inn.

LA MERE BLANC, Vonnas

It was high noon in Vonnas. The atmosphere and general spirit at La Mere Blanc was busy and cheerful. In fact, it reminded me of the small inn that I visited in Iphofen, Germany at the same hour of the day. Waiters and waitresses were hustling and bustling back and forth serving a large luncheon party in one dining room. My table next to the window overlooked a small stream. In the summertime meals are served on the terrace.

The proprietors are Jacqueline and Georges Blanc, third generation innkeepers. I was rather surprised because Georges didn't look more than 25 years old.

The youthful Monsieur Blanc explained that most of the items on the menu were regional specialties and that the menu included six courses. This was the meal that the French eat once a day, either at noon or night.

At his suggestion I ordered the creamed chicken with crepes and, which as he said, "enjoys a local reputation." I've had chicken in various garb all over the world, but I am sure that any chicken would consider it a noble sacrifice to be placed on the table at La Mere Blanc bathed in that truly marvelous cream sauce.

It was, however, the cream cheese that made this visit outstanding. I have never tasted such delicious, creamy, honestly-melt-in-the-mouth fromage. I ate every bit of it and as a result had to pass up the selection of six desserts.

There are several rooms in this small inn, all of them exceptionally well furnished and many with some rather startling color schemes, including lavender. Some of them had a kind of Spanish feeling about them.

A swimming pool and a small park have been recently added, making it a very pleasant quiet overnight stay; however, lunch or dinner would be well worth the short drive from the main Autoroute at Macon.

RELAIS CHATEAU 53, LA MERE BLANC, 01540 Vonnas; Tel. (74) 50.00.10. An 18-room very comfortable hotel with an excellent reputation for food. Breakfast, lunch, dinner. Swimming pool on grounds. Tennis, golf, horseback riding, fishing nearby. Closed December and January. Rates: 80-250 Fr. Family Blanc, Innkeepers.

Directions: Michelin sect. map 91. Exit A6 at Macon (Nord), follow N79 approximately 10 kms. on road to Bourg. Turn right at sign for Vonnas. La Mere Blanc is near the town square.

HOTELLERIE BEAU RIVAGE et l'HERMITAGE du RHONE, Condrieu

I had been in France a few days and was feeling quite comfortable with my growing list of French verbs and nouns when I arrived at Beau Rivage and immediately met another American couple who were on a combination business and pleasure trip. Since they were experienced travelers in France, I asked the husband for his opinion of French innkeeping. This is part of what he said:

"I have traveled in France several times and I have always found the French hotel keepers and their staff extremely accommodating and pleasant, and willing to go to any length to make their guests as comfortable as possible. For example, here

Madame Castaing has been the principal chef for over 30 years, as well as being the owner, and you can see for yourself that she comes out of the kitchen frequently, exchanges a few words of conversation with her guests and radiates the feeling of hospitality."

"Yes," continued his wife, "and did you know that Lyon is the only section in France where there are women chefs? She is one of the most famous in France."

Beau Rivage is right on the banks of the fast-flowing Rhone River as it makes its way south toward the Mediterranean. In the summertime, guests are served on patios overlooking the river and many of the accommodations have a river view.

In addition to the extensive a la carte menu, there are also three set menus. I chose the middle one which included a delicious fresh-water fish served in a very tasty sauce, succulent fresh French beans, and a choice of three main dishes — steak, guinea hen, and lamb chops. There were also scalloped potatoes discreetly seasoned with garlic.

Yves, the headwaiter held a lively discussion with my friends about the features that lovers of good wine seem to hold so dear: the year, the fragrance, the length of time in the bottle, and even the name of the wine grower. "Yes, we French really do get down to the fine points of wine," he said. "The length of time the sun shines on the grapes during the day can play an important role, so that the exposure of the vineyards could be a factor." It was explained to me that wine grapes are gathered in late September because they cannot be picked in the rain.

I learned that many people stayed at Beau Rivage for several days at a time, because there is good fishing, horseback riding, tennis, golf, and the beautiful backroads of the incomparable countryside.

The evening was a marvelous success. Yves, who speaks excellent English, deftly supervised the service. Madame paid us a short visit and we toasted her dinner and her beautiful inn. Then we all resolved to sell our stocks and bonds and move to the Rhone Valley of France where we could meet frequently for dinner at Beau Rivage.

RELAIS CHATEAU 68, HOTELLERIE BEAU RIVAGE et l'HERMI-TAGE du RHONE, 69420 Condrieu; Tel. (74) 59.52.24. A 25-room very comfortable inn on the banks of the Rhone River 60 km. south of Lyon. Breakfast, lunch, dinner. Tennis, swimming, golf, outdoor sports nearby. Closed early January to middle February. Rates: 110-160 Fr. Familie Castaing, Innkeepers.

Directions: Michelin sect. map 93. As nearly as I can determine A6 goes into A7 at Lyon. Follow the road clearly marked Marseille and use the exit (Sortie) marked Condrieu. Proceed south on N86 about 10 km. The inn is on the left between the road and the river.

South from Condrieu

It was Saturday morning along the Rhone. All the people from the little riverside villages were making a holiday of it, visiting the shops and stopping in the town square to exchange some tidbits of conversation with their friends. There were long loaves of delicious French bread carried under arms and colorful shopping bags loaded to the brim.

The towns and cities on the opposite side of the river were a picturebook sight with green vineyards and flower-laden orchards blending into the red roofs.

Following N86 I could occasionally see the remains of an old tower or castle in the distance.

I turned off at St. Paray, en route to St. Romain-de-Lerps, and had my first experience with high hills in France. As the road swung back and forth across little valleys and up into the higher ground, there were increasingly interesting panoramic views of the Rhone Valley. Since it was a promising May day with a warm sun, the industrious French farmers and their families were already working in the fields. To the south and east it was sunny but the clouds and fog still had to burn off to the west.

Now I had reached the village located at the crest of the hills and followed the signs over the rolling Burgundy countryside to Chateau du Besset.

LE CHATEAU du BESSET, St -Romain-de-Lerps

Sitting in the parlor of this 15th-century castle I needed only court musicians playing Vivaldi or Bach to transport me to France before the Reign of Terror. Here were the casement windows, heavily beamed ceilings, rich furniture, tapestries, oils, and acquisitions from several epochs of French decoration and design that provided a clue as to how French royalty might have lived 200 years ago.

From one window I could look out over the fields and down into the valley to the green parkland, an essential feature of many French chateaux. Another window gave me an excellent view of the formal gardens, where with the encouragement of the soft French spring, many varieties of roses were in bud. I am sure that many a French princess has walked the paths of this garden. Today, a small terrace with gay umbrellas invited 20th-century guests to enjoy the blue skies, warm sun, and gentle breezes.

A few hours earlier, approaching the entrance, I realized for the first time that a chateau is really a castle. As in all of the chateaux hotels I visited, the walls were very formidable and high, with towers at some of the corners. The walls were rough and forbidding and the doors quite narrow. Once inside, the interior is a marked contrast to the rude exterior.

There are six lodging rooms in le Besset, all of them carefully furnished in different French periods. It is indeed a French castle hotel of the first class. Great attention has been given to making every room as authentic as possible. Each has a marvelous view of the countryside.

By way of interesting changes, the Tower Room is furnished

in the period of the 1930s. It has a bed with a beautiful suede bedspread, modern lighting fixtures, and tables with glass tops. This chrome and glass did seem a little strange with all the Louis XII, XIV, etc., decor in the remainder of the castle.

I asked some other guests about the food. They replied that, although off the beaten track, le Besset had the reputation of having one of the finest restaurants in France. Menu specialties included rabbit, lobster salad, fresh salmon, and filet of sole. One lady was rather intrigued with the idea that ladies have their own menus without prices.

The Chateau du Besset is an intimate, luxurious experience and deserves more than merely a single night. Active sports — horseback riding, tennis, and swimming are available. The walks in the park and drives around the countryside provide the opportunity to contemplate life in its quiet, graceful, harmonious moods.

RELAIS CHATEAU 81, LE CHATEAU du BESSET, 07130 St-Romain-de-Lerps (near Saint Peray); Tel. (75) 44.41.63. A 6-room exceptionally comfortable 15th-century castle with first class service in the beautiful Burgundy countryside. 15 kms. from Valence. Breakfast, lunch, dinner. Beautiful parkland walks, horseback riding, swimming pool, tennis courts on grounds. Closed Oct. 2 to Apr. 27. Rates: 350-550 Fr. Mme. de Leon, Innkeeper.

Directions: Michelin sect. map 93. Follow N86 south and turn right on D533 at the town of St. Peray. Watch for the signs for St-Romain-de-Lerps and after driving about 10 km. to that village turn left and follow signs back into the country about 5 km. Coming north or south on the Autoroute A7 (sometimes called Autoroute du Soleil) exit at Valence, cross the Rhone River Bridge to St. Peray.

HOSTELLERIE LA CARDINALE, Baix

By this time I had definitely become attached to N86, the road which parallels the Rhone River on the west side and threads its way among vineyards and through small riverside villages.

I drove into the town of Baix and saw the sign for La Cardinale in front of a primary school on the left-hand side of the road. I turned left for about a half a block along the river skirting a large tree growing in the middle of the road. I spied a yellow building with wisteria vines growing on the walls, and a delightful terrace. I was here.

The two gentlemen hosts at La Cardinale, Messrs. Lemasson and Robichow were both accommodating and enthusiastic. As we sat on the terrace enjoying an afternoon cup of tea, I learned something most interesting. La Cardinale was the first of the Relais Chateaux. A number of years ago the owners, Monsieur and Madame Tilloy lived here. They had many guests and the idea occurred to them to transform the house into a hotel. M. Tilloy later saw the advantages of bringing other small inns together so that they could help each other, and the organization was formed.

Properly refreshed, I was ready for a tour of this delightful spot and found its simple homelike elegance most appealing. The sitting room had a collection of very interesting oil paintings and tapestries. The huge fireplace was decorated with roses, and in one corner there was a grand piano with lots of sheet music. The front windows had a view of the Rhone.

A room that had been the kitchen in centuries past was now a small dining room with a huge copper pot full of spring flowers in what had formerly been the bread oven.

The lodging rooms were all simple but generously proportioned, many with a view of the river. They had exposed beams and lots of comfortable furniture. The main part of the house had been built in the 11th century.

It came as a surprise, also, to learn that there is a Residence (which is a French term similar to annex) a few kilometers away on a small promontory overlooking the river and the valley. It has excellent rooms and suites which are not as simple as those in the main hotel. Oddly enough, one of them had a bathroom with two bathtubs!

La Cardinale had a very warm, gracious, informal atmosphere. I think the best word is "natural."

RELAIS CHATEAU 82, HOSTELLERIE LA CARDINALE, 07210 Baix; Tel. (75) 61.88.07. A 15-room very comfortable village inn overlooking the Rhone River approximately 130 km. south of Lyon. Besides lodgings in the main inn, there are also several very comfortable rooms in the Residence which is located outside of the village on a hillside. Breakfast, lunch, and dinner. Private swimming pool. Tennis courts and horseback riding nearby. Closed Oct. 1 to Mar. 1. Rates: 180-280 Fr. Owner Mme. Nelly Tilloy, Innkeepers Messrs. Lemasson and Robichow.

Directions: Michelin sect. map 93. Via Autoroute A7, exit at Loriol. Cross Rhone River Bridge to Le Pouzin and turn south on N86 to Baix. (N86 is an excellent alternative to the Autoroute when following the Rhone Valley south from Vienne to Avignon.)

LE PRIEURE, Avignon

Avignon is one of the showplaces of southeast France. It is rich in history, tradition, scenery. The countryside is dotted with names that are rich in meaning—Arles, where Van Gogh painted some of his sunlit landscapes; Aix-en-Provence, the capital which has been a great artistic center for centuries; Grenoble, which is surrounded by cliff-like mountains; Marseilles, filled with art museums and ancient monuments; and Avignon, itself, the seat of the Papacy in the 14th century which is dominated by the Pope's palace, a fortress sometimes austere and sometimes luxurious, complete with watchtowers and frescoes.

Such historic and artistic wealth makes Le Prieure, located as it is at the double gateway to both Spain and the Riviera, one of the most sought-after accommodations in the south of France.

Located in Villeneuve-les-Avignon, which is a small town across the Rhone River from the much larger city of Avignon,

it is much more quiet and less tourist-oriented than its larger neighbor.

With guests from all parts of the world gathered on the terrace and beside the swimming pool, Le Prieure's atmosphere is decidedly cosmopolitan. Conversations flow in German, English, French, and Japanese, with everyone quite willing to share their travel adventures.

For hundreds of years the inn was a priory; more recently it has become a hotel of the first class presided over by a most pleasant, urbane innkeeper, Jacques Mille, who, like a good many innkeepers, has learned to be affable in any language.

The hotel and gardens are in a setting that reminded me very much of the Alhambra in Granada, with their carefully tended irises and roses, small evergreen hedges, and conical-shaped evergreens that seem to grow everywhere in the Mediterranean country. In the morning, the bees were buzzing among the ivy in the breathtakingly bright sunshine of Provence. The walk to the parking area is through a long, arched rose trellis.

Accommodations for the most part are contemporary in design, and the furnishings in my room with its one glass wall and sliding door leading out to a balcony, which overlooked the swimming pool and tennis courts, had bright modern furniture and draperies. Meals are served in the gardens under the trees.

I took a few moments to walk from the inn to an unusual collection of ancient buildings in Villeneuve, called La Chartreuse, which at one time was an abbey. The courtyards and small lanes were paved with old cobblestones and there were arched doorways and old columns. In the center of one courtyard was an ancient well. Today, La Chartreuse is again an abbey, this time, Benedictine . . . a mixture of the old France and the new, with shops, galleries, and apartments incorporated into the old buildings.

"The old France and the new." In many ways this describes Le Prieure as well.

RELAIS CHATEAU 85, HOSTELLERIE Le PRIEURE, 7 Place du Chapitre, Villeneuve-les-Avignon, 30400 Avignon; Tel. (90) 25.18.20. A 30-room very comfortable inn in the center of one of France's most popular historic and cultural regions. Breakfast, lunch, and dinner. Swimming pool, two tennis courts on grounds. Within a very short distance of the town of Avignon. Closed Nov. 1 to Mar. 1. Rates: 160-350 Fr. Jacques Mille, Innkeeper.

Directions: Michelin sect. map 81, 93. From the north via the Autoroute: note that at Orange, about 10 km. north of Avignon, A7, the main autoroute from Paris to Nice, is a junction for A9 which goes to northern Spain. Use the Avignon exit on either of these two autoroutes and Villeneuve is on the west side of the Rhone River. If using N86 from the North, turn east at Bagnols and follow N580 into Villeneuve.

L'AUBERGE de NOVES, Noves

Monsieur Lalleman, enjoying a respite from his duties as host of this delightful inn just south of Avignon, joined me on the terrace where I was having lunch.

When I remarked about the leisurely service, he responded, "Here at Auberge de Noves there is no hurrying the meal. Even our salads are made especially. They are not waiting in the refrigerator to be served. All of this takes time."

In the meantime, I noticed him keeping a watchful eye on the waiter who was making this selfsame salad of fresh watercress, chopped shallots, and greens all mixed in a handsome silver bowl. Carrots, mushrooms, onions, lettuce, and sliced tomatoes were added. When I remarked that the salad would seem to be a meal in itself, he shrugged and said, "This is only a side dish."

It was a beautiful day in the south of France. The birds in the garden were everywhere chirping, singing, whistling, and fighting. The flowers were already in full bloom. Butterflies were flitting from table to table, and guests having completed their meal, were going for leisurely walks through the quite extensive gardens.

The arrival of some freshly made sliced pate launched M. Lalleman into a short dissertation. "We have many kinds of pate," he said, "in fact, the chef in any good French restaurant is able to make his own particular creation. Ours does wonders with rabbit, duck, and goose liver, but a good pate can be made from many combinations of ingredients." He excused himself for just a moment while I watched the waiter at the next table deftly carve and de-bone two delicious-looking roast ducklings. Seeing my interest, the guests at the table offered me a succulent morsel. It was delicious.

Now adding to a really unforgettable scene, a little girl celebrating her first communion came tripping across the terrace accompanied by her parents, aunts, uncles, cousins, grandmothers, grandfathers, and friends. It was undeniably "her day," and as she flew about the terrace with her white veil trailing behind her, the faces of all the guests were wreathed in smiles.

Following lunch, my host showed me through many of the bedrooms of the inn which were all gaily decorated and he pointed with pride to the swimming pool in the garden which, during less clement days, has a plastic bubble placed over it. There was a view across the meadow to ancient towers in the distance.

My dear friends, Susan and Stephen Bradley in San Francisco, told me that I would be captivated by Auberge de Noves. Indeed I was. I only wish they could have been with me to share such an idyllic day.

RELAIS CHATEAU 106, L'AUBERGE de NOVES, 13550 Noves; Tel. (90) 94.19.21. A 22-room very comfortable Provence manor house a few km. south of Avignon. Breakfast, lunch, and dinner. Swimming pool on grounds. Tennis and fishing nearby. Closed January to mid-February. Rates: 165-320 Fr. Famille Lalleman, Innkeepers.

Directions: Michelin sect. maps 81, 93. From Autoroute A7 use the Avignon Sud exit. Follow N7 across the river, take first right and the next main right. Go about 1 km. and look for sign on left.

DOMAINE de CHATEAUNEUF, Nans-les-Pins

A traveler from Paris to Nice or Cannes on the Autoroutes would do well to stop his headlong flight and remain here for a few days just to let the serenity and tranquillity of southern France envelop him.

The Chateauneuf is surrounded by 250 acres of vineyards and forests and situated in a center of thickly wooded parkland. On the day of my visit, the chestnut trees were in bloom, the birds were singing, and there were white doves restlessly circling the chateau. The courtyard was flooded with sunlight filtering through the leaves and a warm, spring breeze gently wafted its way among the flowers. I could have remained a week.

As my hostess explained, this is an 18th-century chateau which has seen the passing of royalty in France, the horrors of the Terror, and the glories of the Empire. "It is still here now," she said, "as peaceful and as calm as ever."

"Elegant," but "informal" are the words that occur to me. The lodgings are all very pleasant, furnished with very comfortable chateau furniture with many oils and water colors. The dining room overlooks the park and in warm weather meals are taken outside.

Of particular interest to me was a corner room on the main floor with a collection of local crafts: scarves, handkerchiefs, dolls, jewelry, and similar items all presented in a most attractive way.

The two tennis courts were in use while I was there, and the pool had some midday swimmers. It was carefully explained to me that unlike St. Tropez, 80 kilometers to the east, there are separate sunning areas for both ladies and gentlemen in this chateau.

The Domaine de Chateauneuf indeed is quiet and tranquil. It is the south of France the way I hoped to find it.

RELAIS CHATEAU 93, DOMAINE de CHATEAUNEUF, 83860 Nans-les-Pins; Tel. (94) 78.90.06. A 29-room comfortable but simple 18th century manor house with its own beautiful park. 150 km. west of Cannes and 45 km. east of Marseille. Breakfast, lunch, and dinner. Swimming pool and tennis courts on grounds. Horseback riding, golf, fishing, and other recreation nearby. Closed Nov. 3 to Apr. 30. Rates: 115-200 Fr. M. Jacques Malet, Innkeeper.

Directions: Michelin sect. map 84. Exit Autoroute A8 at St. Maximin. Follow N560 south and watch for D80 which leads to village of Nans-les-Pins.

HOSTELLERIE le BAOU, Ramatuelle (St. Tropez)

St. Tropez is one of the glamour places on the Cote d'Azur. This small inn located on the slopes of the hill overlooking the village of Ramatuelle is just a few kilometers from the city of St. Tropez, but well away from the crowds.

Each of the lodging rooms has a terrace with a panoramic view of the valley with the sea in the distance. The open-air restaurant of the inn also shares this striking view.

Pampelonne, one of the famous beaches on St. Tropez, is very close by.

RELAIS CHATEAU 94, HOSTELLERIE le BAOU, 83350 Ramatuelle (St. Tropez); Tel. (94) 79.20.48. A 16-room comfortable but simple hotel a short distance from St. Tropez and the beaches. This section along the Mediterranean is about 100 km. from Nice. Breakfast, lunch, and dinner. Golf, swimming, beaches, horseback riding, and other seaside recreation within a short distance. Closed mid-October to Mar. 10. Rates: 148-246 Fr. M. and Mme. Tydgat, Innkeepers.

Directions: Michelin sect. map 84. Exit Autoroute A8 at sign for Draguignan-St. Maxime. Follow D25 south to St. Maxime, turn left on N98 and then refer to Michelin map 84, locate Ramatuelle approximately in the middle of Cap de St. Tropez.

LA BASTIDE de TOURTOUR, Salernes

For postal purposes this castle-hotel is located in Salernes, which is one of the villages near the larger city of Draguignan. As far as I am concerned, it is located in the extremely scenic village of Tourtour, which, I learned, is pronounced "too-too" (the "r" being silent).

La Bastide de Tourtour is situated in one of the most picturesque and attractive landscapes in Provence . . . on a promontory almost 2000 feet above sea level with a very impressive view of the countryside. The inn sits in the middle of a great pine forest.

While sitting at the pool I learned just how convenient it is to all the scenic attractions in this section of Provence. I struck up an acquaintance with a couple from Atlanta, Georgia, who came for two days and were now extending their stay for a week. "I can't imagine a better place to enjoy the south of France," was one of the most frequently repeated phrases. "It's only about an hour and a half to Cannes, Nice, and St. Tropez, and we took a day trip to the Verdon Gorges and went over to Monte Carlo. We stopped and had lunch at the Chevre d'Or. I hope you will go there." (I did.)

This inn is in a most imposing restored castle whose austere beige-colored walls and towers of native stone belie the luxurious interiors. The heavy stone arches and beamed ceilings in the reception hall, living and dining rooms have all been gracefully accented with golden upholstery and draperies. It is a memorable scene, particularly in the evening when candles are lit on every table.

It is obvious that the owners and innkeepers, M. and Mme. Laurent have taken a personal pride in the lodging rooms, all of which are furnished most luxuriously. Many of them have their own balconies with a panoramic view that stretches for over 100 kilometers.

My friends from Georgia were most enthusiastic about the food, emphasizing the fact that they had already had three dinners, each with a different specialty. "We like to drive around in the daytime and get a lunch of bread and cheese," they said, "but it is such a joy to return here in the late afternoon, go for a swim and then rest until dinnertime. I hope you won't tell too many people about it."

RELAIS CHATEAU 91, LA BASTIDE de TOURTOUR, 83690 Tour-tour; Tel. (94) 70.57.30. A 26-room very comfortable restored castle in the high hills of Var, (Provence), 100 km. from Nice. Breakfast, lunch, and dinner. Swimming pool and tennis courts on grounds. Beautiful walks, back roads, and gorgeous views nearby. Closed October 3 to April 28. Rates: 140-275 Fr. M. and Mme. Laurent, Innkeepers.

Directions: Michelin sect. map 84. From Draguignan follow D49 (spectacular road) to Ampus. Turn left on the road to St. Pierre de Tourtour and Tourtour. Alternate road is D557 out of Dra-guignan to a point outside of Villecroze. Turn right on D51 to Tourtour.

The Marketplace at Draguignan

It was ten o'clock in the morning and the entire plaza at Draguignan was now the weekly farmers' market. Earlier in the day the farm trucks had chugged into the square with loads of carrots, cauliflower, potatoes, beans, enormous green peppers, artichokes, bananas, oranges, strawberries, eggplants, pineapples, and dozens of fresh fruit and vegetables. Stalls and tables appeared almost miraculously, offering cheeses in every flavor and style, poultry, meats, fish, flowers, pastries, and even pet hamsters and rabbits.

It was a gorgeous sunny day and to protect the tables, canopies and umbrellas were quickly put up. Some musicians were holding forth in one corner.

I bought a sweet roll in the bakery and some milk in the butcher shop and sat down on the bench to enjoy the scene. A little French girl in a beautiful blue dress that matched her eyes, came and sat down next to me and solemnly offered me a bite of her delicious chocolate ice cream cone. It was too much to resist, chocolate has always been my favorite.

Throughout my journey in France, I kept thinking about that great Bill Maudlin cartoon showing the American G.I.'s, "Willie and Joe," in the French town surrounded by children. Joe is saying to Willie, "And the amazing part is that they all speak French!"

CHATEAU de TRIGANCE, Trigance

It distresses me to realize that a great many people are going to visit Provence, the Cote d'Azur and the Riviera and not find their way to these magnificent mountains and the truly breathtaking beauty of the Verdon Gorges. A day-trip from Cannes or Nice would be enhanced by a stop at Trigance for lunch.

Not that Chateau de Trigance is undiscovered. Far from it. In looking at the guest list I found that a great many well-known people from all over the world had apparently studied the road maps and found their way to this wild, wonderful country and its 11th-century fortress-castle.

First of all, there is the walk up the steps. The castle was built on the top of the hill to prevent besiegers from reaching it and there is no way of avoiding the climb. However, once reaching the battlements at the top, the feeling of exhilaration is so great that the ascent is soon forgotten. Here I was surrounded by a ring of mountains and I could just imagine what dramas had been enacted on this site for a thousand years.

There are only eight lodging rooms in this fortress; however, all of the conveniences have been added and everything is very comfortable. The main dining room is carved out of the rock, and the atmosphere is definitely medieval.

This is one of the few places I visited where no one spoke English and I had to rely entirely on my sketchy French. I did ascertain that the owners, M. and Mme. Thomas, restored this chateau, which was practically in ruins, and I could imagine that it took years of work, dedication, and lots of money to bring it to this point, beyond even its former splendor.

The day I lunched there, Trigance was being used as a stop for an auto rally. All the drivers had assembled on the terrace and there was much Gallic enthusiasm and arm waving. M. Thomas was cordial, but busy and he gave me carte blanche to walk about the entire castle.

It was during these meanderings that I came upon something that still raises the hair on the back of my head. I walked through the back of the dining room and down some stone steps into a very dark and somewhat gloomy tower. Seeing the sunlight filtering through a narrow window, I stepped into a room, and there in front of me was a woman with grey hair dressed in medieval costume. A very fierce-looking man was standing next to her. They looked so real I was frightened. Then I laughed as I realized they were only papier mache figures.

M. Thomas explained that there was a story connected with them, something to do with a wayward daughter, but I must say that my French was entirely inadequate to understand the details. "It's here for our guests' amusement," he said.

I had to leave in the middle of the afternoon, but I had seen enough to convince me that Chateau Trigance was near the top of my list of places that I wanted to be sure to revisit.

RELAIS CHATEAU 92, TRIGANCE, 83840 Trigance; Tel. (94) 76.91.18. An 8-room comfortable but simple inn located in an ancient 11th century castle near the entrance to the Verdon Gorges. Breakfast, lunch, and dinner. Closed Nov. to Easter. Rates: 72-135 Fr. M. and Mme. Thomas, Innkeepers.

Directions: Michelin sect. map 84. This will take some persistence but it is well worth it. Locate Draguignan on Michelin map #84. Follow D955 north through Montferrat, through the military reservation, north to Riblaquon. Trigance is about 4 km. to the northeast on D90. This is about 10 km. from the Verdon Gorges. Leaving the car in the parking space, carry a minimum amount of luggage and walk the 175 steps up the side of the precipice and along the path to the Reception.

Les Gorges du Verdon

As incredible as it seemed, just a few hours earlier I had been sunning myself on a Riviera beach under a blue Mediterranean sky. Now I was standing on the rim of a high cliff looking down into the depth of the Verdon Gorges in the northern part of Provence. This is an area of absolutely breathtaking views, with bridges soaring over the deep chasms, and villages so precariously perched on the top of rocky precipices that they seem almost ready to topple over into oblivion.

This is a place where even the widest-angle lens does not capture the photograph. The road leads through several tunnels plunging down next to the river and then twisting up treacherously, clinging to the sides of the cliff to the very top of the rim. It reminded me of the volcanic crater on the island of La Palma in the Canary Islands.

HOTEL LE CAGNARD, Cagnes

Talk to anyone who has been to Le Cagnard and invariably they will roll their eyes to heaven and say "Unbelievable." Looking back on it I am not sure that it ever happened. Le Cagnard is part of a medieval fortress called Haut de Cagnes, which overlooks the city of Cagnes and a considerable expanse of the Mediterranean. Viewed from a distance the permutations of towers, bridges, walls, and crenelated battlements exist in a bluish, purplish haze. The amazing thing is that inside this walled promontory are churches, nightclubs, restaurants, art galleries, jazz clubs, hundreds of apartments, an outdoor park, narrow streets in which it is very easy to get lost, hundreds of steps (all of which seem to go up), and a definite shortage of parking spaces.

The hotel is perched precariously, but safely, on the outer walls. My room was on the very top of one of the towers, and its somewhat monastic air was relieved by a white ceiling, blue walls, reproductions of Van Gogh, and red furniture with blue flowers. My casement windows had a glorious view looking down into the town and out across the sea. I sat cross-legged in this window watching early-morning Cagnes come to life.

The dining room looks as if it has been carved right out of the mountain with a vaulted ceiling and a small balcony; when the long Riviera twilight descends and the candles are lit it is indeed very romantic. The specialties on the menu are carre d'Agneaux aux herbes de Provence, and Daurade flambee au pastis. They also serve an impressive bouillabaisse.

Off the dining room there is an absolutely glorious little balcony decorated with geraniums which I shared with several other guests who fell into two categories—people who were visiting for the first time, whose conversation was based on their adventures in locating Le Cagnard, and those blase many-timers who by now knew their way around and had their favorite little shops and small streets. It is very popular with Americans. We all agreed that if you liked it, you liked it a lot.

RELAIS CHATEAU 98, HOTEL LE CAGNARD, 06800 Cagnes-sur-Mer; Tel. (93) 20.73.21. A 14-room comfortable but simple inn located in a castle high above the town of Cagnes-sur-Mer in the Alpes-Maritimes. It is situated about midway between Cannes and Nice. Breakfast, lunch, and dinner served daily. Within a short drive of the Riviera beaches. Closed from Nov. 1 to mid-December. Rates: 130-190 Fr. M. Barel, Innkeeper.

Directions: Michelin sect. map 84. From Autoroute A8 (the main road to Cannes and Nice) use Cagnes Sortie, (exit). Bear to the right at sign for Cagnes-Vence. Do not take the first left that goes up the hill, nor the road to left marked Grasse, but continue on to a roundabout (traffic circle) and follow the road to Vence. This leads through the town of Cagnes. The key word is "Haut de Cagnes." Start looking for this sign on the right when the road to Vence leads up a hill. Turn right and follow a twisting road to the top. There are a few signs for the hotel. Take road as far as you can and walk the rest of the way to the Reception. I had a comically exasperating time locating this place.

LE CHATEAU du DOMAINE ST-MARTIN, Vence

It was a beautiful warm day on the French Riviera. I had taken the road from Cagnes to Vence and following the signs to Coursegoules, could see the Chateau St-Martin high in the hills above me. It looked most impressive. The road wound upward and I found myself at the entrance, which was the well-restored ruins of an ancient drawbridge, now permanently open.

Even before the construction of the drawbridge and original castle by the Knights Templars after their return from the Crusades in the 12th century, St-Martin already had a history, since it was named for a Bishop of Tours and an evangelist to the Gauls who had lived here as early as A.D. 350.

I walked through the courtyard and through the doors

115

leading into the entryway. Inside I found an elegant formal atmosphere with many tapestries, arched windows, rich-looking furniture and many oils and prints. There were several guests enjoying luncheon in the dining room and on the balcony, which had an awesome view from its 1500-foot elevation.

When Harry Truman visited about 20 years ago, he told the owners that they really needed a swimming pool, so they built one and called it the Truman Swimming Pool. There are tennis courts on the estate and the golf course is not far away.

In the main building of the Chateau St-Martin are 17 *très élégantes* bedrooms, most of them reached by climbing the richly carved marble staircase to the second floor. Many of them have views of the town, countryside, and the Mediterranean from their balconies. There are additional lodgings in small, individual Provencal country houses on the estate.

The atmosphere was extraordinarily light, peaceful, and quiet. Fresh summer nights and sunny days make it ideal for a tranquil vacation experience. It is just fifteen minutes from the Mediterranean, and within a very short drive of the old medieval town of Vence with its art gallery with works by Dufy, Carzou, and Chagall. The Matisse Chapel in Vence is world-famous.

In reading the brochure about the Chateau St-Martin

(which incidentally has a four-star luxury category), as nearly as I am able to understand, all of the rates include both breakfast and dinner with no exceptions. It might be well to double-check this while making reservations.

RELAIS CHATEAU 100, LE CHATEAU du DOMAINE ST-MARTIN, 06140 Vence; Tel. (93) 58.02.02. A 28-room exceptionally comfortable hotel with first class service on the heights overlooking Vence and the Riviera in the Alpes-Maritimes. Breakfast, lunch, dinner. Swimming pool and tennis courts on grounds. Golf course a short distance. 30 kms. from Cannes, and 16 kms. from Nice. Short distance from Matisse Chapel in Vence. Closed December and January. Rates: 300-480 Fr. Mlle. Andree Brunet, Innkeeper.

Directions: Michelin section map 84. Follow the road D36 from Cagnes to Vence. In Vence look for signs to Coursegoules and then Chateau St-Martin.

CHATEAU de la CHEVRE d'OR, Eze Village

"This may be the most beautiful view on the Cote d'Azur." It was twilight. Three of us were seated on the patio of Chevre d'Or quietly absorbing the delicate shadings of color as daylight turned to darkness overlooking the Mediterranean. These sentiments were expressed by Judy who, with her husband Alvin, had been traveling up the Italian Riviera into France visiting several attractive hotels en route. "Perhaps it is the night, the company, and our beautiful day all coming together, but I have never seen anything like this before and probably never will again." We all nodded in silent agreement.

Chevre d'Or is located at the top of the highest point of Eze Village which can be seen from some distance away traveling up the Moyenne Corniche. It is, according to the Michelin Green Guide for the French Riviera, "A prime example of a perched village clinging like an eagle's nest to a rock spike towering 1550 feet overlooking the sea." Caution. There are two communities named Eze. One is Eze Mer which is on the edge of the Mediterranean Sea, and the other is Eze Village which is some distance above. Artists and craftsmen have set up stalls and shops in the village and I purchased a very handsome watercolor of Eze.

The innkeeper is Monsieur Bruno Ingold, a sophisticated,

cordial Swiss gentleman. His staff is headed by the headwaiter, Claude, who works deftly from table to table preparing the many French specialties, overseeing the service, and conversing expertly in many different languages.

The few lodging rooms are in a romantic style and, incredible as it may seem, innkeeper Ingold has created a very small swimming pool on the tiny terrace. It is most welcome for a quick plunge during the sunny season.

La Chevre d'Or is always booked considerably in advance for July and August, but between the 20th of August and the 10th of October it might be possible to call the day before and reserve a room. This is an excellent time to be on the Riviera, the sun is still high, the water is still warm, and most important, the crowds are far thinner.

While we were talking, night had fallen completely and the deep blackness was punctuated by the pearl-like pinpoints of moving lights as cars traversed the roadway below. It is all really much beyond my meager powers of description.

RELAIS CHATEAU 101, CHATEAU de la CHEVRE d'OR, 06360 Eze Village; Tel. (93) 41.12.12. A 9-room very comfortable inn clinging by its fingernails to the cliffs high over the Mediter-

ranean, about 12 km. from Nice. Breakfast, lunch, and dinner. Small swimming pool on grounds. Tennis nearby. This is an excellent place to stay (as are all of the others in this section of France), to enjoy the recreation on the Riviera. Closed November to March. Rates: 180-230 Fr. Bruno Ingold, Innkeeper.

Directions: Michelin Sectional Map 84. Eze Village is located on the Moyenne (Middle) Corniche (N7). After reaching Eze Village turn right at the first road after the bus park at a sign that says "Tourist Information." Follow this road to the parking area for the village. Lock your car, don't take your bags, walk up the ancient stone steps through an alley to a sign with a goat's head on it. Bear left through a narrow ancient street that winds around the outside and persist until you reach the front door of the inn. They will send someone back for your bags and tell you how to solve the parking problem.

HOTEL LE VISTAERO, Roquebrune (Cap-Martin overlooking Monte Carlo).

I was on the terrace of the Hotel Vistaero, 1200 feet above the sea enjoying a perfect bird's-eye view of the Principality of Monaco stretched out below me with its high-rise buildings, condominiums, hotels, parks, tennis courts, and marinas. To the east was the arc of the Italian Riviera which extends to Genoa and beyond. It was hard to tear myself away from the view and my ruminations, but the waiter had arrived with a large glass of orange juice and I turned my attention to Vistaero, itself.

The architecture of this hotel is described in the folder as "avant garde." This is accounted for by the fact that it was built fairly recently. The rooms are all furnished individually with a great deal of decorator expertise. Most of them have views of the sea and many have their own balconies. It would be heavenly to have breakfast in your room overlooking the palace of Princess Grace and the expanse of the sea.

It must have been an outstanding engineering feat, not only to build this hotel which is perched on a precipitous cliff, but also to construct the swimming pool which has been carved literally out of the rock.

I spent the afternoon in Monte Carlo looking at the girls on the beaches (properly clothed) and visiting a few hotels. It happened to be a Monday which is one of the best times, because the shops are closed and there are fewer people about.

Monaco, itself, has very pleasantly laid-out parks and beaches, but it is extremely difficult to find a place to park.

Among other places, I visited a few hotels, but did not find anything quite small enough to suit my taste and concluded that Vistaero is just perfect for people who might enjoy the Monte Carlo diversions (which are many), and at the same time welcome the opportunity to be separated from its traffic and crowds.

Vistaero is booked solidly during July and August, the high season times on the Riviera, but the month of June and between September 1st and mid-October, while not as *chic*, would be excellent times to visit.

RELAIS CHATEAU 102, LE VISTAERO, 06190 Roquebrune Cap Martin; Tel. (93) 35.01.50. A 30-room exceptionally comfortable modern hotel with first class service perched on the heights overlooking the Principality of Monaco. 26 km. from Nice. Breakfast, lunch, and dinner. Swimming pool on grounds. Tennis courts and other Riviera recreation just a few moments away. Rates: 250-330 Fr. M. Robert Escach, Innkeeper.

Directions: Michelin sect. map 84. Follow N-7 from Nice through Eze (Moyenne Corniche) and just outside of Eze take the road to the left marked Grande Corniche, continue straight on and the hotel is located at the junction of the road which leads down into Monaco.

More on Cars and Driving in France

Foreigners staying temporarily in France may purchase a new French or foreign car, free of tax, payable in foreign currency; second-hand cars of foreign manufacturers also benefit from this exemption. Valid for one year, this concession allows a car to remain six consecutive months in France. For cars exempt from tax, there is a special "TT plate" and a special registration number. Buyers entitled to this tax exemption must have a permanent residence outside Europe.

It is a French rule of the road that drivers who have been in possession of their license for less than one year must not exceed a speed of 90 kilometers per hour. There are quite likely to be many pedestrians in France, so extra care should be taken and speed reduced at crossings, bends, and on the brows of hills.

Apparently George Gershwin was enchanted by the sounds

of the horns of French taxicabs as illustrated in American in Paris, however, today in Paris and many other French towns, horns must never be used except in emergencies. Dipped headlights are used at night. One last word: according to the book on driving in France, "it is forbidden to dazzle other drivers."

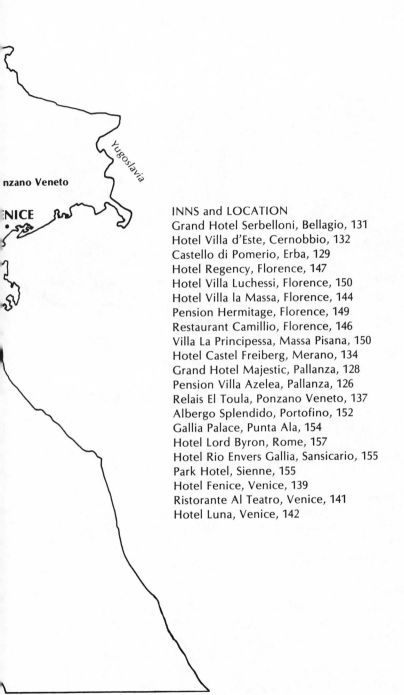

nzano Veneto

NICE

Yugoslavia

TRAVEL SUGGESTIONS FOR ITALY

How to Get There
Alitalia Airlines provides excellent service to Rome and Milan from the U.S. Your Eurailpass is good in Italy.

Country Inns in Italy
In addition to visiting a few of the so-called "Grand Hotels" while in Italy, I found country inn hospitality in villas, country houses, and ancient castles. However, in only a small number did the proprietors actually become involved with the guests.

Reservations
More than half of the inns I visited in Italy belong to the Relais de Campagne Chateaux-Hotels. For full reservation information see "Travel Suggestions for France."

Reservations at other than Relais Chateaux may be made directly or through toll-free New York booking offices as indicated in the final fact paragraph for each inn.

Dining in Italy

Italy has more regional cooking than any other country I visited in Europe. On the coast the specialties are fish and seafood; in the Alpine section it is cornmeal for polenta; farther south, it is rice; and in southern Italy, flour is the base for a great many dishes. Some areas of Italy have extensive grazing lands, so that beef becomes one of the main dishes; however, where there is less pasture, pork and lamb are seen more frequently on the menu.

Italy is a place where individualism plays a great role and this individuality expresses itself most vividly in the preparation of pasta. With all due respect to several Italian-American restaurants I have visited, I never really tasted pasta until I got to Italy. For one thing, it is not a whole meal, it is one course, part of a carefully orchestrated meal. Pasta is the term applied to many different types of flour-based products such as macaroni, spaghetti, noodles, and ravioli, and comes in all shapes, forms, sizes, and names in various regions of Italy. I am sure that every Italian restaurant worth the name serves homemade pasta in all of its many permutations. The sauces alone would fill a cookbook.

As in every country I visited, in all types of food-serving establishments—the ristorante, the albergo, the trattoria, and, of course, the pizzeria—I was assisted by a collection of good-humored headwaiters, waiters, bartenders, and also other patrons. After all, isn't it true that there is a little Italian in all of us?

Car Rentals

Alitalia has many Fly-Drive Plans that include automobiles. Travelers for whom Italy is part of a Continent-wide itinerary should see the section near the front of this book, "Renting a Car for Europe."

Driving Tips

First and most important, gasoline stations in Italy close at 12 noon and open about 3 p.m. Special coins are needed to use the pay telephones.

For information about driving in Rome, see the directions for reaching the Lord Byron Hotel, Rome. The international road signs are described in the Michelin Green Guide for Italy.

My Itinerary in Italy

After a most comfortable Alitalia 747 flight from New York, my trip began north of Milan in the Italian lake district, continued on to the Italian Alps, and thence south to Venice. From there, following in order: Florence, Pisa, Portofino, Grossetto, Sienne, and Rome. To obtain road maps and guides for Italy see the section at the back of the book.

VILLA AZALEA, Pallanza, Lake Maggiore

Enrico Leccardi and his mother are the innkeepers at this exceptionally warm and comfortable inn a short distance from Lake Maggiore in Pallanza. Enrico is an Alitalia steward and, when he is not flying to far-off places, he is the host at Villa Azalea. His mother does all the cooking and her ravioli and fresh pasta that I sampled would make an Italian out of anyone.

The building is most unusual. It sits on the top of a hill in a little forest overlooking an almost perfect park with orange, lemon trees, sequoia trees which were in blossom when I was there, as well as evergreens and palms. There are flowers, shrubs, and bushes in great profusion. It has a wedding cake feeling and the top story is really an oversized cupola which reminded me of the Mainstay in Cape May, New Jersey.

126

There is also a stately mansion in the park, a short distance away, which Enrico and his mother are slowly renovating and refurbishing to provide additional rooms. This is a much more formal building and some of the interior designs, fireplaces, paneled walls, and decorated ceilings are most impressive.

My visit started in the afternoon and continued well into the evening. At dinner I met some very friendly students who were attending college in Pallanza and were quite happy to practice their English. After dinner Enrico turned on the outside illumination which dramatically emphasizes the fountain in the middle of the terrace. All of the bedrooms have very delightful vistas. Enrico explained that July and August are almost always completely booked in advance and anyone desiring a room should make a reservation as early as possible. In May, June, September, and October, a room can usually be obtained without a reservation. As he said, "You can even call the day before."

PENSIONE VILLA AZALEA, 28048 Verbania, Pallanza; Tel. 0323/ 43.575. An 11-room modest inn in the middle of a beautiful park about five minutes from downtown Pallanza. Italian lake country recreation available within a few moments' drive. Breakfast, lunch, and dinner. Closed end of October to Easter. Rates: From 8500-10,000 lire. Famiglia Leccardi, Innkeeper.

Directions: Look for signs for Pension Villa Azalea in downtown Pallanza.

Pallanza

For hundreds of years, indeed thousands, the lakes of northern Italy have meant a mild climate, natural beauty, and peaceful surroundings. They have a romantic, poetic aura. Poets, musicians, and painters like Dante, Stendhal, Manzoni, Ruskin, Toscanini, and Hemingway among many others, found respite and inspiration there.

The Italian lakes have become synonymous not only with mild climate, beauty, and quiet, but with a rich variety of attractions such as swimming, boating, sports, excursions, cultural and social life, folklore, and outstanding cuisine. The traditional boats, with their white awnings, are in themselves symbolic of some of the unchanging customs. The picturesque watercolor effects of the fishermen's villages are much the same as they were in the last century, and the lakes themselves,

bordered by mountains, parks, and vineyards, are always beckoning the visitor to return.

Let us stop for a moment here and say the word "Maggiore"
several times. It is pronounced with a soft "g" and the "a" is
pronounced "ah." Just the sound of the word is soothing and
relaxing and Lake Maggiore is all of that and much, much more.
Say it again: Maggiore . . . Maggiore.

GRAND HOTEL MAJESTIC, Pallanza, Lake Maggiore

I'm not sure what makes a Grand Hotel "grand," but the
Majestic is grand in every possible definition of the word. The
building reminds me of the old John Wanamaker store because
it is built around a hollow square. There are inner galleries
around all four sides at each level and it is possible to look
right down into the reception area below. Everything is massive
and the stairways have broad stone steps with somewhat
faded carpeting.

The terrace which leads off the main drawing room has a
magnificent view of the lake, and people sit for hours watching
the little steamers ply back and forth between Pallanza and the
many islands. The gardens also are right next to the lake,
adjacent to the tennis courts and indoor swimming pool.
Bedrooms are in the size and style that were popular over 100
years ago when the hotel was built; mine was large enough to
accommodate a basketball practice session. Many of them have
a very commanding view of Lake Maggiore.

The Majestic is always filled during the high summer season,
sometimes with guests who stay many weeks. The Majestic
celebrated its 100th year in 1970, and has been host to dozens
of great figures of note in the world of nobility and the arts.
Among the guest both past and present are Sir Laurence Olivier,
the King and Queen of Italy, the Duchess of Genoa, the entire
German imperial family, several Indian princes and maharajahs,
and many other personalities reflecting the colorful canvas of
elegance and splendor which marked the end of the 19th
century.

Even the most pretentious of hotels in North America do not
approximate that particular European style and air of elegance.
True, the Majestic is fading a little here and there, but like
a few others I would see, they remain as symbols of super
hospitality that is slowly disappearing.

GRAND HOTEL MAJESTIC, 28048 Verbania Pallanza; Tel. 0323/ 42453. A 100-year-old sumptuously luxurious hotel overlooking Lake Maggiore. Breakfast, lunch, and dinner. Large park directly on lakeside with private beach, dock for boats, covered heated swimming pool. Tennis and golf nearby. Closed from early October through April. Rates: 20,000-34,000 lire. (U.S. reservations can be made through Jane Condon, New York, hotel representatives, (1) 800-223-5608.)

Directions: The Italian lake district including Lakes Maggiore, Como, and others too numerous to mention are north of Milano. The Hotel Majestic is on the main street of Pallanza on Rte. 33.

CASTELLO di POMERIO, Erba (Lake Como)

My tower bedroom at the Castello di Pomerio was in the oldest part of the castle dating back to the 13th century. One of the windows was very narrow, just large enough to provide a view of the countryside but presenting a very small target for arrows or musket balls by any besiegers. However, a large window overlooked a neighboring villa, and lakes and mountains in the distance. The rough stone walls were partially covered with tapestries and there was a heavy table and chair next to the fireplace to complete the medieval atmosphere. The plumbing, however, was not medieval.

This castle-inn is built around a central courtyard, paved in small stones, in which there are two beautiful mulberry trees. There are wooden balconies around three sides of the square and the stone walls and red-tiled roofs create a quiet, tranquil place, quite unlike anything I had thus far found in Italy. There are flowers everywhere, both indoors and out.

The dining room had very high wooden ceilings supported by heavy beams which contrasted remarkably with the stone walls. There was a large table with a great collection of salads and cheeses and desserts. I saw fresh strawberries, blueberries, grapes, and all kinds of confections.

Restoring and refurbishing this castle has been the work of its owner Madame Lita Donati. As she explained to me: "We have greatly emphasized the necessity for reproducing the naturalness of the past six or seven centuries. Where new windows and walls had to be created we've tried to maintain the graceful arches of the old. We uncovered some absolutely magnificent frescoes in the main dining room hall which had been hidden for many years. This is one of five ancient castles in this vicinity all connected by tunnels."

Our conversation turned to accommodating today's sophisticated travelers: "I think people enjoy staying here very much," she said. "Because this is one of the oldest castles in northern Italy and because we have added some of the recreational facilities that travelers have come to expect. There is a swimming pool, two sponge-surface tennis courts, an outdoor grill area, and a sauna.

"Many of our guests stay here for quite a few days and travel by car to all of the points of interest and beauty in the lake district. We are just a few moments, literally, from the shores of Lake Como."

In the main lounge there was some electronic equipment indicating that although this may be an old castle, there was very modern entertainment. That night, a young man played classical selections on the piano with great fervor and sincerity.

Madame Donati was kind enough to take me to visit the Museum of Ancient History which is located in the nearby village of Erba. Even in that brief tour, I was able to understand more fully, perhaps, the succession of prehistoric eras which have traced the progress of European man.

RELAIS CHATEAU 231, CASTELLO di POMERIO, 22036 Erba, Como; Tel. (031) 611516. A 30-room restored ancient castle with modern conveniences in the middle of the Lake Como district. Breakfast, lunch, and dinner. Swimming pool, tennis courts, sauna on grounds. Golf, horseback riding, touring Lake country all nearby. Open all year. Rates: 20,000-30,000 lire. Mme. Lita Donati, Innkeeper.

Directions: Erba is located on the road which runs from Como to Lecco. Look for sign for Castello di Pomerio on the north side of this road. It is well marked. Do not go into the town of Erba.

GRAND HOTEL VILLA SERBELLONI, Bellagio, (Lake Como)

"You must go to Bellagio, even in the rain, it is beautiful." Lita Donati at the Castello di Pomerio was insistent. "It is a beautiful, unspoiled village and you definitely should see Villa Serbelloni!"

Signora Donati was right. Bellagio *is* beautiful in the rain and the Villa Serbelloni belongs to another world in another century. It is situated in one of the most romantic settings imaginable, almost at the point where the two arms of Lake Como join. There is a sandy beach, swimming pool, and beautiful gardens, all adjacent to the lake. The drawing rooms, dining rooms, and lounges have marvelously painted frescoes and ceilings and an airy openness that is unexpected in a building constructed over 100 years ago.

I was told that Americans don't find their way to Bellagio very frequently, and that for many years it has been a favorite of the English. I am sure that Shelley and Byron walked these shores, and drew inspiration from the mountains, lake, and sky.

The Villa Serbelloni has been owned by Rudi Bucher and his family for many years. Although it was a busy day for him, he took a few moments to point out some of the more attractive aspects of both the hotel and the town. "There are many wonderful day-tours here in the Lake District," he said, "we suggest that our guests take the demi-pension which leaves them free to make the noontime meal optional. Most of the time they return in the middle of the afternoon to enjoy the tranquil view of the lake and the mountains and to walk in our gardens."

On beautiful Lake Como the Grand Hotel Villa Serbelloni is a leisurely look backwards into the 19th century.

GRAND HOTEL VILLA SERBELLONI, 22021 Bellagio, Lake Como; Tel. (031) 950.216. A 120-room luxury hotel, literally at the heart of Lake Como. Breakfast, lunch, and dinner. Heated swimming pool, private lake beach, tennis courts, boating, water skiing on grounds. Golf nearby. Open April 10 to October 10. Rates: as with all hotels of this nature in Europe there is a wide variety of rooms and eating plans. There are special reductions for children, rooms for servants and chauffeurs, rooms with a park view and a lake view. Cost for two people for one night in an average room including breakfast and dinner averages about 47,000 to 70,000 lire. Rudy Bucher, Innkeeper.

Directions: Lake Como is shaped like an inverted "Y." Bellagio is at the confluence of the two arms of the lake. It is also accessible from Varenna and Cabenabbia by ferry. About 1 hour from Milan.

GRAND HOTEL VILLA D'ESTE, Cernobbio (Lake Como)

Villa d'Este is one of the world's most famous hotels. With 160 rooms, I would not call it a country inn, but anyone who visits the Lake Como area should at least stop for lunch or dinner. This is exactly what I was doing when I met another American couple from Cleveland who were making their first return visit after spending their honeymoon at Villa d'Este 25 years ago. We were seated on the terrace overlooking the lake, and naturally I asked them if it had changed very much.

"We were worried about that," she said, "we thought perhaps it might have been 'modernized' as so many other things are, but it is almost exactly as we remembered it. We found our favorite spot in the gardens and we were actually able to have our old room again—the food is still exceptional. We are planning to come back for our fiftieth!"

Villa d'Este has a most intriguing and unusual history. It was built in 1568 by one of the wealthy families of Italy. In the 18th century it was renovated by a former La Scala ballerina who married an Italian nobleman. During this period, the gardens were perfected by an avenue of cypress trees bordering a cascade of fountains. This same lady made a second marriage to a young, handsome, Napoleonic general, and since she feared he might suffer from military nostalgia, she had a series of simulated fortresses and towers built on the slopes overlooking the

gardens where he and his friends could play war games. They are still here.

Unquestionably the most interesting chapter in the history of the Villa centers around Caroline of Brunswick-Wolfenbuttel, Princess of Wales and the future Queen of England. This unhappy lady discovered Lake Como in 1814 and devoted the next five years of her life to adorning and decorating it. All of this put a great strain on her resources and she returned to London in 1820 hopefully to take her place on the throne beside her husband, King George IV, but a scandalous divorce action filed against her by the King, was thought to have caused her to die broken-hearted in 1821.

In 1873, the estate became a luxury hotel providing hospitality for European nobility and wealthy guests from all over the world.

Today Villa d'Este is indeed a swinging place. The parade of Roll Royces has been augmented by rented Fiats and Renaults. Things are still done in the grand manner, but it is not stiff or formal. Every imaginable resort facility is available, and there is both a discotheque and a night club. It is very popular with Americans.

Caroline of Brunswick-Wolfenbuttel, wherever you are, your beloved Villa d'Este is in good hands.

RELAIS CHATEAU 230, GRAND HOTEL VILLA d'ESTE, 22010 Cernobbio, Lake Como; Tel. (031) 511.471. A 180-room exceptionally comfortable resort-inn with first-class service located on the western shores of Lake Como. This is a complete resort facility including indoor and outdoor swimming pools, private beach, motor boating, sailing, water skiing, surfing, tennis, golf, discotheque, and night club. Rates: 45,000-74,000 lire. Mario Arrigo, Innkeeper.

Directions: Cernobbio is just a few kms. north of the town of Como near the southern tip of the western arm of Lake Como.

This part of Italy is as much Austrian as it is Italian. When asking directions in the city of Merano, I had answers almost entirely in German. I stopped in two places to determine the location of Castel Freiberg; in one, a waitress took me outside and pointed in the general direction, and in the other, the proprietor took me to one of his guests who spoke English and who, in turn, made a marvelous map with extremely good directions. To double-check myself before heading up the mountain, I stopped once more and asked directions from a lady who was selling cold drinks in the street. Before I knew it we had drawn a crowd of people with helpful suggestions. Everyone was extremely friendly and cooperative.

HOTEL CASTEL FREIBERG, Merano (Fragsburg)

I was strolling around the walls and grounds of what was, for the moment, my own castle thrust high into the blue skies of northern Italy. Circling me on all sides was a ring of mountains, whiteclad sentinels announcing the first snowfall of the season. The view from this side was of rolling green upland meadows where a herd of cattle placidly grazed. I could hear the tinkling of the bells even at this distance. At the far end farmers were making the last hay crop of the season.

I left the crenelated battlements that might have protected the men-at-arms in earlier days, and passed a young gardener who had paused for his morning snack of round brown bread, some meat, and a bottle of wine. He was responsible for the gorgeous array of flowers that were sending forth their divine message.

Now, I came to a grassy terrace on which was located the outdoor swimming pool, tennis courts, and a few swings and slides for children. The view from here was of the city of Merano, and on this clear, fall day everything in the valley seemed to be miniaturized, and I felt almost as if I could step into space.

The interior of Castel Freiberg is rather formal with a series of drawing rooms, including a card room with color television, heavy castle-type furniture, and floors of mellowed terra cotta. The beige walls have been amply decorated with pieces of armor and other war-like reminders of earlier days. Everything is beautifully kept with great style and grace.

The castle dates back to the 14th century, and has an extensive history that includes several noble Italian families. As is the case with many European castles, it fell into disrepute and disrepair; rescued by the present proprietor in the 1960s, it was opened as a hotel in 1973.

Castle Freiberg is not a place where one meets the proprietor. The contact for everyone is the concierge who, in this case, is a very affable, smiling, well-informed person. He has everything to assist his guests in making the most out of a holiday in the Italian Alps, including maps, recommendations for lunch, and road reports.

I met no Americans among the other guests, but there were quite a few people from over the mountain in Austria and Germany. I am sure they felt quite at home in Merano and the vicinity, because this is still very much a part of Austria although it is within the boundaries of Italy.

*RELAIS CHATEAU 232, HOTEL CASTEL FREIBERG, 39012 Merano,
Tel. (0473) 44196. A 40-room very comfortable castle inn located
at 2400 ft. in the Italian Alps. Breakfast, lunch, and dinner.
Swimming pool, tennis courts on grounds. Fishing, horseback
riding, water skiing, mountain climbing nearby. Closed November through March. Rates: 24,000-43,000 lire. Signora Bortolotti,
Innkeeper.*

*Directions: Merano is located high in the Italian Alps a relatively
short distance from both Switzerland and Austria. First get
directions to the Scena (Schenna) section of the city. The inn is
located in a small community called Fragsburg. Once in Scena
look for the signs to Castel Freiberg or Fragsburg. Passing the
Hotel Angelica look for sign at a bridge on the right that says
Laberz. This will also have the hotel and Fragsburg signs. Turn
right over the bridge, head up the side of the mountains. There
are street lamps and the road is very twisty. To the right will be
the sensational view of Merano. If necessary, reassure yourself by
stopping at a small restaurant on the right-hand side of the road.
Persist, have faith, believe the signs. Once you have arrived at the
top of the mountain, ignore the parking lot and drive to the left
on a brick roadway which eventually will lead to the entrance.
Park car, leave bags, check with concierge who is amazingly
informed and I will leave everyone in his hands.*

A Day in the Italian Alps

*I was headed out of Merano in a northeasterly direction
toward Passo di Giovo. The clouds gathered at the tops of the
mountains, but the valley was quite sunny as the sun filtered
through. There were many apple orchards in full fruit and apple
sellers along the road.*

*The floor of the valley with its meadows and farms is as
appealing as the upland meadows and pastures with small
houses set high above. There are numerous single cable lifts
which valley farmers use to bring bales of hay down from the
upper pastures. The architecture is Italian Tyrol, which means
the top floors in the old houses are often wooden with white-
painted stone and plaster ground floors. Hundreds of flowerpots
suspended from the overhanging roofs splash their bright colors
against the beautiful, weathered wood and white walls. The
overhanging roofs provide shelter against rain and snow. Some
of the older houses have stones on the roofs.*

Here the cow is queen of all she surveys, as the road signs imply, and twice a day the traveler is apt to find cattle being driven across the main road. There is something about looking into the eyes of a Tyrolean brown cow that apprises one of the true order of things.

Now the road begins to hug the mountains with a series of linking S-turns, and there are many waterfalls coursing down from the very tops of the mountains like silver ribbons tracing their way among the various shades of green trees. Jagged mountains cut into the skyline with their saw teeth, while occasional old barns and houses cling to their sides. It is a countryside that is verdant and challenging, with massive vastness of gentle meads, rushing rivers, and thousands of shades of green with an occasional accent of red or beige.

It is a place where small kittens sit sunning themselves on stone walls and cattle placidly munch their way through the meadows—a place where waterfalls seem to emerge from the sides of the mountains; where barnyards have fat roosters and goats; where the wash is hung out in the sunshine and the wind; and where birds lift the hearts and spirits of all who hear their full-throated, joyous songs.

RELAIS EL TOULA, Ponzano Veneto (Treviso)

It was dinnertime at El Toula. My repast began with some very thinly-sliced ham and an excellent house paté, and was followed by a beef marrow placed on a bed of fresh sauteed tomatoes.

The third course was a delicious pasta in the form of a thin spaghetti cooked to a perfect degree of firmness and over which the waiter sprinkled freshly grated cheese. I found that in Italy there was nothing to compare with homemade pasta in any form.

Next came a small piece of beefsteak served with an unusual herb sauce and local endive. Dinner ended, or at least I thought it did, with a delectable creme bruleé—the second ending came in the form of a piece of local cake, which was like a very large Scotch shortbread cookie.

Almost on cue, the owner of El Toula, Alfredo Beltrame entered. "You have enjoyed dinner. Yes?" I responded in the same rhythm. "I have enjoyed dinner, yes!" Alfredo and I talked at length about the joys of Italian innkeeping and I learned that he was also a partner in a restaurant in Rome, as well as in some resort inns in Sardinia.

My room at this beautiful villa had two full-length windows with balconies overlooking the terrace and the fields in the rear. There was a small swimming pool which I was sure would be most welcome in the Venetian summer. The theme of the original villa was carried out with antique furniture and painted ceiling beams.

In the morning looking out of the windows towards the small forest, I saw many different colors of autumn leaves. The stunning red of the New England maples was missing, but otherwise it could have been the view from my bedroom at home in the Berkshires.

The entrance to El Toula is impressive. Turning off the main road, I drove for at least a kilometer between vineyards where the vines had been trained on an arch-like trellis over the road so that I was driving literally through a tunnel of grapes, which were being harvested at the time of my arrival. Alfredo informed me that these grapes supply the house wine.

Once inside a big gate, I found myself in a very large courtyard paved with small black and white stones. The main house was a Venetian villa, and in recent years had been flanked by new additions which stretched out on each side like large wings. There were flowers and plants everywhere, many in huge earthenware pots which were being watered by a very colorful-looking lady wearing a straw hat.

El Toula is less than an hour's ride from Venice. Many guests commute daily preferring the quiet of the countryside evenings to the somewhat hectic tourist-oriented pace of the city.

RELAIS CHATEAU 235, EL TOULA, 31050 Ponzano Veneto, Venice; Tel. 0422-96023. A 10-room exceptionally comfortable villa hotel with first-class service, located about 1 hr. north of Venice. Breakfast, lunch, dinner. Swimming pool on grounds. Open every day of the year. Rates: 30,000-50,000 lire. Dorino Sartor, Innkeeper.

Directions: Leave the Autostrada at Treviso Nord, turn right after toll gate and follow that road about 6 km. to Hwy. 13 at Pontebbana. Turn north to the 30 km. mark which is also the first traffic light. Turn left into Postioma Road. Relais El Toula is about 5 km. from traffic light.

HOTEL LA FENICE ET DES ARTISTES, Venice

I am indebted to Lynn and Charlie Henry, whom I met on the Rialto bridge, for referring this hotel to me and I think it was a great find. In fact, I might well term it the "Algonquin of Venice." For one thing, it is just around the corner from the Teatro el Fenice and the artists appearing there are quite likely to be booked at the hotel. I browsed through several guest registers with fascinating signed photographs and compliments from singers, actors, and conductors. Like the Algonquin, it has that artistic ambience.

La Fenice consists of two buildings — the old section which does not have a lift (there are bellmen to help with luggage) and a newer section with a lift. Both buildings are air-conditioned, and every room is furnished with great individuality in the "romantic style," and all have baths.

Because these are very old buildings, there are some interestingly shaped hallways and rooms, with views out of corners into hidden courtyards overlooking the canals. Seven rooms have their own terraces, and provide an ideal place to rest in the late sun after a lovely day in Venice.

I found it very easy to get information and assistance at the main desk here. The concierge, Mr. Saccoman, is at home in several languages and has a good sense of humor in many of them. The director, an imposing man with the equally imposing name of Dante Apollonio, says of La Fenice, "We have an atmosphere of intimacy. All of our guests become our friends."

Breakfast, the only meal served, is taken during clement weather in a secluded L-shaped garden, and at other times in a small dining room located between the two buildings. There are two restaurants just a few steps away, both of which are highly recommended.

As Dante Apollonio pointed out, "It is 385 steps to the Plaza San Marco, however, we are quite out of the way and very quiet."

HOTEL LA FENICE et des ARTISTES, 1936 San Marco, Venice; Tel. 26.403-32.333. A 75-room hotel of the second class, centrally located a short distance from the Plaza San Marco. Open all year. Rates: 35,000 lire for two including continental breakfast.

Directions: From Grand Canal Station at Parking Garage, take either water taxi or ferry to Pier #15 (taxi fare approx. $10, ferry cost 10¢ but do be certain to have a complete understanding with the water taxi driver as to cost in advance). Porters will be available at Pier 15 to carry luggage to hotel.

Twilight in the Plaza San Marco

Idling away the hours in the San Marco Plaza is a continuing preoccupation in Venice—the tables and chairs of the various cafes are filled from 10 a.m. until midnight. At noon, the orchestras appear in the cafes, and there ensues a battle of the bands with at least three different groups playing at the same time; however, the result isn't cacophony, since they are some distance from each other. The orchestra for my cafe struck up a medley, not of Vivaldi or Puccini, but of "Oklahoma," for which they received a smattering of applause. Shadows were getting long now, and the sun had dropped behind the palaces. Sweaters and coats were being put on and the sunny afternoon was changing into a fall twilight. The huge metal figures on top of one of the buildings have drawn back their hammers to let the world know that it is, indeed, five-thirty. A toddler from a nearby table climbs up on the chair next to mine and dips a finger into my hot chocolate—what a look of instant pleasure comes across his little face as he tastes this heavenly concoction.

The pigeons which enliven the Plaza by day have all but disappeared; maybe it's because the people selling corn have folded their little carts and traveled home for a Venetian dinner.

The first of the many artists have returned to the center of the Plaza to set up their easels and show their work once again, and the crowds at the cafe become more numerous as twilight deepens into evening. Now, a man selling yo yo's with lights in them comes strolling by, followed by the usual group of young people. At the far end of the Plaza, they are playing with Frisbees—but mostly the San Marco Plaza is people: people walking arm-in-arm, solitary strollers, people visiting for the first time, and others who know exactly where they are going.

Ah, San Marco! One day I shall return to the pigeons, to hear your beautiful music and watch your wonderful people.

RISTORANTE AL THEATRO, Venice

I had several recommendations for this restaurant which is just a short distance from the Hotel la Fenice. Lynn and Charlie Henry mentioned it first and their recommendation was backed-up by the concierge and director of the hotel. The word was that this restaurant, in addition to being a regular family-style Italian restaurant, also had some of the best pizza in Venice.

There were different types of dining rooms. I ate in one

where there were fish nets and other fishing gear hanging from the ceiling. Mounted securely on one wall was a Venetian gondola.

The headwaiter was very helpful. We settled on pizza with anchovies and a small salad. However, the rest of the extensive menu was most enticing. The dessert cart which is wheeled around in most Italian restaurants for everybody to "ooh" and "aah" over was particularly tempting.

There was also a more elegant dining room located on the top floor of the building. This is called La Mansard, which started out as a club, but is now open to anyone. It is richly appointed with beautiful furnishings and paneled walls; in one corner a pianist was playing Gershwin.

Here was an opportunity for me to see Italians in a totally unselfconscious atmosphere. There were several families with children and it was a very gay, happy, inviting place. I enjoyed not only an unusually good pizza with fresh mozzarella cheese, but also the fun of watching people at other tables having a good time.

RISTORANTE AL THEATRO, Campo S. Fantin 1917, Venice (located a few steps from La Fenice Hotel). Tel. (041) 37.214-21.052. A good restaurant in the middle price range located a short distance from the Plaza San Marco. No rooms available. Open every day.

HOTEL LUNA, Venice

The Hotel Luna has the advantage of being just a few steps from the San Marco Plaza, and the water taxi from the Plaza Roma stops right outside of the hotel. It is very convenient to everything in that section of Venice and seems to be quite popular with Americans and American tour groups. I had the opportunity at breakfast to talk with them and discuss first impressions of Venice with other enthusiastic Americans. We all agreed that the Plaza San Marco is "the place."

My single room with a bath on the fourth floor was very clean and the window overlooked the red-tiled roofs of Venice.

I had a rather interesting experience at the Luna, and I presume there is a lesson in it somewhere. When I arrived in the middle of the afternoon, I washed my socks so they would dry overnight. Since the sun was shining on my window, I hung them on the inside of the wooden shutters. Subsequently, leaning out the window, I accidentally brushed against my socks and they fell to the next balcony, where they landed very neatly on the railing. Meanwhile, I watched the plastic hanger plummet downward and eventually shatter into 1048 pieces on the street below. Immediately, everyone looked up and I popped my head inside the window. What to do? Almost simultaneously, the maid came in my room to turn down my bed for the night, and I took her to the window and pointed to the balcony below (using sign language) and asked her if she could retrieve my socks. She replied in kind that she could, and disappeared. About 2½ minutes later, one of the gentlemen from the main desk arrived with my socks in his hand saying, "Are these yours?" I had to confess. "Well, signor, do not in the future hang your socks in the window. Hang them in the bathroom, because the police came and we had to explain."

This was, for about thirty minutes, possibly the most embarrassing moment of my life. I'm just grateful that no one was struck in the head by the falling hanger, and that I got off with merely a reprimand from the gentleman at the desk.

HOTEL LUNA, 1243 San Marco, Venice; Tel. (041) 89840. A clean comfortable hotel about 50 steps from the San Marco Plaza. Water taxi comes to hotel door. Breakfast, lunch, and dinner served. Open year round. Rates: 25,000 to 54,000 lire (U.S. reservations can be made through Jane Condon, New York, (1) 800-223-5608).

Directions: Use either the ferry (10¢) or the water taxi ($10) from the Parking Garage to San Marco Plaza. Porters are available at the landing, if needed.

FLORENCE (FIRENZE)

Florence, like Rome and Venice, is one of the main cultural tourist attractions in Italy. Between visits to several small hotels and inns, I did manage to see the Duomo — the great cathedral in the city, as well as the famous doors on the Baptistry which were created by Ghiberti. I walked across the Ponte Vecchio, the bridge over the Arno, which is traditionally the center of the gold and silversmith shops, and also visited the truly inspirational Uffizi Museum.

For full details on everything in Florence, I recommend the Michelin Green Guide to Italy which has devoted 10 pages to Florence (see section on maps and guides in the back of the book).

HOTEL VILLA LA MASSA, Candeli Firenze (Florence)

It was a beautiful October Sunday morning at Villa La Massa on the Arno River just a few kilometers from Florence. Bells in the nearby village were joyfully peeling out the good news that church doors were open and everyone was invited to attend.

I was in the garden overlooking the river, watching a solitary fisherman who had three poles working at the same time. The Arno takes a bend at this point, so it was possible to look in both directions for some distance. The mist was rising from the water as the sun rose on a cloudless blue Florentine sky.

Florentine is indeed the mood, because the city is such a short distance away and all the artistic delights are readily available to Villa la Massa guests. The hotel has a mini-bus that goes in and out several times a day. On this particular morning there was a number of U.S. and European fashion buyers staying at the Villa to attend the yearly display of new Italian fashions in the city. Apparently this was a return visit for many of them and there were several reunions. Everyone was saying, "Why are we going to be spending the day inside when we could be staying here."

The main building of the Villa is built around an open three-story square, and the entry to the lodging rooms is from inside galleries that circle each floor. All of the rooms are furnished in a comfortable villa style.

Saturday night we all had a good time in the main dining room with a pianist who enticed dancers onto the floor with his repertoire of all the old and new songs. The menu was relatively simple with a reasonable number of choices in each category and the service was friendly and helpful.

I am sure that every guest staying at Villa la Massa is not only impressed with the beauty of the gardens and the tranquil atmosphere, but also with the extremely accommodating air of the staff. The pace for all of this is set by Mariella Garonetti, the general manager, an attractive woman with laughing eyes and a disposition to match. The concierge is one of the most affable that I encountered in Italy. Villa la Massa was one of the earliest members of the Relais de Campagne in Italy. Even before I arrived, many people said, "Oh, you will love Villa la Massa."

Love is part of the theme here. The very atmosphere inspires warmth and affection, and to illustrate the point, two people who were sitting in the garden enjoying the sunshine suddenly looked at each other, smiled and embraced. Ah, amore!

RELAIS CHATEAU 238, HOTEL VILLA la MASSA, 50010 Candeli, Florence; Tel. (055) 63.00.51. A 44-room very comfortable inn located in a 16th century villa on the banks of the Arno River, about 20 minutes from downtown Firenze (Florence). Breakfast, lunch, and dinner. Swimming pool on grounds; tennis, fishing, golfing, and horseback riding nearby. Open year round. Rates: 38,000-43,000 lire. M. et Mme. Bocchini, Innkeepers.

Directions: From Autostrada (A1) use Firenze Sud Exit and proceed through the village of Bagno a Ripoli. Follow signs for Candeli. At the river, still following signs, turn right on Via Villa Magna which is the principal way from Candeli to Florence, a distance of about 10 kms. Keep a careful eye out on the left-hand side of the road for Villa la Massa.

RESTAURANT TRATTORIA CAMMILLO, Florence

Frederick and Christine Boes from Dusseldorf were the two people I saw embracing in the gardens of Villa la Massa. We became acquainted and they suggested that I join them for dinner at the Trattoria Cammillo. "This is not a so-called 'exclusive' restaurant," said Frederick. "It is a place where Florentians enjoy a family meal."

We took a taxi to the center of the city, walked over the famous Ponte Vecchio Bridge and within a few moments were at the door.

The Trattoria Cammillo is not elegant in any sense of the word. Fortunate guests, (those *with* reservations), stand inside the front door and wait for a table to become available. The waiters deftly carry the trays over their heads and good-naturedly work around the anxiously waiting, hungry, expectant, would-be diners. "Don't let all this bother you," said Frederick, "believe me, it is well worth it."

Finally the owner informed us that our table was ready and we were unceremoniously seated and the fun of choosing from the menu began. From my chair I could look right into the kitchen where there were many shiny pots and pans and busy chefs exchanging bandinage.

Briefly, the evening at the Restaurant Cammillo was a great success. We all sampled each other's choices and pronounced them delicious. My opening course was spinach mixed with cheese and tomato sauce. For the main dish I had veal scallopini —thinly-sliced veal in a most marvelous sauce. Frederick had chicken breasts baked just right, topped with some cheese and basil.

Dinner moved on in what was now a leisurely pace as there were no more diners waiting. At the cheese course, I had Bel Paesa for the first time in Italy. It was a very delicate cheese, and I was to order it several times in the future. Another very good, inexpensive, local cheese is called Pecorina.

Dessert was baked pear, a house specialty. Other specialties on the menu were Scaloppine Capriccio, scampi with curry and wild rice, and Florentine tripe.

Frederick, Christine, and I resolved we would write a book on the small, little-heralded restaurants in Italy. It would take 1000 years and begin with Trattoria Cammillo.

RESTAURANT TRATTORIA CAMMILLO, Borgo S. Jacopo, 57, Florence; Tel. 21.24.27. This is an excellent, moderately-priced family restaurant. Not certain whether it is closed on any nights during the week. Telephone ahead for reservations and then be prepared to wait.

Directions: Trattoria Cammillo is located about two blocks from the Ponte Vecchio on the south side of the Arno River. It is a few squares from the Pitti Palace.

HOTEL REGENCY, Florence

Florence is a busy, bustling city . . . one of the great tourist objectives in Italy. Naturally, with this kind of reputation and with so much to see and enjoy, finding accommodations that are peaceful and quiet (and with a convenient place to park) can sometimes present a problem. The Regency answered all of these conditions.

The director is Arturo Secchi, a most accommodating and well-informed man with lovely Florentine manners that put me immediately at ease. "We used to be called the Umbria," he said, "but now we are the Regency. We have only 31 rooms, but all of them have a bath or shower, radio, air conditioning, and everyone enjoys the lovely private gardens between the two buildings."

There is a park in front of the Regency with dozens of beautiful sycamore trees and a place for children to play. It is in a very quiet section of Florence and provides quite a change from the busy downtown area.

My first impression, once inside the front door, was of hundreds of fresh flowers. They were placed everywhere—in the sitting rooms, lobby and in the dining rooms.

Arturo took me on a brief tour which included lodging rooms, most of which had high ceilings, harmonizing curtains and wallpaper; many overlooking the garden or the park.

Over lunch, he talked about the food on the Regency menu

which is "homemade and natural." One of the interesting house specialties is a T-bone steak which comes from the fat cattle in the Tuscan countryside.

The Regency is that quiet corner in Florence that many people will find delightful.

RELAIS CHATEAU 237, HOTEL REGENCY (formerly the Umbria), Piazza M. d'Azeglio 3, 50121 Florence; Tel. 587.655.602. A very quiet 31-room conservative hotel, conveniently located to all the Florentine museums and beautiful churches. Parking facilities. Breakfast, lunch, dinner. Rates: 37,000 lire includes Continental breakfast. Half pension and full pension rates available. Open all year. (New York Reservation tel. # 800-223-5581.) Arturo Secchi, Innkeeper.

Directions: Arriving by car in Florence, inquire for the Piazza D'Azeglio which is a small park. The Regency is about six squares from the Duomo.

Counterpoint on the Ponte Vecchio

In the middle of the bridge called Ponte Vecchio, which spans the Arno between the Pitti Palace and the Uffizi Gallery, there is a bronze bust of Benvenuto Cellini, who was the master craftsman of Florence.

Today, a few centuries after Cellini, the Ponte Vecchio is more than a bridge, it is actually the street of the gold sellers where, in addition to the shops, there are young people who spread out on blankets their designs and crafts in leather, silver, jewelry, ceramics, and paintings.

In the very middle of the bridge on a Sunday afternoon, a group of young people can be found singing to guitars and bongo drums. From time to time, their friends drop by and "sit in," singing the choruses softly after the main singer and guitar player have done a few verses.

The passersby also create a good show ... sightseers of all ages in all types of garb, conversing in many languages and accents . . . some of them, perhaps themselves Florentines, strolling in their Sunday best after the noontime meal ... young ladies in knee-high white boots and cotton dresses, and others wearing black cotton socks and black dresses . . . there are Germans and Scandinavians with long hair and blue jeans — sometimes it is impossible to tell the nationality.

I am not sure what Signor Cellini is thinking about all this. His bust faces the young people in the street, but his eyes seem to be raised to heaven. I think that's just perhaps an accident of design; I would like to think that Benvenuto appreciated this kind of a good time as well.

PENSION HERMITAGE, Florence

"The Hermitage is just like a private club." These are the words in which Jim Mellow of St. Louis described this unusual accommodation in the center of Florence. "You don't even realize you are in a small hotel."

His recommendation was backed up also by Malcolm Frager, my concert-pianist neighbor, who was also most glowing in his praise. Thank you, gentlemen.

The Hermitage is located literally a few steps from the Ponte Vecchio and is just around the corner from the Uffizi and Pitti Museums as well as the Duomo.

An elevator carries guests to one reception room on the fifth floor which also has the dining room with a rooftop view, and a living room with a very cozy fireplace. Just one flight above is a roof garden with many flowers, and even more inviting views of the town. Accommodations are in small but tidy rooms.

Dinner is a set meal each night in a most homelike atmosphere. During the summertime breakfast is served on the terrace.

149

High season at the Hermitage is from March to October and fortunate, indeed, are the guests who are able to obtain accommodations during this time.

PENSION HERMITAGE, 1, Vicolo Marzio (Ponte Vecchio) 50122 Florence; Tel. 28.72.16. A 16-room intimate inn in the heart of old Florence within walking distance of all of the main attractions. Breakfast, lunch, and dinner. Probably closed during November. High season is from March to October but anyone writing in advance will receive a room confirmation. Rates: Reasonable.

Directions: The Hermitage is about 20 steps to the famous Ponte Vecchio Bridge. Park as close to the Ponte Vecchio as possible, proceed on foot until you find Vicolo Marzio. There is a brass plate on the side of the building. Take the elevator to the fifth floor where the reception desk is located.

PLAZA HOTEL LUCCHESI, Florence

The Plaza Hotel Lucchesi is located directly on the banks of the Arno River within a pleasant walking distance of the center of the city. The management and the staff seem to be particularly adept at handling the number of tour groups. I must also commend them for efficiently and courteously tracking down two sweaters which I left inadvertently in the wardrobe of my river-view lodging room. The Plaza Lucchesi is an excellent example of a large hotel that manages to maintain pleasant contact with its guests.

PLAZA HOTEL LUCCHESI, Lungarno della Zecca Vecchia 38, Florence 50010; Tel. 298-856. A 105-room modern hotel overlooking the Arno River, a 12-min. walk from center of city. Breakfast, lunch, and dinner. Garage on premises. Open year round. Rates: 23,500 to 40,000 lire. (Reservations may be made through Jane Condon, New York, N.Y. 800-223-5608.)

VILLA LA PRINCIPESSA, Massa Pisana (near Pisa)

Dinner at Villa La Principessa was over; I returned to the living room where there was a crackling fire sending out a welcome warmth against the mild chill of a Tuscany October evening.

A very attractive Italian couple invited me to share their

delicious roasted chestnuts, and while we were getting acquainted the last piece of wood was put on the fire, so we asked the porter to replenish the supply. He replied, "The wood was burning too fast." This started a series of jokes about fireplaces, and wood, and darkness that had us all laughing in both English and Italian. Another bundle of wood arrived and the laughter and good conversation continued well into the late hours of the evening. All of this played against the rather impressive background of the villa: the main living room has an extremely high ceiling and the walls are adorned with a large collection of oils from a variety of Italian periods, mostly portraits of noblemen. They all seemed to be gazing approvingly at an elaborate coat-of-arms over the fireplace.

Villa La Principessa is set in the midst of a very lovely park with a terrace on two sides. The view from the swimming pool offers a panorama of the Tuscany hills.

Lodging accommodations are quite luxurious; the furnishings more modern than traditional.

We all met for breakfast the next morning as the sun streamed in the windows of the dining room. The gardener was already preparing for the oncoming, relatively mild winter. This is a quiet part of Italy, although the city of Pisa with its famous leaning tower is just a short distance away.

RELAIS CHATEAU 239, VILLA LA PRINCIPESSA, 55050 Massa Pisana, Lucca; Tel. (0583) 379.136. A 44-room very comfortable inn in a beautiful villa approximately 25 minutes north of the city of Pisa. Breakfast, lunch, and dinner. Swimming pool on grounds; tennis, golf, horseback riding, and visit to Leaning Tower of Pisa nearby. Open all year. Rates: 41,000 lire, breakfast extra. Giancarlo Mugnani, Innkeeper.

Directions: Use Lucca exit from Autostrada (A11). Follow signs to Pisa. Villa la Principessa is on the right about five km. from Autostrada exit. Massa Pisana is not on many Italian maps. It is a wide place on the road on Rte. 12 between Lucca and Pisa.

Portofino
One look at the brochure on Portofino and I was enchanted beyond measure. Portofino is an old fishing village at the end of a small peninsula which thrusts its way into the Mediterranean and is reached from Santa Margherita by a magnificent winding

coastal road which is considered to be one of the most beautiful drives in the world. On a brilliant fall afternoon the sea was blue and the flowers and trees were in their final burst of glory. Best of all, because it was not the height of the season, the traffic on this road had been reduced to a minimum.

The village of Portofino is clustered about a national harbor, and although it is a prime objective of tourists, the main business is fishing, an occupation that has persisted for several hundred years. The crescent-shaped harbor is surrounded by small cafes, restaurants and curio shops which attract many sightseers. The brochure on Portofinio can be obtained by writing the Tourist Office, 16034 Portofino.

ALBERGO SPLENDIDO, Portofino

I was savoring a lunch of fresh Gorgonzola cheese, Italian bread, grapes, and some small, very tart Italian oranges and luscious pears. The view from the terrace at Albergo Splendido, overlooking a portion of the harbor at Portofino and the Mediterranean Sea beyond, was so enchanting that it brought a lump to my throat.

Before me in the wonderful Riviera afternoon boats were bobbing on a blue harbor, beyond which was an ice cream cone-shaped, green, forested hill at the top of which was a most appealing villa. Here was a scene that had been enjoyed by Phoenicians, Roman nobles, and tourists from all parts of the world for many centuries.

The mid-October sun was so strong that I spent most of the afternoon at the pool, getting a light tan and alternating between reading a novel and looking at the hilltop skyline, which was replete with the wonderful silhouettes of the green trees against the blue horizon.

Later, I walked from the hotel down the hill into the narrow streets of the village and out into the harbor area. I arrived at five o'clock to the accompaniment of two different sets of church bells. On a bench by the water, I idled away an hour watching the fishing boats returning with the day's catch, and then I wandered back into town to enjoy a hot chocolate at one of the outdoor cafes.

My dinner at the hotel was enlivened by the company of two English people—we sat outside on the terrace and chatted until well past midnight. A piano played lightly in the background, and in the semi-darkness, the soft voices and occasional laughter of other guests created a warm feeling of belonging.

Down in the harbor, the riding and cabin lights of the boats were bright punctuation points in the blue velvet of the night, and the street lights of the town seemed like an enchanted pearl necklace disappearing around the small hill.

In the bright sunshine the next morning, again there was breakfast on the terrace, a conversation with some tennis players, and a reluctant goodby to my friends of the previous evening. They were on their way north and would stay near Nice that evening. "Oh, we stop here every year," they said, "sometimes for two or three days. It is on the road to Rome."

The Albergo Splendido was what I was looking for on the Italian Riviera. The rates are in the luxury class, but considering its comparatively small size and romantic setting, I think it is worth it.

RELAIS CHATEAU 236, ALBERGO SPLENDIDO, Salita Baratta 13, 16034 Portofino; Tel. 0185-69195. A 67-room exceptionally comfortable inn with first-class service overlooking the exquisite harbor of Portofino. About 1 hr. south of Genova. Breakfast, lunch, and dinner. Swimming pool and tennis on grounds. Fishing, water skiing, golf, horseback riding, and exceptional Italian Riviera scenery. Closed early November to late December. Rates: 30,000-60,000 lire. Half and full pensions available. All rooms face the sea. Tito Pinchetti, Innkeeper.

Directions: Portofino is just off Autostrada (A12) using the exit for Rapallo follow signs through Santa Margherita. Before reaching Portofino village watch carefully for signs to Albergo Splendido leading up a precipice road on the right.

GALLIA PALACE HOTEL, Punta Ala (Grosseto)

"If you are driving from Portofino to Siena, you must certainly stop and see Gallia Palace even though we are closed at this time." Hans Herzig, who was so very helpful in planning my itinerary in Italy was most enthusiastic about this resort hotel which is located in the southern portion of the Italian Riviera. His advice in directing me to several other beautiful inns in Italy had been excellent, so I was quite willing to follow it once again.

I drove down the Tirrenic coast to Grosseto which faces the Island of Elba. The Gallia Palace had an ideal location on a sandy beach overlooking the sea with a background of high cliffs and pine woods. On this warm day in late October the lawns were still green and the flowers were in great profusion.

For the sports-minded vacationer there is an 18-hole golf course, horseback riding, tennis, hunting, and even polo. The sheltered harbor provides lots of water sports.

RELAIS CHATEAU 242, GALLIA PALACE HOTEL, 58040 Punta Ala (Grosseto); Tel. 92.20.22. A 100-room very comfortable resort on the Mediterranean Sea a short distance from the town of Grosseto, facing the Isle of Elba. About 100 km. from Pisa. All manner of vacation diversions available including swimming pool, sea bathing, tennis, golf, horseback riding, water skiing, polo, sailing, gardens, etc. Closed from early October to late May. Rates: 23,000-55,000 lire. Hans Herzig, Innkeeper.

Directions: Punta Ala is located on a country road (Aurelia) which leads from Follonica to Grosseto. It is near Castle della Pescaia.

HOTEL RIO ENVERS GALLIA, Sansicario (Turin)

Oddly enough, my visit to the Gallia Palace came at a time when it had just closed, and the other hotel under the direction of Mr. Herzig was not yet open: the Hotel Rio Envers Gallia in Sansicario, which is located in the mountains northwest of Milan near the border of Italy and France.

Here the great sport is skiing and there are many ski lifts within a short distance of this winter resort-hotel. Both half and full pension are available as well as weekly rates. The scenery is magnificent and the skiing, I am told, is excellent.

RELAIS CHATEAU 227, HOTEL RIO ENVERS GALLIA, 10054 Sansicario (Turin); Tel. (0122) 89296/89328. A very comfortable resort-hotel in the mountains 220 kilometers northwest of Milan and 90 kilometers from Turin. Skiing, indoor tennis, swimming nearby. Closed from April 1 to Dec. 20. Rates: 20,000 to 41,000 lire. Hans Herzig, Innkeeper.

PARK HOTEL, Siena

I believe that the man from New Jersey on the American Express tour summed up the Park Hotel very well: "We never expected to be staying in a place like this ... a real castle. We have been on this tour for about a week now, starting in Paris and going to Rome and Naples. We're on our way back through

Switzerland to Amsterdam. This had been the most impressive place we have visited."

The Park Hotel occupies an old 15th-century Tuscan castle that has been thoroughly modernized. Built in the form of an "E" with about 60 lodging rooms, it is on a piece of high ground on the outskirts of Siena and is very quiet. The hotel is surrounded by olive groves and vineyards, both of which enchance the menu—vegetables and fruits for the table are grown also in the fields below.

Besides this feeling of being set apart, perhaps the most impressive feature of the hotel is the gardens. One is a formal garden of carefully trimmed hedges and trees that I have seen pictured in the paintings of the Italian masters. The other is a carefully tended flower garden that even in mid-October was a riot of color. A gardener was busy cutting, trimming, and tying back.

Adding to the naturalness of the scene, the vines, which grow in profusion over the beige walls, were turning the many hues of autumn. A small park immediately adjacent to the castle, has paths which have been used for centuries to meander among the old trees.

The center of activity is the main desk where the concierge and the secretary speak many languages. Between them they have all the information necessary to make the traveler's sojourn in Siena and Tuscany doubly memorable.

The exterior of this castle has remained unchanged in recent centuries. The architecture is typically Tuscan. For the most part, all of the bedrooms and the interior public rooms have contemporary furniture with an occasional sprinkling of traditional paintings or tapestry. Castles differ in various parts of Europe, and perhaps this one would be better described as a palace.

I became acquainted with the people on the bus tour, and finding an upstairs lounge with a piano, we spent the evening singing old songs. By this time everybody had become good friends and they were having a wonderful time. Here is an interesting point: when I first saw them in the hotel dining room, being unable to distinguish the language they were speaking, I couldn't tell what nationality they were. Aren't we all really the same?

I saw them off at a sleepy eight o'clock the next morning as they headed for Florence. Just as she was leaving, one lady from

Atlanta, Georgia turned back for one final look at the Park Hotel saying, "I just can't get over it, a hotel in a castle."

RELAIS CHATEAU 240, PARK HOTEL, Via Marciano 16, 53100 Siena. Tel. (0577) 44.803. A 52-room very comfortable inn located in a 15th-century castle with a panoramic view of the city of Siena. Breakfast, lunch, and dinner. Swimming pool and tennis on grounds; horseback riding, fishing, golf nearby. Open all year. Rates: 23,000 to 35,000 lire. Mario Pescini, Innkeeper.

Directions: Siena is in the heart of the Tuscany area of Italy. The Park Hotel is on the east side of the city.

HOTEL LORD BYRON, Rome

I was up to my neck in bubbles in one of the world's deepest bathtubs. The water was soothing to my tired muscles and exhausted emotions. What a day it had been! At eight-thirty in the morning I had taken the tour that leaves the front of the hotel and had "done" just a small section of the sights and attractions of Rome in the morning. Returning for lunch, I had followed up with another tour in the afternoon. I had seen St. Peter's, the Capitoline Hill, the Coliseum, the bridges of Rome, the fountains, and many of the ruins. In the normal course of events it would take another four days to see everything. Now I was luxuriating in this beautiful bathroom with its mirrored walls, scented soaps and great fluffy towels.

A hotel like the Lord Byron is what every traveler needs in Italy. Rome is one of the most energetic, frenetic cities in the world—a fantastic mix of the old and the new in every possible sense. It is certainly one of the most popular tourist attractions because of the presence of the Vatician and all of the incredible ruins of the Old City. After a day on the buses, on foot, bicycle, taxicabs, or what-have-you, it was a pleasure to return to the quiet, efficient service at this small, conservative hotel.

It is conservative by some standards, although I think that the dining room's white walls and ceilings with recessed lamps, white rattan furniture, pink couches, red carpets, and many mirrors were an interesting change from the traditional antiques that I had seen elsewhere in Italy. The Lord Byron is located on a residential dead-end street which means practically no traffic— and traffic is the one thing that impresses everyone visiting Rome.

I cannot praise the front desk, the concierge, and the management enough for all of the services that they provide for their guests, because one thing that everyone needs when they come to Rome is information, advice, and directions.

There are many large hotels in Rome catering to the innumerable crowds of tourists that seem to be there in all seasons of the year, but in the many conversations I have had since my return, and sharing experiences with people who have been to Rome, I now know that it was a very fortunate day for me when Hans Herzig, the innkeeper at the Gallia Palace in Punta Ala, insisted that I stay at the Lord Byron. "It is," he said, "your kind of place."

He is right, it is.

RELAIS CHATEAU 243, LORD BYRON HOTEL, 5, Via de Notaris, 00197 Rome; Tel. 360.9541. A 55-room exceptionally comfortable modern hotel with first-class service in a very quiet section of Rome on the outskirts of the Villa Borghese and near the Via Veneto. Breakfast, lunch, and dinner. Open all year. Rates: 32,000-48,000 lire. (New York reservation number Tel. 800-223-5581.) Amadeo Ottaviani, Innkeeper.

Directions: Arriving by air: either take a taxi directly from the airport to the hotel (15,000 lire), or take Air Terminal bus which goes to the middle of Rome, and then take taxi to hotel. In either case, before paying taxi fare, check with Lord Byron concierge to make sure it is a fair amount.

Note: Don't pick up a car at the airport if you are going to be at the Lord Byron. The car company will bring car to your hotel. The traffic in Rome for the first-time visitor is unbelievable.

Arriving by car from north: Exit Autostrada (A1) and follow signs that say Salaria, which is one of the main avenues in Rome. Stay on Salaria (if you have a map of Rome you will notice a large green area to the north of the city, this is Villa Borghese). The most sensible thing to do when you arrive in this area is to hire a taxi and follow him to the Lord Byron. It is not far, but complicated enough so that this procedure is advisable.

SOUTHERN GERMANY

INNS and LOCATION

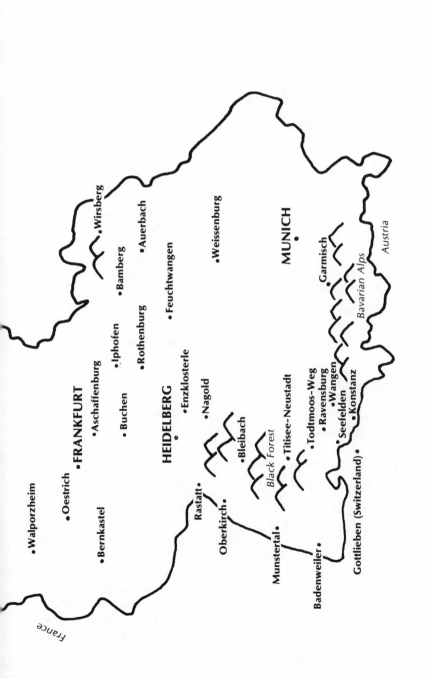

TRAVEL SUGGESTIONS FOR GERMANY

How to Get There

Lufthansa Airlines provides excellent service from many U.S. cities to several gateway cities in Germany. Your Eurailpass is good in Germany.

Country Inns in Germany

Innkeeping in Germany is a highly-respected and traditional occupation. While visiting small hotels, I found three, four, and even five generations of family-owners, and where the ownership has passed through the wife's family, her maiden name has also been retained, linked by a hypen with that of her husband's. For example: Familie Sachs-Stern.

The inn buildings are frequently rich in architectural heritage since many have been in continuous use for centuries. Dining rooms are especially attractive with many handpainted designs lovingly applied to the mellowed wall panels and chairbacks. There are almost always splendid wood carvings as well.

The service is excellent and cheerful both in the dining room and in the house, although I had to adjust to the idea of frauleins carrying my bags; there are many sons and daughters sharing the responsibilities. Almost everyone speaks English, but I found it fun to practice my German, sometimes with hilarious results.

Visiting these small family-owned hotels provided me with a rich opportunity to learn more about Germany and the Germans themselves. The experience was similar to that of visiting country inns in North America.

Reservations

Most of the accommodations I visited in Germany are part of a promotional group called "Romantik Hotels of Germany, Austria, and Switzerland." In this book I will refer to them by the Romantik Hotel numbers which appear on our map. These Romantik Hotels have a "Plan As You Go" travel plan which includes a voucher for seven overnight stays and longer. The first night's accommodation is booked in advance; the following stays can be reserved by each Romantik Hotel. Your travel agent can book this plan through the Lufthansa-Europcar Fly-Drive Plan at no additional cost to you, or you can make reservations yourself by contacting Romantik Hotels, Box 1144, D-8757 Karlstein/Main, Germany (Tel. 061/88-5020, Telex 4784).

Dining in Germany

What wonderful treats are in store for the visitor to Germany who loves to eat! Here are a few of the Hauptegerichte (main courses) that I enjoyed at the small hotels:
Bayerischer Linsentopf (Bavarian lentil casserole with smoked pork and spices); Hasenlaufe in Jagerrahmsauce (rabbit in a hunter-style dark cream sauce of mushrooms, shallots, white wine, and chopped parsley); several different kalb (veal) dishes, including sweetbreads poached in white wine; veal meatballs, and fricasseed veal. There are many varieties of sausage, sauerbraten (a beef pot roast that has been marinated several days in vinegar with vegetables and spices), and Zigeunerschnitzel (a gypsy-style preparation of veal cutlets sauteed in tomato sauce with thin strips of pickled tongue, red peppers, mushrooms, and possibly truffles).

The Germans prefer to linger over their delicious pastries

and desserts in the late afternoon during the coffee hour. In this case the konditorei (bakery also serves as a cafe. Two of the most important words on the dessert menu for me were schlagrahm (whipped cream) and schokoladen (chocolate). The varieties of strudels would stretch from Munich to Frankfurt.

Car Rentals

The "Plan As You Go" Program includes an automobile. The traveler for whom Germany is part of a Continent-wide itinerary should see the section in the front of the book, "Renting A Car For Europe." I had an Auto Sixt car on my trip. They have been renting cars since 1917. The main office is in Munich (89.22.33). They also have a limousine service with English-speaking chauffeur-guides. These can be booked through Auto-Europe in New York.

Maps and Guides

As an added convenience, a special road map of Germany, Austria, and Switzerland, showing the location of all the Romantik Hotels by numbers, is available to our readers. Please refer to the section in the back of the book marked "Maps and Guides."

Driving Tips

German roads are excellent; even the secondary and back roads are well-marked and well-constructed. The thinnest lines on the map lead through beautiful farming and mountain country with very little traffic. They may not have route numbers, but the villages are clearly shown.

The International road signs are described in the Michelin Green Guide for Germany.

My Itinerary in Germany

For traveling in Germany, I have provided a group of five different itineraries, starting from Frankfurt and going in many directions. Travelers from Luxemburg, Berlin, Netherlands, Switzerland, or Austria also will find these suggestions helpful.

Itinerary #1: *From Frankfurt northwest through the Rhine and Mosel River Valleys.*

These suggestions can also be used by travelers from Luxemburg, Belgium, and the Netherlands. It leads through the beautiful wine country of both the Mosel and Rhine River Valleys.

HOTEL SCHWAN, Oestrich im Rheingau, (Rhine)

It was a beautiful morning on the Rhine and I was faced with the problem of getting bathed, shaved, and dressed as rapidly as possible, and at the same time keeping an eye on the ever-changing parade of river traffic. Occasionally there would be a barge with an automobile perched on it, a popular way to take both car and driver up and down river.

The setting of the Schwan would be worthy of an operetta. Below me were the white tables and gay awnings of the terrace, with the maple trees in bloom. There were already some hotel guests wandering along the river banks, perhaps to look at the old crane which used to be operated by foot power to lift casks of wines to barges. At a table on the terrace, a young couple I had seen in the dining room were sitting close to one another, and I had a feeling they were in the bridal suite. If they had cared to, they could have had breakfast in their room.

Now something new was added as a company of local firemen came down to the river apparently to test their hoses and pumping equipment, and soon there were three or four silvery streams of water arching into the river.

The date on this hotel is 1628, and my host, Dr. Wenckstern, remarked that things have remained the same for a great many years. "We are now, through my wife's family, in the fifth generation of innkeepers and with few exceptions it has been in the family since it was built." We were joined by Jens Diekmann, and even though he had been here many times, he said that he was learning some things about this beautiful old hotel. We visited the historic wine cellar where there were long rows of wine casks and dust-covered bottles of the Rhineland's most famous product.

On the second floor there are conference rooms which have been used in times past by important members of the government, among them Kaiser Wilhelm.

There was one lodging room on the top floor with six windows that had an absolutely smashing view of the river in both directions which my host said had been described by the famous travel writer, Temple Fielding, as resembling the bridge of an ocean liner. I wish I'd said it first.

Because the Schwan is within a very reasonable distance of the Frankfurt Airport, for many people it is either the first or last night in Germany.

ROMANTIK HOTEL 22, SCHWAN, 6227 Oestrich im Rheingau; Tel. 06723/3001. A 60-room rambling hotel directly on banks of the Rhine River. Breakfast, lunch, and dinner served daily. Rhine River excursions in either direction available at hotel landing. Many beautiful drives through the wine country. Rates: 90 Dm. Familie Winkel-Wenckstern, Innkeepers.

Directions: Oestrich is located on Rte. 42 between Mainz and Koblenz.

RESTAURANT WEINHAUS SANKT PETER, Walporzheim/Ahr (Rhine)

I was seated under the famous chandelier of St. Peter's-wein church. In front of me was the magnificent stained glass window showing St. Peter holding two keys in his hands, protectively taking care of all the guests.

I couldn't help but be impressed by the interior of this ancient building which, tradition says, was built in 1246. The simplicity of the white plaster walls provided a dramatic background for the black wrought-iron work. The main dining room is two stories high with a small balcony traversing the upper story.

The Weinhaus St. Peter, along with a few others I visited in Germany, has a reputation for gourmet cooking. The owner, Herr Brogsitter explained that many of the important members of the government in Bonn hold frequent luncheon conferences here, and the restaurant guest book certainly bore him out with some very flamboyant signatures, photographs, personal business cards, and even a cartoon. The Weinhaus St. Peter has obviously played host to a considerable number of political and artistic people.

It was the Saturday midday meal (midtag), and for the most part the guests were families enjoying the holiday with their well-mannered children seated around the big tables, obviously enjoying, as children do everywhere, the fun of "eating out."

A light repast was all I wanted, and the headwaiter suggested a local fish which was enhanced by a delicious sauce. One of the young waiters brought a gigantic board holding at least 28 kinds of cheese; I chose a few and ate them with the usual excellent German bread.

Walporzheim is a small village next to the larger walled-town of Ahrweiler. It is 145 kilometers (about 4 hours) from Bernkastel, through the countryside west of the Rhine by way of the famous Nurburgring, the well-known race track, which is the scene of professional automobile and motorcycle races. This section is known as the Eifel and is a most attractive ride. The St. Peter is an excellent luncheon stop between Bernkastel and Oestrich.

ROMANTIK RESTAURANT 19, WEINHAUS ST. PETER, 5483 Walporzheim/Ahr (Bad Neuenahr); Tel. 02641/331. A most attractive restaurant open from 11 a.m. until 11 p.m. daily. Closed for holidays and January and February. No lodgings.

Directions: Weinhaus St. Peter is located on Rte. 266 which runs east and west from the banks of the Rhine at Linz. Walporzheim is adjacent to the larger walled-town of Ahrweiler which is on most maps.

HOTEL ALTESTE WEINSTUBE, Bernkastel-Kues, (Mosel)

It was about 10 o'clock on a gentle April evening. I stood in the middle of the bridge at Bernkastel looking out over the water and pondering, for a moment, the generations of people who had lived in this valley, fought its wars, raised their children, and nurtured their hopes. Above me, on a promontory overlooking the bend of the river was one of the hopes that had gone by the board ... an ancient floodlit castle that seemed to be hanging like a yellow satellite in the sky.

I had taken an extra long stroll to offset the effects of indulging in a dinner at the Alteste Weinstube that seemed almost a work of art. It started off with a most delicious, homemade, fresh asparagus soup which was garnished by small bits of shrimp and very thin slivers of ham.

The main course was another artistic achievement ... eels from the Mosel River, a local delicacy that simply cannot be duplicated elsewhere. These were served in a rich, creamy sauce and accompanied by small yellow potatoes and three cresent-

shaped pastries; all were arranged on the blue plate to present an eye-pleasing picture including the garnish of a small leaf of lettuce upon which was placed a thin wedge of tomato and some fresh parsley.

The dessert was a little cake with a hole in the middle, liberally doused with brandy, and then set aflame. After the flame had dissipated, two scoops of vanilla ice cream were added and the entire melange was covered with delicious fresh strawberries.

After dinner I had a long conversation with Henry Krebs, the chef and owner. He is a ninth-generation innkeeper and the inn is, indeed, the oldest wine shop in the town. He took me on a tour of the dining rooms, which included an examination of the old family Bible (which recorded the marriages of countless of his ancestors), the baptismal bowl and the official family crest. All of these are kept in a case in the very attractive breakfast room on the second floor. Henry's mother had painted the floral designs on the highly varnished panels in this cheerful room.

My bedroom was on the fourth floor, furnished in the traditional manner, and the window with circular panes opened out over the roofs of the town.

I visited Bernkastel during the last week in April, and while the weather can be a bit chancy at that time, this little town on the banks of the Mosel was absolutely enchanting, especially since all the fruit trees were in blossom.

169

ROMANTIK HOTEL 25, ALTESTE WEINSTUBE, 5550 Bernkastel; Tel. 06531/2443. A 26-room inn in a small town on the banks of the Mosel River. This is a popular resort area with many outdoor activities and sports available such as motor boating, sailing, and water skiing, plus walks and drives through the Mosel wine country. Breakfast, lunch, and dinner served daily. Rates: 70 Dm. Familie Krebs, Innkeepers.

Directions: Bernkastel and Kues are two cities separated by the Mosel River. They are south of Koblenz and north of Trier. The hotel is located about one kilometer up the steep street which starts at the bridge.

Itinerary #2: *From Frankfurt south via Heidelberg, the Black Forest to Switzerland.*
This itinerary includes some of the most popular vacationing sections of Germany.

Heidelberg

Ah Heidelberg! A romantic city where the Student Prince in Lehar's operetta caroused and sang with his fellow students and

fell madly in love. Michelin gives it three full pages with an extensive description of the Heidelberg Castle and the other impressive sights within the city and its environs.

Heidelberg is the oldest university town in Germany and the university and the students play an important role in its ambience. There is a student jail (studtenkarger) which was used between 1788 and 1914 to allow certain too-uproarious students to cool their ardor. To be so incarcerated was considered by many of them a mark of distinction. They have left timeless reminders of their tenure with inscriptions and drawings on the walls. It is one of the principal tourist sights in Germany, particularly with thousands of young people finding their way there with guitars and backpacks. I saw quite a few American college T-shirts, although these are sold in stores everywhere in Europe.

The pedestrian section of the old city which is cordoned off from automobile traffic is a conglomeration of stores with a blatant appeal to tourists situated cheek-by-jowl with oriental rug shops, banks, jeans stores (everywhere), ice cream stands, meat markets, bakeries, restaurants, pizzerias, discotheques, and motion picture theatres. It is a meeting of the old ways and the new. As one Scottish boy responded when I asked him why he came to Heidelberg: "Why mon, this is where it's at!"

HOTEL ZUM RITTER, Heidelberg

Now Heidelberg and the Zum Ritter! It is hard to imagine Heidelberg without the Zum Ritter.

There are two most uplifting experiences at this hotel. The first is to stand on the street and to become absorbed in the truly magnificent facade. The other is to ascend to the roof garden and enjoy a leisurely view of this historic, romantic city on the Neckar.

The hotel derives its name from the statue of a young Roman knight (ritter) which is poised on the uppermost gable of the many-storied facade. Each of these five stories is supported by carved pillars on which are depicted a variety of figures from Roman history and mythology, as well as representations of the nobility of Heidelberg in the 16th century. The intricate designs of each section could be studied for hours at a time.

The Zum Ritter is in two sections; the oldest part was built in 1592 by master builder Carolus Belier, and was spared the ravages of a siege 100 years later. It was the only structure in Heidelberg to survive, everything else was burned to the ground.

On the first floor there are high vaulted ceilings and rather formal dining rooms and sitting rooms which have fragments of sculpture and carvings, including a bust of the builder of the house who is further commemorated by two large oil paintings.

On the floors above, the rooms in the original section have been furnished with traditional pieces—the honeymoon suite, for example, is positively lavish and has two alcoves overlooking the church across the street. Oddly enough, there is a cradle in the hallway in front of the door. Other traditionally furnished lodging rooms have a holiday feeling.

The rooms in the newer section are undergoing, I am told, a gradual redecorating.

The innkeeper, Georg Kuchelmeister, is an avid hunter and on the day before my arrival had been hunting in the nearby Odenwald, a beautiful forest just across the river. He explained to me that he provides some of the venison and small game that is served frequently in the hotel dining room. A specialty of the house is Heidelberg Schlossplatte, a beef, calf, scrambled eggs, and vegetable dish.

The view from the roof garden puts it all into perspective; I could see that the city nestles at the foot of the mountains on both sides of the Neckar. The ancient castle still towers above the city, its ruins a continual reminder of bygone centuries.

The Zum Ritter, a late Renaissance masterpiece, is one of the important sights of the city. The Church of the Holy Spirit, which is just across the cobblestone street; the Heidelberg Castle and gardens which tower over the city; and the Philosopher's Walk, are all points of interest.

Heidelberg and the Zum Ritter are, indeed, well-matched.

ROMANTIK HOTEL 32, ZUM RITTER, Hauptstrasse 178, 6900 Heidelberg; Tel. 06221/24272. A 36-room historic hotel in the center of the old part of Heidelberg adjacent to the university, the Old Bridge, and within a short walk of the cable car to the ruins of Heidelberg Castle. Breakfast, lunch, and dinner served daily. Rates: 86 Dm. Margarete and Georg Kuchelmeister, Owners.

Directions: The Zum Ritter is located in a section that is cordoned off from auto traffic from 10 a.m. until 6 a.m. the following morning. Find the way to the street just to the right of the Neckar River. Follow this street to a point just before the Old Bridge which you will see from a distance distinguished by its two classic towers. Turn right at the Blue Alta gas station. Then turn right on the one-way street that leads to the Holy Ghost Church. Park your car as near the chain across the street as possible, walk to hotel and they will give you information on parking and send someone to help with your bags. The front desk people all speak English and understand your problem.

RESTAURANT KATZENBERGER'S ADLER, Rastatt (near Baden-Baden)

I'm finally "one up" on John Ashby Conway, the distinguished gourmet, owner, and chef of the Farmhouse Res-

173

taurant in Port Townsend, Washington, for I have enjoyed a meal at Rudolf Katzenberger's restaurant in Rastatt, and John has yet to enjoy that magical experience.

Rudolf Katzenberger looks like a favorite grandfather. He is a very gentle man with a courtly manner and smiling eyes. He is certainly one of the most active grandfathers I have ever met. He works in his restaurant side-by-side with his wife, his daughter, his son-in-law, and his grandson.

Mr. Katzenberger joined me at a corner table for a few moments, and we had a lively talk which was frequently interrupted by his greetings to new guests, and good-byes to those departing. During the course of this conversation I assured him I would be quite satisfied with something very light for lunch, and he assured me that he had just the answer to my needs.

Shortly thereafter, a cup of delicious soup was set before me which, he told me, is served once a year and tells us "that spring is definitely here."

This was followed by two tasty dumplings topped with two small shrimp and accompanied by three crescent-shaped pastries. One bite and I was transported. I ate everything on the plate, and then felt that it would be sensible to order a small dessert.

That's when Isolde, Mr. K's daughter came with a large platter containing a noodle omelet and veal cutlets. When I protested that she must be at the wrong table, she replied, "Oh no, you have only just started. Besides that, you must also eat your salad."

I restricted myself to a few bites of the noodle omelet and the veal cutlet, although it took a very firm effort on my part not to consume everything on the plate. Isolde returned and I told her I was finished, but she shook her finger at me and told me I should eat more. Before she could take the plate away, Mr. K. came back and looked very upset because he thought I didn't care for the food.

I assured him that it was ambrosial. Well, so much for my eating adventures at this exceptional restaurant run by such an exceptional man. I hope that perhaps in some way I have conveyed the inherent pride and concern that are expressed here. I would say that Rudolph Katzenberger enjoys a reputation in Germany somewhat akin to that of a cabinet minister, and certainly his tenure has been much more enduring. Many other innkeepers told me that he was the dean of chefs in Germany and possibly Europe.

As for John Ashby Conway, I would love to introduce him to Rudolph Katzenberger and then just sit down and listen to both of them talk.

ROMANTIK RESTAURANT 38, KATZENBERGER'S ADLER, 7550 Rastatt; Tel. 07222/32103. A distinguished restaurant located at #7 Josefstrasse. Luncheon and dinner served daily except Monday. No lodgings. Rudolf Katzenberger, chef and proprietor.

Directions: Josefstrasse is the first street to the left after crossing the river on Rtes. 3 and 36 in Rastatt. Do not go into the center of town.

The Black Forest (Schwarzwald)

The three sections of the Black Forest contain some of the most popular resort and recreational areas of Germany. The Michelin Green Guide devotes five pages to it. I visited several Romantik Hotels in which it would be a pleasure to spend an entire vacation.

The Black Forest has beautiful lakes, high mountains, vineyards, great rivers, graceful bridges, farmhouses crouching under sloping hip roofs, and perhaps one of the continual challenges to photographers: old towns with crooked lanes.

For the active sports-minded vacationer there is downhill and cross-country skiing, horseback riding, tennis, fishing, sailing, hiking, and back roads to content the most lively heart. At various times of the year there are special festivals where traditional costumes are worn and there are many displays of arts and crafts. Black Forest hospitality has a tradition of centuries, and the cuisine in the area features venison, rabbit, and other wild game. Black Forest cake in its many variations is known the world over.

HOTEL POST, Nagold (Black Forest)

Kurt Scholl was translating from a most fascinating book written in 1841 about the various hotels in Germany. He turned to the page which had information about the Hotel Post. "In former times the Hotel Post was called the Hotel Sonne. The innkeeper was also the manager of the post office. The hotel is located on the road from Stuttgart to Strasbourg. It has 12 bedrooms with very good furniture and stables for the horses. Concerning the cellar and the kitchen we recommend it as one of the best restaurants in this area. The service is very good, the bill is not too high, and it can be recommended for travelers in all walks of life."

"Nothing has changed," I said. "Except that your father is not the postmaster of Nagold." The moment was punctuated by the arrival of Kurt's father, Karl, who joined in our laughter. "You might be surprised," he said, "at the number of recipes that have been used in the kitchen since the 19th century."

"My great-great-great-grandmother was the chief cook and was known as a woman with a very strong mind. The King of Wurtemberg was having dinner here during a very hot period of the summertime and there were a great many flies. He ordered my venerable ancestor to prepare a table for the flies. Naturally, she was rather indignant, but she complied with his demands and then returned to him and said, 'Your Majesty, the table for the flies has been prepared. Please order the flies to sit down!'"

This was only one of several most amusing anecdotes that Karl told throughout the evening.

Kurt, who is majoring in economics at a university in Switzerland, is very proud of the family heritage of innkeeping. He pointed out that since Nagold is so close to France, it is inevitable that there would be an emphasis on French cuisine — for example, there is saddle of hare, marinated in juniper sauce, and served with potato croquettes and a chicory salad garnished with nuts. There is also a stuffed leg of lamb which is cooked in a pastry jacket, and served with potatoes au gratin and kidney beans.

In its role as both post office and inn, the old hotel has flourished, and the older sections, including the paneled dining rooms, have been admirably preserved. In recent years, a more modern annex has been constructed, which also provides guest parking. All of the bedrooms in this section have been modernized throughout.

Besides the King of Wurtemberg, other distinguished guests of the house have been Napoleon, Otto von Hapsburg, Prince Louis Ferdinand of Prussia, and Juliette Greco.

The pride in the tradition of innkeeping expressed by this family is typical of what I found throughout Germany. I am sure

that the now-unknown travel writer of 1841 would endorse the improvements that have been made, but would also agree that the really important things have remained unchanged.

ROMANTIK HOTEL 43, POST, Bahnhofstrasse 2, 7270 Nagold; Tel. (07452) 4048. A 42-room city hotel at the northern border of the Black Forest. Parking available for guest cars. Breakfast, lunch, and dinner served daily.·Rates: 74 Dm. Lore and Karl Fr. Scholl, Innkeepers.

Directions: Nagold is southeast of Karlsruhe and Heidelberg and southwest of Stuttgart. The hotel is located in the Centrum.

HOTEL WALDHORN POST, Enzklosterle, (Black Forest)

Enzklosterle is a quiet resort area about 40 kilometers southwest of Baden-Baden. Those particular 40 kilometers are through some outstanding and picturesque Black Forest country.

The Hotel Waldhorn Post was originally built in 1968 with some new additions in 1974. The dining rooms, wine rooms, and reception area were decorated and furnished in the German traditional style, including several paintings that are identified with Black Forest animals, birds, and fishes. There were many mounted deer horns on the walls, and paintings of Black Forest guides.

On the second and third floor, the lodging rooms had the appearance of a modern American motel.

The Waldhorn Post also has an indoor swimming pool that is larger than usual, a sauna, a solarium, and massage facilities. For the outdoor-minded guests there is tennis, golf, fishing, hiking, and skiing nearby.

ROMANTIK HOTEL 41, WALDHORN POST, 7546 Enzklosterle; Tel. 07085/411. A 60-room resort hotel in the northern end of Black Forest. Swimming pool and tennis courts on grounds. Golf and all other sports available nearby. Breakfast, lunch, and dinner served daily. Rates: 84 Dm. The Schilling Family, Innkeepers.

Directions: Enzklosterle is between Nagold and Baden-Baden.

HOTEL OBERE LINDE, Oberkirch (Black Forest)

One of my lasting impressions of this tidy hotel located in the central Black Forest is that the names of all the innkeepers dating from 1659 have been painted on one of the rows of beams of its classic half-timbered construction. That means it has been an inn for over 300 years!

The hotel has two recently restored buildings connected by a small, second floor gallery. One building houses the dining rooms and the principal public rooms, as well as a few bedrooms; the other is entirely occupied by bedrooms.

Located on the main street a few squares from the town center, it is a popular hotel particularly in the height of the vacation season, and it is also a very important town meeting place—for example, the Rotary Club meets here every week. The hotel dining room and gardens frequently have an interesting cross-section of both visitors and town people. In the rather spacious basement there are two bowling alleys which are slightly different from the American variety. Several local bowling clubs have matches there every week.

The two attractively decorated main dining rooms have a collection of lanterns, rolling pins, ceramics, copper, and pewterware displayed on plate rails. Also on display was a large collection of photographs of young people ... children and relatives of the owners, no doubt—this practice is quite common in Germany.

I arrived at lunchtime and after looking over the extensive

menu, chose a bowl of soup and a piece of delicious homemade Black Forest cake. Accompanied by an ice-cold glass of milk, this chocolaty, creamy concoction was close to divine.

Oberkirch is a small, attractive town and, because of its quite mild climate, it is a center of strawberry growing. There is a strawberry market in town which is the largest in Germany, where a strawberry festival is held every year. There is also a sizable outdoor swimming pool and park. During the summertime there are frequent concerts.

In many ways, the Obere Linde in Oberkirch, Germany reminds me of the Red Lion Inn in Stockbridge, Massachusetts. Each has definite community ties while at the same time providing warm hospitality to travelers.

ROMANTIK HOTEL 42, OBERE LINDE, 7602 Oberkirch; Tel. (07802)/3038. A 34-room family-style inn a few squares from the center of a German town in the Black Forest. Breakfast, lunch, and dinner served daily. Closed for two weeks in February. Rates: 70 Dm. Familie Dilger, Innkeepers.

Directions: Oberkirch is on Route 28 which runs east and west from Freudenstadt to Strasbourg.

I took a few hours to explore some of the scenic views and mountains of the Rhine Valley and even got lost. While I was leaning over the radiator of the car examining the map, a man stopped his car and asked me if he could help. He not only showed me the way on the map but then suggested that I follow him so that I would not lose my way. I had many such instances of courtesy and consideration in Germany. I find it extremely touching.

HOTEL-RESTAURANT STOLLEN, Bleibach (Black Forest)

I will always remember this little crossroads inn for its flowers—there were flowers at every window, on all the balconies, and throughout the dining and sitting rooms. The tasteful arrangements bespoke a lover of flowers who, I am sure was very happy in his or her work. The blooms, many of them geraniums, were set off beautifully against the whitewashed exterior walls and, on the inside, against the traditional brown carved beams, and posts, and the white walls, and ceilings.

As is the custom in this part of Germany, on the first floor there is a wine room which usually accommodates guests who wish to have light refreshments or the German version of a simple snack. There were also two more formal dining rooms, one decorated in red and the other in shades of yellow. I saw the familiar corner fireplace.

The 14 lodging rooms on the second and third floors were furnished either traditionally or in a contemporary mode. They looked very comfortable and pleasant.

The innkeeper and chef, Herr Jehli explained that the inn had been built in 1847 and had been in his wife's family for many years. "She and I are the fourth generation of innkeepers," he explained. Unfortunately, his wife was not present that day and he had to excuse himself to return to the kitchen, However, he generously invited me to wander around in the hotel at will.

Bleibach is just a few kilometers north of Freiburg which is one of the centers of recreation and entertainment in the Black Forest.

ROMANTIK HOTEL 44, STOLLEN, 7809 Bleibach; Tel. 07685/207. A 14-room crossroads inn kept in the Black Forest tradition. Breakfast, lunch, and dinner served daily. Rates: Reasonable. Familie Jehli-Kiefer, Innkeepers.

Directions: Bleibach is a few kilometers north of Freiburg on the upper road to Offenburg (look for Route 294).

HOTEL ADLER-POST, Titisee-Neustadt, (Black Forest)

The Titisee area is one of the most popular recreational areas in the Black Forest. The main reason is a very beautiful lake which offers a considerable number of additional dimensions to vacation pleasures. From its shores I could look to the tops of some of the great mountains nearby, and when I was there in April the ski lifts were still running. During the summertime there was sailing, tennis, golf, bicycling, swimming, horseback riding, and the ever-present thermal baths.

Let me explain that there are two towns. One is Titisee, which is located on the lake, and the other is Titisee-Neustadt just a few kilometers distant. The "Neustadt" part means "new town." It may well be that a town was built here about 500 years ago and has been known as the new town ever since.

Titisee-Neustadt is a business town, and bustles with the air of a prosperous Midwest American community. Both the town

and the Adler-Post reminded me very much of the Durbin Hotel in Rushville, Indiana.

Although this squarish stone building seemed rather conventional, I was surprised to find a reception area that was quite rustic in design and furnishings. The twisting staircase to the second floor, with its carved woodwork and painted decorations, reminded me of a similar staircase at the Glen Iris Hotel in Castile, New York.

There were several surprises at the Adler-Post. For one thing, on the second floor there is a small swimming pool, sauna baths, solarium, and a few unobtrusively placed pinball machines. (Excellent for rainy day entertainment and practicing body balance.) There was also a massage parlor and I was assured by the assistant manager who had visited Texas, that any similarity to the kind we have in America is in name only.

Bedrooms furnished in the traditional manner were quite handsome with parquet floors and hand-decorated beds. As usual there was also a number of rooms furnished in a more contemporary manner.

The Adler-Post is another example of a good, smallish German hotel that, because of its location in a resort area, has a mixture of both vacationers and business travelers. An outstanding feature of its menu is the many different cuts and preparations of venison. "There are many ways to prepare it," said my host, "and I believe our chef knows most of them."

ROMANTIK HOTEL 45, ADLER-POST, Hauptstrasse 16, 7820 Titisee-Neustadt; Tel. 07651/5066. A 35-room intown hotel located just a few minutes away from the resort town of Titisee. Indoor swimming pool, sauna, solarium, massage are located in the hotel. Breakfast, lunch, and dinner served daily. Rates: 85 Dm. Familie Ketterer, Innkeepers.

Directions: The Titisee area is in the upper Black Forest, 28 km to the east of Freiburg. Titisee-Neustadt is about 3 km. east of the town of Titisee on Route 31.

HOTEL SPIELWEG, Munstertal, (Black Forest)

Bright sunshine bathed the gentle spring morning with its warming goodness. I paused for a moment to breathe the marvelous Black Forest air and look out over the brook, across the deep valley and up the steep mountain where a little girl was leading a cow along the mountain path. The sounds of the cow bell were clearly audible.

"Is it not beautiful?" I turned to look into the blue eyes of a very beautiful lady who introduced herself as the mother of the innkeeper of the Hotel Spielweg. She suggested that we have breakfast together while she told me about the history of this attractive resort hotel.

"This is a very old house," she said. "It has been here since 1650. We built the new section about seven years ago." (In Germany I discovered that almost all of the innkeepers refer to a hotel or inn as the "haus," or house.) "My son, his wife, and I are trying to preserve the very best of the old ways, while at the same time making improvements and progress with new methods. For example, here in the original building we have maintained the traditionally furnished rooms with painted doorways, antique beds, chests, and other furniture. In the new building, where you are staying, each accommodation has its own balcony or terrace overlooking the brook and the mountains. We know that a great many of our guests relish that wonderful feeling of being close to nature, so one whole wall of every room is of glass. However, perhaps you have noticed that the ceiling in your bedroom is wood and the beds are decorated with the traditional Black Forest flowers and other designs." (I will add a footnote here that my bathroom was an absolute joy.)

"Here in this building, we've made very few changes. That's my favorite pewter displayed on the plate rail and I'm very particular about even the smallest detail. We place fresh flowers throughout the hotel, and our waitresses wear aprons and blouses made in the same styles that were worn in the middle of the last century."

She continued: "The holiday preferences for the average European family have changed considerably during the last 25 years, and so we have changed with the times. I have been here for many years, and I sometimes cling to the old ways— fortunately, my son and his wife have joined me and they have shown me that new ideas make for better innkeeping ... I think that we make an ideal threesome."

"For example, the alpine and cross-country skiing nearby bring enthusiastic families who must be provided with recreation after a day on the slopes. That's why we have the game rooms and television rooms, and why we also built an indoor swimming pool, as well as one outdoors."

After a most pleasant breakfast, we parted and I went out into the clear Black Forest spring morning to pack my bags and continue my travels through Germany. I am already looking forward to my return trip.

ROMANTIK HOTEL 46, SPIELWEG, 7816 Munstertal; Tel. 07636/ 218. A 42-room resort-inn in the heart of the upper Black Forest Region. Indoor and outdoor swimming pool on grounds. All Black Forest sports and outdoor activities within a few minutes drive. Breakfast, lunch, and dinner served daily. Rates: 84 Dm. Familie Stemmle-Fuchs, Innkeepers.

Directions: Locate Freiburg on map and then move your eye carefully south to look for "Belchen"—this is one of the highest Black Forest mountains. Munstertal is just above it.

HOTEL SONNE, Badenweiler (Black Forest)

According to my friend, Jens Diekmann, Badenweiler is an ideal place to recover from everyday stress and enjoy a good vacation. "It is the spa" he said, "where knowledgeable Europeans go who wish to have a quiet, tranquil vacation along with the thermal baths."

"Let me advise you in advance that you cannot park in the middle of the town. There are free parking centers on the outer edges of the town, and one takes a bus into the centrum where it is so pleasant because there is no traffic."

I was now riding the bus and enjoying a conversation with another traveler who seemed to be quite informed about this resort community. "The most popular activity is the thermal baths," he said, "although I am sure that many people who visit here never go near them, as there are other things to do. There are some beautiful shops showing the latest fashions, and several restaurants and hotels." As we got closer to the centrum, I realized that Badenweiler was a very sophisticated town, in many ways similar to Highlands, North Carolina.

The Sonne Hotel is located near the Rathaus (Town Hall) and is distinguished from the other hotels and pensions because of its traditional design—the building is 200 years old. The Fischer family, fourth-generation proprietors, reflected the sophisticated spirit of the town, and were most accommodating when it came to explaining the hotel and the ambience of the area. "It is so easy to drive most any place in the southern Black Forest within a short time," explained Frau Fischer, "and there are many bus tours that leave on a regular schedule from Badenweiler to dozens of nearby points of interest."

The Sonne Hotel appears to be very comfortable. In particular, I was impressed with the large lobby that had many, many chairs and tables arranged to encourage conversation. The main dining room was rather formal; however, the two side dining rooms were decorated in the traditional Black Forest manner, and the wooden chairs even had hearts carved in their backs.

The rooms, most of them with balconies, overlooked the garden to the rear and there was also a terrace for sunbathing. As I recall, plans were in the works for an indoor swimming pool.

The Sonne Hotel appeals basically to people who are looking for a rest, and perhaps a few days in and out of the famous baths which are just a few steps away. Frau Fischer explained that it is indeed a very lively place with concerts, films, theatre, folk singing, and many other types of live entertainment scheduled in the town on a continuing basis.

ROMANTIK HOTEL 47, SONNE, 7847 Badenweiler; Tel. 07632/ 5053. A 42-room hotel located in one of the Black Forest's famous spa areas. Breakfast, lunch, and dinner served daily. Rates: 84 Dm. Familie Fischer, Innkeepers.

Directions: Badenweiler is located at the southwestern edge of the Black Forest. It is a short distance north of Basel (Switzerland) and is accessible from the Autobahn running next to the Rhine

SCHWARZWALD HOTEL, Todtmoos-weg, (Black Forest)

Uta Poppe and I were looking at two photographs of the Schwarzwald Hotel—one of them pictured gay umbrellas on the terrace with many flowers and flower boxes, and the lamp post had flowering vines climbing up to the light. The other showed the same scene in winter with snow piled high on the slanted roofs and the terrace completely enveloped in white. In the background I could see skiers going up the ski lift and some young children sledding.

"Yes, we are really an ideal place for people who enjoy vigorous outdoor sports," she said. "In the summertime we have tennis, horseback riding, and a swimming pool. Naturally, everybody enjoys walks and hikes in the Black Forest. Our sauna bath and solarium are popular in the winter, especially after a day of downhill and cross-country skiing. We even have some snowshoeing."

Uta and her husband are excellent examples of today's young German innkeepers. They are an enthusiastic, sports-minded couple who enjoy the pleasures of living in the Black Forest; in fact, the day I was there Herr Poppe was out fishing.

Nearly all of the bedrooms were done in knotty pine, and many had enclosed parlors and balcony extensions. Uta explained that originally the buildings had all been part of a Black Forest farm.

Like many hotels and inns in the resort sections of Germany there are various lodging plans available which include two and three meals a day.

Incidentally, there are two towns in the area with the same prefix name—Todtmoos. I failed to note this and went into the village of Todtmoos and visited a hotel with a similar name. I was soon redirected by some very friendly people.

The Schwarzwald looked like a wonderful place to spend a few days in either the summer or the winter, especially if one happens to be a vigorous outdoor sports enthusiast.

ROMANTIK HOTEL 49, SCHWARZWALD, 7867 Todtmoos-weg; Tel. 07674/273. A 28-room mountainside hotel with a beautiful panoramic view of the Southern Black Forest. Breakfast, lunch, and dinner served daily. All winter and summer sports available. Rates: 70 Dm. Familie Poppe, Innkeepers.

Directions: Todtmoos-weg is northwest of Waldshut.

Itinerary #3: *Frankfurt southeast via Aschaffenberg, Buchen, and the Romantic Road. This itinerary includes some of the most picturesque and famous old towns of Bavaria.*

HOTEL POST, Aschaffenburg, (Frankfurt)

Like others in Germany, the Hotel Post has a history as a stagecoach stop, and this background has set the theme for some of the interior decorations in the inn. For example, in the main

dining room where I was enjoying my first lunch in Germany with Jens Diekmann and Innkeeper Karl Seubert, there are many reminders of earlier days, such as several prints of old coaches and paintings of them on ceramic tiles. One of the most striking features is the *half* (actually) of a stagecoach which has been built into one corner of the main dining room. As innkeeper Seubert explained, "The whole coach would take too much space, so we split it in half and put it here for everyone to see." It is possible to open the door and step up on the driver's seat.

The outstanding menu of the Post has won a gold medal, not only for the rich and unusual design, but also for the orderly and easily understandable contents, most of which are in both German and English. It has 16 pages with a center spread of extremely intricate paintings done in the Bavarian style. The richly decorated pages are done in the manner of an illuminated medieval manuscript.

Here are a few of the menu items that caught my eye. In the hors d'oeuvre section there was corn on the cob, smoked trout, frogs' legs, smoked salmon, and caviar. International soups, included Hungarian goulash, turtle soup, Russian borsch, and

Indian hotchpotch. There were several different types of salads; many egg dishes; and fish dishes, including river trout and sole meuniere. The meats included pork cutlets, rump steak (very popular in Germany), leg of lamb, and several others. There were also venison and chicken.

After my first meal in Germany, we took a tour of the hotel which included an unusual dining room dedicated to Holland, because the innkeeper and his wife had been married there. In it were Dutch wooden shoes, Delft china, and ceramic figurines. The window paintings on glass were done after the manner of Rubens, Franz Hals, and Breughel.

This hotel has still another unusual feature—an indoor swimming pool. Two of the walls had saucy murals depicting life in medieval Bavaria.

The lodging rooms looked very comfortable and tidy, and somewhat contemporary in furnishings; although, as was the case everywhere I traveled in Germany, I found the traditional goosedown-filled comforters which in turn are covered by a sheet which is changed after each guest's stay.

ROMANTIK HOTEL 23, POST, 8750 Aschaffenburg; Tel. 06021/ 21333. A 100-room midtown hotel about a half-hour drive from the Frankfurt Airport. An excellent, quiet accommodation for Frankfurt visitors. Breakfast, lunch, and dinner served daily. Indoor swimming pool. Rates: 80 Dm. Karl Seubert, Innkeeper.

Directions: From Frankfurt Airport: Follow autobahn east to Aschaffenberg exit.

The Romantic Road

The Romantic Road links the River Main and the Bavarian Alps by way of some extremely picturesque old medieval towns. There is a complete description of it in the Michelin Green Guide to Germany and I am certain that the German Tourist Offices in North America will be happy to supply folders in English about this area and the other tourist areas in Germany.

I have described Romantik Hotels, either on or near this road which is a much-traveled highway for Europeans heading south on vacation trips.

The Romantic Road begins in the old cathedral town of Wurzburg and continues through Rothenberg, Feuchtwangen, Dinkelsbuhl, Donauworth, Augsburg, and Landsburg, finally coming to an end at Fussen in the foothills of the Bavarian Alps.

HOTEL PRINZ CARL, Buchen, (Romantic Road)

I'll always remember the Prinz Carl, not only for the fact that it was where I spent my first night in Germany, but because we all had such a wonderful, laughing time together. There was Jens Diekmann, Innkeepers Werner and Elizabeth Ehrhardt, and Ilse and Bettina, their two very attractive young daughters. A third sister, Baltraut, was unable to be with us. We all quickly became acquainted and they were most courteous in attempting to speak English as much as possible. I, in turn, taught them two ersatz German-American words with which they were not familiar: "schuss-boomer" and "sitzmark." Everybody thought this was most hilarious.

Furthermore, I am now a member of the famous *Goldener Kanne* Club. Jens Diekmann and I were both inducted by innkeeper Ehrhardt in a very touching ceremony which took place in the main dining room, amidst the congratulations and bravos of the other assembled guests and friends. In order to supply proof of membership, I now possess a scroll on which Herr Ehrhardt has written my name, and I am officially entered in the club rolls. In addition, I have a miniature golden *kanne* (stein) with a flip top.

The Ehrhardts have kept the Prinz Carl these 27 years, and Werner is the chef. He is particularly well known for the preparation of a saddle of venison and for a range of pastries that includes tarts made from sour cherries.

That evening my dinner started with a tasty duck liver pate and then followed with their famous "green wheat" soup which is also a house recipe. The next course was delicious French fried shrimp with a Bernaise sauce in which tomatoes had been mixed. The main course was medallions of veal served with artichokes, and we finished with everybody sampling two delicious desserts: a chocolate mousse, which is one of my favorites, and a very scrumptious ice cream cake.

The Prinz Carl was a post station for many years. Today it is a most interesting combination of the old and the new. The dining room and the main reception hall are furnished in a traditional manner, as are several of the lodging rooms on the second floor. However, a new section has very attractive contemporary furniture which is reminiscent of Scandinavian style. My room, #22, was a studio room overlooking the roofs of the town.

When I left the following morning, the entire family

189

gathered in the center hallway to speed me on my way. I was to have many a warm welcome and companionable experience at German inns for the next several days; however, none would exceed the enjoyable time I had at the Prinz Carl.

ROMANTIK HOTEL 29, PRINZ CARL, 6967 Buchen/Odenwald; Tel. 06281/1877. A 26-room village inn, 50 km. south of Frankfurt. Breakfast, lunch, and dinner served daily. Riding, indoor and outdoor swimming, walks through the forest, boat rides on the River Main, and many castles nearby. Rates: 74 Dm. Familie Ehrhardt, Innkeepers.

Directions: Locate Frankfurt on the German road map and then Heidelberg about 50 km. to the south. Buchen is east on Rte. 27. From Frankfurt the road through Miltenburg and Amorbach is very scenic.

HOTEL MARKUSTURM, Rothenburg ob der Tauber (Romantic Road)

"What is Stammtisch?" I asked Marrianne Berger while the two of us were seated in the reception hall of the Hotel Markusturm. We had just completed a brief tour of the many different lodging and public rooms of this truly old hotel. It was just a few moments before dinner.

"Stammtisch, oh you will see that in just a moment. I am sure that you will like it very much."

Her husband, Otto, and her daughter Gabriella and son Stephan, joined us and we stepped into a most attractively decorated dining room. The waiters wore green vests, flowery white shirts, red ties, and black trousers. Otto explained that this was the Empire-style which was worn to commemmorate the first 700 years of the freedom of the town. "This was celebrated in 1974," he explained, "but we decided that the men would continue to wear the costumes and the waitresses would wear theirs only on special occasions. Marrianne sewed eight costumes that year and they are all very beautiful and elaborate."

The Hotel Markusturm was constructed out of the first fortified wall of the city of Rothenburg and is located where St. Marc's Tower, built in 1204, and the Roeder Arch (1330) formed one of the romantic corners of this medieval city. It is one of the most historic buildings in the town. The hotel served as barracks for soldiers who were assigned to duty in the tower. In later years

it was both a brewery and a gasthaus.

Our meal started off with one of the specialties of the house called "Ratsherrimspiel." It consisted of various kinds of meats, onion, sausage, bacon, and other succulent things served on a skewer with potato croquets. It was served on a special plate that is only used for this particular dish. Gabriella and Stephan, who were studying English in school, explained to me that there were many other plates designed for special menu items at the Markusturm. "We have eight cooks in our kitchen," explained Stephan very proudly.

For dessert I had a local cheese which was very strong and peppery and comes wrapped in a napkin. However, Marrianne insisted upon my sampling some sliced apples which had been dipped in a batter of meal and beer and then dropped in hot oil. They were delicious.

It was during this meal that I learned about the German custom of the "Stammtisch." While we were discussing the history of Rothenburg, one of their friends came to the edge of the table and knocked three times. Otto and Marrianne smiled and said, "Hello," and the man sat down at the table and lit his pipe. A few minutes later, another man did the same thing. About ten minutes later, a few more men came over, knocked, and we moved a little closer together so that everybody could sit down. Each time I was introduced briefly and we went on with our conversation, while some of them started their own.

Marrianne looked at me with a gay smile and said, "Now you know about the Stammtisch. It is a custom at almost every hotel in Germany that there is a table where friends and the people of the town come to sit and talk and gossip, or just to be together. Instead of everyone standing up and shaking hands, which you know all Germans love to do, the newcomer simply knocks on the table and everyone says hello and he takes his place."

Before the evening had ended we had a dentist, a factory manager, a folk singer, a bricklayer, a couple from another town (who used to live in Rothenburg), and a bookseller.

A marvelous custom is "Stammtisch."

ROMANTIK HOTEL 33, MARKUSTURM, ob der Tauber, Roder-gassel 8803 Rothenburg; Tel. 09861/2370. A 30-room village inn. Breakfast, lunch, and dinner served daily. Sauna, solarium, garage (if desired). Rates: 75 Dm. Familie Berger-Reinwald, Innkeepers.

Directions: Rothenburg is in central Germany south of Wurzburg and west of Nurnberg. The Markusturm is about three squares from the town hall. (Hallestadt.)

Rothenburg ob der Tauber

Rothenburg is a walled town, and like Maastricht in the Netherlands, as the town expanded and more walls were built, a series of walled rings were created around the city. Today, so zealous are the townspeople in preserving the ancient atmos- phere and quality that any construction or remodeling in the old part of the town must conform to the old architecture. No modern buildings may be built.

The town history started around 900 A.D. and continued through fire, earthquake, and wars. One of these was the Thirty Years' War (1618-1648) when the town was besieged and conquered by three different armies. A play, the "Meister-trunk," which is performed each year in Rothenburg at Whitsun-tide (Pentecost), commemorates a most unusual event which took place during one of the occupations. According to the story, General Tilly, the victorious commander, was considering the execution of four of the city councilors. The hangman was called, but meanwhile the general was offered a mighty bumper of Franconian wine (three-quarters of a gallon). On what was obviously a whim, Tilly promised mercy to all four if one of the councilors could empty the bumper in one draft. The past mayor drank the wine in less than ten minutes, Tilly kept his promise and the population shouted and danced with joy.

There are many other yearly events celebrated in the town including the historic Shepherds' Dances, when members of the Shepherds' Guild meet in the afternoon to perform the historic dances in front of the town hall, the performance of farces, plays by the famous, 16th-century shoemaker-poet, Hans Sachs, which are also presented at Whitsuntide. Among other special occasions is the Freetown Festival which takes place during the second weekend in September; and from Christmas Eve to the Epiphany, the town offers its visitors a delightful program of a series of contemplative, historical, and romantic productions, and lively entertainments.

Rothenburg has gates, churches, castles, fountains, muse-ums, and old houses—all incredibly beautiful and well-pre-served.

One of the unusual sights is known as the "Alte Rothenburg Handwerkerhaus," a remarkably restored and preserved house of a Rothenburg tradesman built in 1270. It contains 11 rooms from the ground floor to the attic, all furnished with original medieval furniture and shows most graphically how large families, including grandmothers and grandfathers, lived and worked a few centuries ago. The furniture, utensils, stoves, fireplaces, toys, and clothing have all been thoroughly re-searched by the Berger family who are the owners of the Hotel Markusturm. It is truly a glimpse into life in the Middle Ages.

HOTEL GREIFEN-POST, Feuchtwangen, (Romantic Road)

I was standing in one of the dining rooms of this very old hotel, and Brigette Lorentz was explaining the meaning of one of the five murals.

"The first one shows Kaiser Karl who was out hunting in this area around 700 A.D. He became thirsty and saw a pigeon and followed it to a fountain. He was so enchanted that he caused a Benedictine monastery to be founded on the spot. There you can see King Karl and the pigeon and the fountain."

Other important turning points in the history of the region are also depicted in the murals, and in the final scene I saw a typical 14th-century marketplace scene when Feuchtwangen flourished as a trade and corn market.

Brigette and Edward Lorentz are continuing in the inn-keeping tradition of Edward's grandfather who transformed the inn, which has been here since 1599, from a brewery gasthaus to a hotel. Most of the old feeling has been retained and there are walls with many exposed half-timbers on the second and third floors.

I discovered that the Greifen-Post is two hotels with a second-floor bridge connecting the Greifen to the Post. In the Post, the rooms are furnished in the traditional manner, whereas in the Greifen, more modern furniture has been used.

Feeling as if I were stepping back into the Middle Ages, we

returned to the main hallway and reception area, where Brigette pointed out a scroll inscribed with names of such renowned early guests as Emperor Maximilian, who stayed here; Queen Christina of Sweden, who stopped on her way to Rome (probably disguised as a man). The mother of Queen Victoria of England was a guest in 1844, and Jenny Lind, the famous Swedish nightingale, also stopped off for lunch, during a tour. Immediately next to the scroll was a notice that the chef at this hotel had won a medal at a recent exposition for preparing what Brigette called a "farmer's dish."

We walked into the front dining room and discussed the various regional specialties on the menu, like the homemade soups, Bavarian liver and dumplings, goulash-and-garlic creamed soup, which was a recipe of Edward's grandmother.

"We cook everything with butter and cream, and only use fresh things," she asserted. Other regional specialties include mushrooms in cream on toast with Bavarian cheese, and Franconian sausage served with sauerkraut.

Brigette took me to one corner of the dining room where there was a mural showing a man in the forest confronting a wild boar. She translated the German saying just above the mural: "I would rather be with the wild pig in the forest then to be at home with my scolding wife."

ROMANTIK HOTEL 36, GREIFEN-POST, 8805 Feuchtwangen; Tel. 09852/9133. A 50-room hotel located on the market plaza. Breakfast, lunch, and dinner served daily. Rates: 64 Dm. Edward and Brigette Lorentz, Innkeepers.

Directions: Feuchtwangen is on Rte. 25, a few km. south of Rothenburg.

HOTEL ROSE, Weissenburg, (Romantic Road)

If glamour is supplied by having guests who are theatrical and political celebrities, then the Hotel Rose in Weissenburg certainly qualifies as being glamorous. I took a look at the rather elaborate guest book under the watchful eye of its owner, Edgar Mitschke, and on the very first page I found that Chancellor Konrad Adenauer had been a guest here in 1957. There was also a most impressive number of television, theatre, and musical stars, many of whom included their photographs as well as appropriate sentiments. It reminded me of the registers of old inns from the 19th century in the United States in which itinerant theatrical troupes took advantage of the opportunity to do a little advertising.

Although Weissenburg is not a large city, the Hotel Rose has a "big city" atmosphere with a certain air of elegance about it. Some of the bedrooms, particularly those facing the square are rather elaborately furnished. The single and double rooms in the back of the house were somewhat austere.

The ratskeller in this hotel dates back to 1320, and the arched brick ceilings have been whitewashed and decorated with animal skins. The light, furnished from candles, created a romantic atmosphere, and in one corner was a small, private fireplace which could supply extra romance for four people.

Over a cup of delicious hot chocolate with whipped cream, Herr Mitschke and I sat in the main dining room and discussed his elaborate menu which, in addition to offering local German specialties, apparently caters to international tastes as well. He explained that there are certain weeks in the year when they feature a particular kind of cuisine, such as French, Hawaiian, or Swiss.

ROMANTIK HOTEL 37, ROSE, 8832 Weissenburg/Bayern; Tel. 09141/2096. A 37-room midtown hotel in a very busy central Bavarian town. Breakfast, lunch, and dinner served daily. Rates: 84 Dm. Edgar Mitschke, Innkeeper.

Directions: Weissenburg is on Rte. 2 south of Nurnberg and east of Feuchtwangen via many back roads. (Bring magnifying glass for map.)

Itinerary #4: From Frankfurt east through Bemburg, Wirsberg, Bayreuth, Auerbach, and Munich.

HOTEL ZEHNTKELLER, Iphofen (Romantic Road)

I have visited inns both in North America and Europe with many unusual features, but this is the first time I have ever visited an inn where an opera was written! A well-known German composer, Hans Pfitzner composed it while a guest in this hotel in 1932.

I learned all this from Henry Seufert, the young innkeeper who, with his father and grandfather, have owned this hotel since the late 19th century. Henry is a very interesting man in his early 30s, unmarried, and very proud of the fact that he not only has vineyards, but a winery as well. I found Henry's wine in other Romantik hotels in Germany.

The entrance to the Zehntkeller from the road is through an arched gate, and in the early German spring there were pansies and daffodils growing in pots and an old wooden wheelbarrow.

Inside the massive door I approached the reception desk which, with wonderful practicality, is right next to the service bar so that the elder Herr Seufert, in attendance, could be in two places. In fact, I found this arrangement rather common in Germany. While he spoke very little English, the elder Herr Seufert conveyed the message that his son would be on the scene in very short order. Meanwhile, I walked about the inn, which at noon had a distinctly bustling air. The waitresses were hurrying back and forth with platters of delicious-looking food with tantalizing aromas. There were two rather small, but very attractive, dining rooms both of which had paneling halfway up to the ceiling topped with the characteristic plate rail with pewter, silver, and ceramics.

Henry appeared, and since he had very good English, we plunged into history..The old building was originally a monastery dating back to 1250 and later was occupied by the town tax collector. At the turn of the century it was acquired by the Seufert family.

We talked about the menu, and the specialties of the house included chicken in wine, mixed grill, venison, and duck. There are also several veal dishes. For dessert at lunch I had sliced apples which had been lightly sauteed in flour and cinnamon. I later tried them in my own kitchen.

Henry explained that this was an excellent stopover for people from Belgium and Holland and northern Germany headed for Austria or Italy. Many guests returned several times on these trips. Most guests stayed for just a single night. Slightly off the highway, it has a very restful air about it.

In the guest book of the inn, the composer of the opera did something rather novel—he wrote a few musical notes and the legend "Here you have what you want." I have a feeling that many people have found a restful atmosphere, good food, and the warm hospitality of the Zehntkeller exactly what they want.

ROMANTIK HOTEL 27, ZEHNTKELLER, 8715 Iphofen; Tel. 09323/ 3318. A small village inn about 1 km. off main highway. Breakfast, lunch, and dinner served daily. Rates: Reasonable. H. Seufert, Innkeeper.

Directions: About 25 km. south of Wursburg. (Rte. 8)

RESTAURANT MESSERSCHMITT, Bamberg (Bavaria)

Bamberg is a rather sizable, attractive city with colorful old buildings, a river running through the middle of the town, and a shortage of parking spaces. Although I wasn't certain of the location of the Messerschmitt, I took my chances and rode right into the centrum—and there it was! I joined the rest of the German drivers and parked on the sidewalk.

The restaurant has a look of antiquity about it with wood-paneled ceilings, elaborate chandeliers, substantial furniture, many plants, and gleaming white tablecloths. The menu had quite a few specialties, including different varieties of soups and fishes, as well as steaks and veal dishes; among an extensive selection of French and international entrees was Mexican rump steak.

The most tempting and largest dessert menu I think I have ever seen was called "La Dolce Vita" and featured all kinds of ice cream dishes, including banana splits, and quite a variety of crepes; also coffee with heavy cream, and chocolate. It was tantalizing to someone with a sweet tooth like mine.

It all looked very inviting, and if the opportunity presented itself, I would certainly return again to enjoy lunch or dinner at the Messerschmitt — unfortunately, my visit fell between meals.

ROMANTIK RESTAURANT 26, MESSERSCHMITT, 8600 Bamberg; Tel. 0951/26471, Lange Strasse 41. A well-known restaurant and weinhaus in the center of a small, attractive German city. Lunch and dinner served daily. Familie Pschorn, Innkeepers.

Directions: Reaching Bamberg, follow signs to center of city (Centrum) and ask directions.

HOTEL POST, Wirsberg, (Swiss Franconia; Bavaria)

Frau Herrmann and I were seated *in* a beer barrel. She was recounting the history of this hotel, which is high in the Swiss Franconia resort section of Germany just a few kilometers north of Bayreuth. "My grandfather and grandmother came here and planted the oak tree across the street in front of the church," she said. She showed me some photographs of the inn at the turn of the century, and also of her father and mother who continued in the innkeeping tradition — just as she and her husband have.

"I was born in Room 2," she said, and then added with a big smile, "why that is the room you are staying in." Room 2 overlooks the triangular-shaped plaza of the town, around which are several shops. In one corner is a church whose bells peel every quarter-hour for twenty-four hours a day; I was a bit shaken at this information, but she assured me I would not hear them after I had gone to sleep, and I did not.

The hotel is furnished with both romantic and contemporary furnishings. My bedroom, as did most, included a television, a small honor-system refrigerator, and a bathroom heater, which I made good use of on a chilly April morning.

At dinner, I enjoyed sliced venison served in a gravy-laden casserole with red cabbage and apple. Frau Herrmann's son was active in the kitchen, and she was very proud of some of his creations. "We have dishes from Alsace, Yugoslavia, and Mexico," she said. "We also have special weeks where we feature

unusual international dishes."

She joined me for breakfast the following morning, and we continued my education on Germany. I enjoyed her very interesting observations which were expressed in a combination of English and German. She suggested that I take a walk around the village and also the gardens of the modest castle which she and her husband were restoring.

Now, how did we happen to be seated in a beer barrel? Because, in one of the dining rooms, a booth which accommodates at least five people has been fashioned from a beer barrel. A decorative lamp hangs from the top, and seat cushions make it very cozy and comfortable.

ROMANTIK HOTEL 24,POST, 8655 Wirsberg; Tel. 09227/888. A 40-room village hotel in the high hills about 20 miles north of Bayreuth. Breakfast, lunch, and dinner served daily. Wirsberg is in a very pleasant high elevation with many narrow but excellent roads for car touring and miles and miles of walking in the forest. Indoor swimming pool being built, outdoor swimming pool is nearby in the hills. Rates: 71 Dm. K. Herrmann, Innkeeper.

Directions: Wirsberg is a few miles west of the Berlin-Nurnberg Autobahn (E6). On the map look for Bayreuth and Kulmbach; Wirsberg is just off Rte. 303.

HOTEL GOLDNER LOWE, Auerbach (Bavaria)

I was seated in the Knappenstube with Elizabeth Ruder. It was like having lunch in a coal mine—overhead were rough beams and planks supported by massive posts from which the bark had been stripped. The walls were of rough, raw rock with the streaks of orange iron ore plainly visible.

"We here in Auerbach are very proud of the heritage of the iron miners," said Elizabeth, who with her fair hair and 22 years would be most out of place in an iron mine. "So, we have decorated this dining room to resemble the tunnels in the mines below the city. The word 'knappen' is the German word for iron miners." She pointed out the many miners'lamps and tools, and even a big cart from the mines which had been used to bring up the ore in the mine shafts. Now it was gaily decorated with greens and Easter eggs, a reminder of the holiday just passed. There were several wrought-iron lamps and candleholders. In one corner was a statue of St. Barbara who, I understand, is the patron saint of iron miners.

The Goldner Lowe has been in existence since 1144, and until 1898, when a disasterous fire destroyed a great deal of the town, has occupied the same building. It was rebuilt on the same site, and there are some very interesting primitive paintings in one of the dining rooms showing both the old inn and the new. The Ruder family has owned it for almost 100 years.

There are some excellent primitive wooden carvings of miners in the reception hall, showing the great strength of those men who worked beneath the earth.

Alfons Ruder, Elizabeth's father, joined us and explained some of the original Bavarian dishes on the menu which included salted brisket of beef served with horseradish, pigs' knuckles, fresh trout, which is kept in a tank in the kitchen. For a rather unpretentious hotel, there were some surprisingly sophisticated dishes on the menu; I never cease to be amazed at the versatility of many of the chefs in these middle-class hotels who are able to prepare dishes from all over the world.

One interesting dish on the menu is called "Knappen Toast," which is pork steak, horseradish, and anchovies.

Several rooms in the Goldner Lowe are furnished in both traditional and modern styles; in addition to a roof terrace with a view of the town, there is also a bowling alley in the basement. Everything is clean and wholesome-appearing.

Auerbach is not far from the city of Bayreuth which is the site of the famous music festival, and the Goldner Lowe would make an ideal quiet place to stop for a few days.

ROMANTIK HOTEL 28, GOLDNER LOWE, 8572 Auerbach/ Oberfalz; Tel. (09643)/352. A 20-room village inn in an old, middle-ages town. Breakfast, lunch, and dinner served daily. Roof terrace. Rates: 74 Dm. Alfons Ruder, Innkeeper.

Directions: Auerbach is a short distance south of Bayreuth about 10 km. east of the Berlin-Nurnberg Autobahn (E6). Exit is marked Forcheim-Amberg.

HOTEL VILLA SOLLN, Munich

This small hotel, which is about 15 minutes from downtown Munich, had about 22 rooms, all with baths, direct-dial telephones, radios, T.V.'s, and an inside swimming pool with a sauna. I found the rates most reasonable and the quiet rest very welcome.

HOTEL VILLA SOLLN, Wilhelm-leibl str. 16; 8 Munich 71; Tel. 792091. The Villa Solln Hotel is not a part of the Romantik Hotel group so all communications have to be made directly with them.

Itinerary #5: *Munich south to the Bavarian Alps and east to Lake Constanz.*

This itinerary includes part of the famous Alpine Road where the traveler may continue into Austria. It leads from Garmisch through Oberammergau, skirting the northern edge of the mountains and continuing into Vangen and Lake Constanz.

CLAUSING'S POSTHOTEL, Garmisch-Partenkirchen (Bavarian Alps)

What a beautiful, sun-drenched, blue-skies morning in Garmisch! What a remarkable contrast to the day before when snow fell upon the Bavarian Alps in mid-April just as it does in mid-winter. Certain roads had been closed and it had been necessary to arrive in Garmisch by a different route.

I was having breakfast on the heated terrace at Clausing's Posthotel, where the hot spring sun had re-exerted its customary role and was beginning to melt the ten inches of snow that had accumulated on the tabletops and chairs of the outdoor section.

Visitors and townfolk alike were following the beckoning sounds of Sunday church bells.

I joined some new friends from Iowa whom I had met the night before, who were also traveling in Europe during the off-season.

The waitress brought me tea and a basket of assorted breads along with a plate of sausage and cheese slices, and pots of honey and marmalade. She explained my egg would follow. After a week in Germany I had come to enjoy these German breakfasts very much.

Clausing's, as it is called, is a busy, well-run hotel with a sophisticated, international, yet definitely Bavarian, flavor. My room was comfortable, but probably scheduled for remodeling in the future, and I saw several others that had a similar appearance.

There were a few quixotic touches. For example, during dinner a lady came through the dining room selling flowers, and hot on her heels was a man in a business suit wearing a Bavarian hat taking photographs of the guests on request.

Young Henry Mike Clausing, the son of the innkeeper, and himself a fourth generation hotelier, explained that about 85% of all the people who came to Garmisch each year are from Germany, although there is a U.S. Army rest and recreation center here. Clausing's is very popular for American service families. It isn't large enough to accommodate the bus tours so, by and large, most of the guests are in groups of two and four. There were several families in the house enjoying the un-expected bonus of a weekend of skiing. On Saturday night the discotheque nightclub had been running at full capacity and I was happy to see that cheek-to-cheek dancing was still alive and well in Garmisch.

Clausing's has been many things to many people for many years—a place for honeymooning, anniversaries, and holidays in all seasons. Best of all, I think it is fun.

ROMANTIK HOTEL 53, CLAUSING'S POSTHOTEL, Marienplatz 12, 8100 Garmisch; Tel. 08821/58071. A 45-room intown hotel located in one of Germany's most famous resort towns. Break-fast, lunch, and dinner served daily. Rates: 88 Dm. Familie Clausing, Innkeeper.

Directions: Garmisch is about an hour and a half from Munich with a choice of several roads on the map. Also about three-quarters of an hour from Innsbruck, Austria.

Saturday Night in Garmisch

It was six o'clock on an April evening in Garmisch. The sun, which had been hidden behind the heavy snow clouds all day, was now providing us with some marvelous shots of gold on the top of the snow-clad mountain peaks which completely sur-round this Bavarian alpine town.

An unexpected heavy snowfall provided Garmisch with another full weekend of skiing, and mingling with the German families dressed in traditional Bavarian garb were American servicemen pelting each other with snowballs.

There is lots of traffic on a Saturday evening in Garmisch, including Mercedes-Benzes with Munich plates, Porsches with U.S. Army plates, local town buses, and many taxis that shuttle back and forth to the train station.

The big attraction in Garmisch is the mountain peaks like the Zugspitze at nearly 9000 feet, the Dreitorspitze and the Alp-spitze at 7500 feet, and the Osterfeoderkopf at 6000 feet. All of them have many ski lifts, tramways, and cable cars. The 1936 Winter Olympic games were held here, and since then Garmisch has been one of the ski capitals of the world. There is also bobsledding, ice skating, and extensive cross-country skiing.

In summer there are the ubiquitous climbing, walking, and

excursions. *During the warm weather, lakes provide swimming and boating and the famous castles Linderhof and Neuschwanstein are nearby, as is also the village of Oberammergau where the famous Passion Play is held.*

I came to Garmisch in the spring hoping for a glimpse of summer, instead found a generous helping of winter. It was like Christmas on the 4th of July!

HOTEL ALTE POST, Wangen (Bavarian Alps)

Herr Veile is a man who loves to smile and laugh. As far as I could see he had a great many things to smile and laugh about. For one thing, he and his wife Louisa have been keeping this hotel for the past 27 years and it apparently has been prospering under their direction. It is located in a beautiful section of Germany, well within sight of the peaks of the Bavarian Alps and only a few kilometers from Lake Constance which has many beautiful drives, homes, castles, and churches.

After meandering through the Bavarian Alps from Garmisch on a beautiful Sunday afternoon, I arrived in Wangen, a baroque walled town, as the bells were tolling six. The bells of Wangen are still another story. I heard them ring many times, but couldn't make any sense out of them. One seemed to toll four times every hour, and in turn found a response in another deeper-toned bell that tolled the hour correctly. As soon as this duet was finished, a soprano bell took up the message, apparently just marking time.

The Alte Post, which was once a post stop, is located just outside one of the town gates which has a very impressive clock tower. After a most refreshing bath and a short rest, I found my way to the second-floor dining room where quite a few people from Wagen were enjoying dinner. The atmosphere was very pleasant.

After being shown to a table, I was joined by a German businessman and his wife who shared the table with me. We became acquainted quite easily, and again I was pleased with the custom in middle-class European restaurants of guests sharing tables when there are no other vacancies.

After a most satisfying dinner which wound up with the specialty of the house, an ice cream cake with slivered almonds, I had a long visit with Herr and Frau Viele and learned that there is an annex about a half-mile away on an elevation overlooking the town. We made an appointment to look at it in the morning, and after a short tour of the guest lounge and the hallways where I found many extremely interesting and attractive pieces of antique furniture, I enjoyed a good night's sleep under my down comforter.

The following morning Herr Viele showed me around the remainder of the house and modestly pointed out the fact that he had received an award as a "Kuchmeister" which meant that he was a master of the kitchen.

The Alte Post Hotel is a beautifully decorated, well-furnished accommodation. It has an interesting history that goes back to 1409 which is 200 years before the formation of the German postal system in 1670.

Yes, Herr Viele has much to smile about.

ROMANTIK HOTEL 51, ALTE POST, 7988 Wangen im Allgau; Tel. 07522/4014. A hotel with 50 rooms included in two locations. The main building is located next to one of the walls of the town. The annex is on a slightly higher elevation. Breakfast, lunch, and dinner served daily. Rates: 70 Dm. Familie Viele, Innkeepers.

Directions: Wangen is on Rte. 18 approximately 30 km. from Lake Constance. It is 2-2½ hrs. from Munich.

HOTEL WALDHORN, Ravensburg (Lake Constance)

It was Monday morning in Ravensburg. The streets were enlivened by housewives with their shopping bags, and gentlemen of commerce were busy with the affairs of the day.

In the Hotel Waldhorn, the main affairs of the day seemed to be clean, clean, clean! In the front dining room, there was a young lady standing on the table dusting off the plate rail and picking up every piece of pewter and china to give it a good swish. She even opened every decorative beer stein and wiped out the inside. Fresh flowers were being arranged on every table, the sweepers were sweeping, the vacuum cleaners were vacuum cleaning.

I was enjoying a cup of tea in one of the dining rooms when I felt something jump on the bench next to me and wag a friendly tail. "His name is Bimbo," explained my hostess, "he is also part of the family." The "family" in this case includes the innkeeper, Herr Dressel and his wife, along with his son and daughter-in-law.

I was shown to the second floor by Frau Bouley-Dressel where the hotel was hosting an exhibition of chocolate manufacturers from Switzerland. I have never seen such an incredible collection of fanciful chocolate. I walked around several of the tables aching to pocket many of the tantalizing morsels.

We progressed to a series of bedrooms most of which were very pleasantly furnished and several had television sets. We returned to the ground floor and I was asked to sit and have some refreshments where I could watch the activities of the morning.

The young son joined me and we had a brief discussion about some of the specialties of the newly remodeled kitchen, which was a splendid example of cleanliness and good organization. He explained that one of the policies of the house was to serve only fresh vegetables. "Nothing frozen or in cans," he said. Consequently, the menu is constantly changing according to the season. One of the popular dishes is chicken Bresse, which is cooked in a Burgundy wine sauce and served with Gruyere cheese. There is also lamb Bretaigne and many fresh fish dishes. I sampled the homemade goose liver pate and truffles which are grown in the Strasbourg region a little to the north.

Now Bimbo and I were seated at what I learned was the "Stammtisch" table in the front dining room with its paneled ceilings and walls and interesting carvings and ceramics.

Jan Lindstrom's line drawing which includes a handsome stove, catches the spirit very well.

ROMANTIK HOTEL 48, WALDHORN, Marienplatz 15, 7980 Ravensburg; Tel. 0751/23017. A 20-room hotel in the center of a fairly large town. Quite convenient for many excursions both to the Lake Constance region and the Alps. Breakfast, lunch, and dinner served daily. Rates: 70 Dm. Familie Bouley-Dressel, Innkeepers.

Directions: Ravensburg is about 35 km. north of Lake Constance via Routes 30 or 33.

HOTEL LANDGASTHOF FISCHERHAUS, Seefelden (Lake Constance)

A rooster was crowing. Soon another responded and for awhile it was a contest of wills and lungs. Roosters have been crowing, chickens clucking, and spring has been coming to this farmland for centuries. It is a gentle place on the shores of Lake Constance in southern Germany and much of it today is still being farmed or is in vineyards. The father and mother of innkeeper Roland Birkenmayer farmed it for many years and had a small inn nearby. In 1963, according to Roland's sister Ella, who, along with her brother and his wife, is an innkeeper at this quiet, restful resort hotel, the parents closed their smaller place in favor of the new Fischerhaus. It is next door to a farm and there are other farms and villas along the northern shore of the lake.

The hotel has three-and-a-half stories with typical German half-timbers and white plaster both inside and out. The two front dining rooms have benches around the walls and one has a corner fireplace. They are low-ceilinged rooms with appropriate farm utensils decorating the walls.

Above stairs, the 15 lodging rooms have been recently redecorated with gay curtains providing a marked contrast to the pristine white plaster walls and exposed beams. The rooms were most pleasantly furnished and had a view either of the lake and the flowering fruit trees in the front, or the hills in the back of the house.

When I remarked on the beauty of the birch trees, Ella replied, "Yes our name 'Birkenmayer' actually is a reference to birch trees. Those were all planted about ten years ago."

In addition to lake sports, the principal one of which is

fishing, guests at this farmhouse-hotel also enjoy sailing on the lake and swimming in a heated outdoor pool. There is tennis, walking, and much touring of the area. It is excellent for families with children, everyone gets acquainted very easily.

Roland is not only the hotelier, but also the only cook. The specialties of the house naturally include fish from the lake such as perch, pike, trout, and eel. He also makes the desserts which include chocolate mousse, apple cake, and cheese cake.

It was a warm, spring afternoon when I bade farewell to Ella and Roland and their 300-year-old farm which is now a resort inn. It was a very happy place.

ROMANTIK HOTEL 50, LANDGASTHOF FISCHERHAUS, 7772 Seefelden/Bodensee; Tel. 07556/8563. A 15-room, 35-bed resort hotel on Lake Constance. Breakfast, lunch, and dinner served daily except Monday. Swimming pool on grounds. Sailing, fishing, touring, walking nearby. Rates: 82 Dm. Familie Birkenmayer, Innkeepers.

Directions: Seefelden is located on B31 which runs along the northshore of Lake Constance. The road east from Meersburg is marked "Uhldingen." From Switzerland, take the Konstanz-Meersburg Ferry and go west 7 km. on B31.

RESTAURANT STEFANSKELLER, Konstanz, (Lake Constance)

Bertold Siber is both the chef and the owner of this side-street restaurant (not a part of the Romantik group) which is adjacent to St. Stephen's Church in this southern German city on the banks of Lake Constance. He unabashedly told me that his is the sixth best restaurant in Germany, and that in spite of his youth he has received a great deal of training in France and Scandinavia.

I arrived in the middle of the afternoon only to find that it would not open until 5:30. I returned at 5 o'clock, and although I could see waiters and others on the inside, they did not answer my knock. I went around and entered through the kitchen. This was bad etiquette and did not gladden the heart of Bertold (who is a man of some imposing appearance with black hair and an equally full beard). After I had properly introduced myself, we did find a place by the window and he turned on the charm, which was considerable.

He explained that he cooked the "new French cuisine."

Everything was fresh and cooked to order, even the sauces. We went over the menu as well as we could in his rather rusty English and my completely disintegrating French. There is a small a la carte menu, but for the most part guests choose from one of two set menus. One for 50 Dm had four courses, and the other, five courses for 100 Dm. I would have been willing to invest in the 50 Dm dinner, although the 100 Dm dinner was entirely out of my range. The decision, however, was very simple because I already had a dinner engagement and several kilometers to travel.

Although I did not sample the food, I was sold on everything else—the fresh flowers, the art collection, the highly polished brass cooking utensils—the general appearance all added up to enjoyment. Bertold, himself, is worth the price of the hors d'oeuvres.

RESTAURANT STEFANSKELLER, 775 Konstanz am Bodensee, Stefanplatz 41; Tel. 07531/23566. A most interesting restaurant officially designated a wine shop. Luncheon served daily except Sunday and Monday from 11:30 to 2:30. Dinner served daily except Sunday from 5:30 to midnight. Expensive. Bertold Siber, Owner and Chef.

Directions: In Konstanz ask anyone for the location of St. Stephen's Church. Restaurant faces church. Parking nearby a problem.

HOTEL KRONE, Gottlieben, Switzerland (Lake Constance)

It was raining on the Rhine. Yes, it rains in Germany, or perhaps I should say Switzerland in this case, because Gottlieben is a small town just outside of Konstanz, Germany, about 7 kilometers into Switzerland. In this rain, the flowers which were abundant in Gottlieben, seemed to burst from their buds. The pots of pansies, daffodils, and other flowers on the terrace in front of the Hotel Krone, which directly overlooks the river, were persisting gaily in spite of the grey sky. There were ducks and swans swimming in the river.

The only person who spoke English at the Krone was a very pleasant waitress named Chrystal—Frau Tschudi, who is both owner and head cook, smiled at me benignly but Chrystal did all the talking.

At dinner, she and I decided on a small steak cooked in a horseradish sauce with generous amounts of black pepper and

211

homemade noodles. Delicious. For dessert I asked for something with chocolate and the couple at the next table
suggested in German that she bring me a large goblet containing
three scoops of vanilla ice cream and a pitcher of hot chocolate
on the side. I ate every last bite.

I struck up a conversation with my benefactors. He was a
businessman who preferred to stay at the Krone when he came
to Konstanz because, he said, "It is very tranquil." He was a
friend of Frau Tschudi's and apparently they were having some
kind of celebration because there was a great deal of
examination of wine labels and tasting of dishes and much
fluttering about by the Frau.

All of the lodging rooms in this hotel have recently been
converted from the old-fashioned romantic theme to a more
contemporary feeling. They are quite a contrast with the
traditional furnishings in the public rooms.

I wandered around before dark and found Gottlieben to be
a very pleasant, quiet town. There was a fascinating boatyard just
a few steps away from the hotel where large luxury boats are
built, apparently for use on the Rhine. Gottlieben is also a stop
on the regular Rhine River boat lines.

*ROMANTIK HOTEL 1, KRONE, 8274 Gottlieben, Switzerland;
Tel. 072/96130. A 25-room hotel on the banks of the Rhine near
Konstanz, Germany. Contemporarily furnished lodging rooms*

are clean and comfortable. Breakfast, lunch, and dinner served daily. Rates: Reasonable. Frau Tschudi, Innkeeper.

Directions: From Konstanz, Germany follow Gottliebstrasse through the Swiss checkpoint approximately 10 km. to Gottlieben. Turn left at river to hotel.

My trip to Germany was particularly successful through the efforts of Jens Diekmann, the executor director of the Romantik Hotels. His encyclopedic knowledge of Germany, Austria, and Switzerland was most helpful, and I'm certain that readers contacting him in Karlstein will share my enthusiasm.

My very short stay in Munich was made most enjoyable by Hermann and Ellen Sendele, who showed me some of the interesting sights of this fascinating city by night.

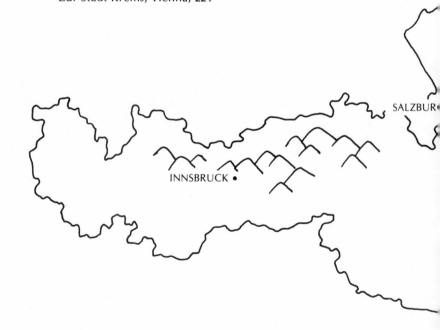

SALZBUR

INNSBRUCK •

AUSTRIA

LINZ •

VIENNA •

Baden •

Wr. Neustadt •

Semmering •

Bruck •

GRAZ •

TRAVEL SUGGESTIONS FOR AUSTRIA

How to Get There
Pan American has direct flights from the East coast to Vienna. Vienna is also a very popular charter flight city. Eurail-pass is good.

Country Inns in Austria
Austrian country inns are delightful. Some are simple, less expensive pensions offering the opportunity to know Austrians more readily. The somewhat austere, but pleasant, clean, and comfortable rooms usually have two beds and a wash basin, with wc's and bathrooms "down the corridor." Almost all overnight stays in a pension include a breakfast of rolls, butter, jam, tea or coffee. Many offer an evening meal (full pension), and special rates are available for longer stays.

Reservations
When a reservation is made for an Austrian accommodation, the agreement is very clear. The hotel owner or pension proprietor must hold the room, and the guest (unless he cancels) is positively obligated for the cost of the room. This is the law of Austrian innkeeping.

Reservations for accommodations in this book can be made by mail (a deposit helps) or by telephone.

Car Rentals

See section in front of book entitled: "Renting a Car for Europe."

Driving Tips

Driving in Austria is the same as driving in Germany. Once again the back roads are beautiful and driving in the Austrian Alps is a marvelous experience.

My Itinerary in Austria

I flew directly by Pan Am to Vienna where I spent about six days sightseeing and eating. I took the train to Graz, Semmering, and Baden. To obtain road maps and guides to Austria, see the section at the back of the book.

Vienna Nights and Days

In every European city there are always "musts." In Copenhagen it is probably Tivoli Gardens; in London, the Changing of the Guard. In Vienna, the list is so long that there is a temptation to try and see everything. There is the Spanish Riding School, the Vienna Boys' Choir, and the Opera. There are almost endless art galleries and museums. There are also the Vienna Woods, the many gardens, castles, memorial sites, and libraries.

There is also the Prater, over 1300 acres on an island in the Danube River. It is easy to find because it has a 210-foot-high

ferris wheel and the ride is something no one ever forgets. *Some of the fun rides in the Prater are the most unusual ever devised by the minds of amusement park operators. It is said that Johann Strauss used to play at the various restaurants and his melodies are heard continually.*

One of the most fascinating things about Vienna is the fact that the visitor can go almost everywhere by streetcar or public transportation. At 5 p.m. there were people in evening clothes riding the streetcars toward the center of the city to go to the Opera, and at 11:30 p.m. the same people were riding back to the suburbs.

It is possible to go most everywhere in Vienna and nearby on really well-organized sightseeing tours.

HOTEL ROMISCHER KAISER, Vienna

This hotel belongs to what is called a "voluntary association of small historical hotels and restaurants which has been formed to provide an alternative to the standardized facilities offered by the large hotels and catering groups." It is located in the center of the city not far from the Opera and St. Stephen's Church.

I liked it immediately and was very happy to meet the young manager and his wife who showed me proudly through many different rooms and the restaurant.

Some of the bedrooms were most romantic indeed with ornately carved beds and rather plush furniture. The building is quite old and therefore has higher ceilings and larger rooms than I found in some of the more recently constructed hotels.

I happened to drop by there again about 11 o'clock in the evening where I found the night manager babysitting for two of the guests' children. He was a most affable man and explained that this was part of the informal service provided by the hotel.

ROMANTIK HOTEL, 1, ROMISCHER KAISER, Anagasse 16, A-1010, Vienna. Telephone: 527751. A 50-room hotel in the center of Vienna. Rates: 480 to 680 schillings per person.

SAVOY HOTEL, Vienna

This hotel is located one block from the main shopping area. It has a rather small lobby with some very interesting

St. Stephen's Church

prints. The only meal served is breakfast. It was here that I first saw an eiderdown comforter. Almost everywhere in Austria this is the standard type of blanket. They usually have sheets that are buttoned around them.

The general appearance of the Savoy is slightly more austere than the other two I visited.

SAVOY HOTEL, Lindengasse 12, A-1070, Vienna. Telephone: 934646/012491. A 43-room hotel just a short distance from downtown Vienna. Rates: 300-500 schillings per person (includes breakfast).

HOTEL KAISERIN ELISABETH, Vienna

Here is another small center-city Vienna hotel that is quite plush and elegant. The lobby is furnished with beautiful antique rugs, wall hangings and elegant furniture. The hotel has been in existence since the 14th century and has a very impressive history of famous visitors.

The lodging rooms are both modern and traditional.

HOTEL KAISERIN ELISABETH, Weihburggasse 3, A-1010, Vienna. Telephone: (0222) 522626. A 127-bed hotel in central Vienna. Rates: 200-550 schillings per person (includes breakfast).

Dining in Vienna

Briefly, Viennese restaurants can be divided into several categories: first-class, middle-class (or restaurant "bourgeois"), the gasthaus or inn, the pub, the cellar, restaurants bon marché (for cheap meals), and specialty restaurants. Out-of-towners in Vienna can always be seen with two items in their hands — a Viennese restaurant booklet and a map of Vienna. I have discussed Viennese food more completely in describing my visits to various restaurants.

CAFE LANDTMANN, Vienna

It was chilly in the late afternoon and I was happy to succumb to the beckoning blandishments of the Cafe Landtmann which is across the street from City Hall Park in the center of Vienna. It has marble-top tables and very spacious booths of different sizes. Everything has a turn-of-the-century look with

A back street in Vienna

walls of inlaid wood and ornate hanging brass lamps.

The cafe menu listed at least eight different kinds of coffee and they also served tea, chocolate and milk. The menu, as in most restaurants, was printed in several languages. I ordered a cup of marvelous hot chocolate served in an old-fashioned cup. There is also a theatre in this building and I looked at the playbill which indicated that there was a new play offered every two or three nights.

Occasionally the head waiter would bring around a most delicious selection of cakes and pastries with great amounts of mocha filling and mocha cream icing.

Now the tables were filling up and more people were coming in. It was the end of the day and the beginning of a gay Viennese evening.

CAFE LANDTMANN, Dr. Karl Lueger Ring 4, A-1010, Vienna. Telephone: 630621. A typical Vienna cafe open daily from 9 a.m. to 11 p.m. Immediately across the plaza from Town Hall (Rathaus).

WIENER RATHAUSKELLER, Vienna

I left the Cafe Landtmann and wandered across the park to the Town Hall which is known as the "Rathaus." It was built between 1872 and 1885, and has carved figures all around the fourth story of the building. A huge clock was pointing at six o'clock.

The doors opened promptly and I went downstairs into the Rathauskeller which is one of the famous tourist restaurants in Vienna. I was in the cellar with a vaulted ceiling, beautifully carved chairs, many murals and the sound of music in the background. There were various dining rooms off a long hallway, some of them decorated for parties. In the middle of this hallway I saw a large glass tank filled with fish.

One of these rooms is known as the Gringskeller where there are most unusual wine decanters that look like gigantic medicine droppers at each table. The music I heard was coming from the four musicians at the other end of the dining room. I was told that the atmosphere made this room very popular with Viennese and visitors.

The menu was typical of many Viennese restaurants with quite a few schnitzels and other Austrian dishes featured.

WIENER RATHAUSKELLER, Rathausplatz, A-1010, Vienna. Tele-phone: 421219. A popular "middle class" tourist restaurant in the cellar of the Vienna Town Hall. Open for lunch and dinner. Closed Sundays.

The Vienna Opera House

THE THREE HUSSARS, Vienna

I had been told that this was one of the supreme restau-rants, not only in Vienna but in all of Europe. It is located just off the main shopping plaza not far from St. Stephen's Church, which along with the Opera House is the center of Viennese downtown activity.

I did have a chance to talk to Mr. Egnon Fodermayer, a very handsome gentleman of considerable restaurant experi-ence who confessed modestly that the Three Hussars was, in fact, the number one restaurant in Vienna.

Here was genteel Vienna at its very best. The restaurant was rapidly filling up with well-dressed, confident-looking people, both Viennese and visitors, all of whom seemed very much in place in this rather elegant atmosphere. My table was decorated with a small plant and a lighted candle.

The one thing that everyone always talks about when the Three Hussars enters the conversation is the hors d'oeuvres. There must be at least fifty different varieties and they are all expertly moved by a waiter from table to table on a series of four carts.

I eventually settled for a delicious chicken served Hungarian style, which is one of the specialties of the house. For dessert I had something that probably could only be born in Vienna. I am not sure it has a name but it consisted of fresh peaches and strawberries intermixed with chocolate whipped cream and nuts.

The Three Hussars is a great adventure in Viennese eating.

THE THREE HUSSARS (Zu den 3 Husaren), Weihburggasse 4, A-1010 Vienna. Telephone: 521192. A "first class" restaurant especially famous for its hors d'oeuvres. Dinner only. Closed Sundays.

GRIECHENBEISL, Vienna

I visited this very old restaurant in the market district of Vienna on a Sunday morning after church. There was a wedding party in progress with gay accordion music and everyone was having a very good time.

I was shown to a small table in one corner where I had a vantage point to watch all of the people arriving for the noontime meal. All around me were coins embedded in the walls and here or there was a hole where apparently someone had acquired a souvenir.

The restaurant is made up of many different rooms, some with very low doors in which it is necessary for tall people to stoop as they enter. The furniture, tables, chairs, and fixtures all give the appearance of being antique.

Long before I visited it, I heard it mentioned as the place Mozart frequented. I discovered that not only Mozart but Beethoven, Schubert, Wagner, Strauss, Brahms, Mark Twain and Count von Zeppelin had also been guests.

Naturally a restaurant like this is well known and quite a few visitors find their way to it during a visit to Vienna. I had an excellent cup of hot chocolate and a piece of Viennese pastry for lunch.

The little booklet in English which was distributed to each

patron indicates that apparently there has been an inn on this site since 1447. It was once built into the high wall of the outer defenses of the city against the Turks.

GRIECHENBEISL, Fleischmarkt 11, A-1010, Vienna. Telephone: 631977. A "middle class" restaurant located two blocks behind St. Stephen's Church. A well-known tourist attraction. Open every day from 10 a.m. to 1 p.m.

ZUR STADT KREMS, Vienna

Two-star restaurants in Vienna are known as "Das Gasthaus" which incidentally translates out to "the inn." Generally the innkeeper's wife does the cooking and traditional Viennese dishes are served. Frequent guests are known as "regulars" and are therefore entitled to special services.

This little restaurant of two stars was a dandy experience for me. For one thing it had great numbers of young people enjoying dinner. This is located in the university area and it was obvious that they were students. The food was exactly what I had seen on the menus of other Viennese restaurants but considerably less expensive.

It is quite common in a restaurant of this type to be joined at the table by other people if other tables are filled. In my case I was joined by a very nice Austrian couple who spoke enough English to combine with my rather frayed German so that we were able to have a good conversation about Vienna, Austria, traveling, the United States and many other subjects.

The lady explained to me that she and her husband come here frequently but they also enjoyed other restaurants in the area. She felt that they were a typical retired couple who ate out at a modest restaurant three or four times a week. She said that the food here was very good.

By the time the evening had wound up we had had several conversations with the students at the next table who were very fascinated by the idea that I was writing a book that might include my Austrian experiences in country inns. Some of the students who lived outside of Vienna made some good suggestions.

At this restaurant I had my first sampling of Hungarian goulash and I am certain that it is served in no other place as it is in Vienna.

ZUR STADT KREMS, Zieglergasse 37, A-1070, Vienna. Telephone: 937200. A pub or bistro restaurant featuring family-style food. Also popular with students. Dinner only. Closed Sunday and holidays.

Graz — The Natural City

Almost from the moment of my arrival I felt that Graz had been a great choice of Austrian cities to visit. It was an almost completely "natural" city, neither self-consciously preening itself for tourists nor dominated by some tremendous scenic attraction such as high mountains or picturebook lakes. I found that it had dozens of extremely interesting scenic and cultural attractions, but on the whole it was relatively undiscovered, as far as tourists are concerned.

Graz is the capital of the province of Styria and the second largest city in Austria with about 250,000 inhabitants. It is situated at the eastern border of the Alps on both sides of the River Mur, about three hours southwest of Vienna by train.

My guide was a young woman who was a student at the

University. Incidentally, this guiding service is available at all times through the Graz Tourist Office.

We walked across the river into the Old Town, and immediately I was struck by the many different architectural styles. As she explained, Graz is actually one of the oldest cities in Europe and has one of the best preserved Renaissance environments.

We walked into the town square where there were a number of market stalls selling hot chestnuts, soft drinks, fruit, fish, produce, candy—just about everything. Around the square I saw some extremely interesting houses, many of them with handpainted facades. There were all kinds of small cafes and sweet shops around the plaza and on nearby streets.

One of the most impressive sights in Graz is the Landhaus which was built in the middle of the 16th century. Its striking three-story inner courtyard is the scene of many pageants.

We walked up the castle hill to the famous clock tower, the Uhrturm, which is the symbol of Graz and from the vantage point of the Herberstein Gardens, the panorama of the city stretched out below us. By this time we were both ready to take a few moments rest and enjoy a cup of hot chocolate.

Later that evening, I walked back into the Old Town again, through the town square. The stalls were all shuttered and the stores were all closed. It was a very quiet and peaceful time. The fire engines came through the pedestrian plaza without even sounding their sirens.

I paid a visit to one of the cafes, and once again had the experience of having people join me at my table when all the other tables were filled. We all started talking to one another almost immediately, the accordion player struck up a few tunes and quite a few people began to sing. It was a fitting conclusion to an enjoyable day.

GRANDHOTEL WIESLER, Graz

It was a warm, sunny early spring day when the train arrived in Graz. I inquired at the Tourist Information Office of the station about the best way to get to the Grandhotel Wiesler.

A few minutes later I had registered and met the innkeeper, Peter Wiesler. He invited me to one of the spacious parlors of the hotel to spend a few minutes before lunch. I liked this very generous and outgoing man immediately. He is the seventh

The Landhaus, Graz

generation of his family to own the hotel and they are one of the oldest innkeeping families in Styria, which is the name of this province of Austria.

The dining room had a high ceiling with exposed beams and graceful paneling halfway up the wall. A plate rail had many old decorative platters, plates, and pictures. All the waiters were dressed in black suits and starched white shirts and black ties.

The menu for the midday meal, which is quite substantial, had quite a number of Austrian specialties and a surprising number of international dishes as well.

For lunch I decided on a beef dish served with a delicious horseradish sauce and German fried potatoes. Peter explained that this was one of the favorite dishes of Emperor Franz Josef.

There are 88 rooms in the Grandhotel. Those on the top floor were remodeled and modernized about three years ago. They have a striking view of the famous Graz Tower and the Old Town (Graz).

Other rooms have high ceilings, parquet flooring, and old-fashioned furniture. About two-thirds of the rooms have private wc's.

That evening I joined the other hotel guests as well as some of the town people in the hotel coffee shop for a light meal.

That night, after settling down into my comfortable bed, and reviewing the events of the day, I was convinced that Graz was one of the most interesting experiences I ever had.

GRANDHOTEL WIESLER, Graz, 8020. Telephone: 913240. A very comfortable family hotel well within walking distance of most of the sights and attractions of Graz. Rates: Double room 500-700 schillings (includes Continental breakfast).

PARKHOTEL, Graz

This very pleasant hotel is located in a quiet section of the old city within easy walking distance of the Opera Theatre, the University, and the Music and Fine Arts Academy. It has been almost completely modernized in a comfortable re-strained style. My guide and host was a very knowledgeable young man named Mr. Florian and he explained that he, and his mother and father, Elizabeth and Herbert Florian, were the owners of the hotel. He has just finished his law studies as well as the hotel school of Vienna.

True to its name, the hotel overlooks a very pleasant park. On the same spot where it has been standing for more than 400 years. It was known for centuries as the Golden Pear.

We sat for some time in the tastefully furnished coffee shop talking about the many cultural opportunities and advantages in Graz. Then we went for a short tour of the hotel.

The first floor has a lobby with contemporary furniture and one of the living rooms opens out into a garden where meals are served during warm weather.

Lodging rooms were quite large and most of them have windows overlooking the park in front or the garden in the rear. Mixed in with contemporary furniture were suits of armor and old tapestry. It made for an interesting blend.

I liked the spirit of youth and vitality here. Like the Grand-hotel it would be an excellent place to stay during a visit to Graz.

228

PARKHOTEL, A-8010, Graz. Telephone: 0316/33511. A 60-room hotel with mostly modern furnishings. Rates: 420-660 schillings (includes breakfast).

Semmering—My Own Hidden Place

Austria will always have a very special niche in my memory. It was the first country I visited in Europe, and Vienna was the first large city. Graz was the first "natural city" and now Semmering was the first "country" experience.

I arrived on a sunny morning after an overnight snowfall. The train ride from Graz had been through the beautiful alpine foothills with those remarkable little Austrian villages built along the sides of rushing streams and upland pastures.

I was the only passenger to alight at Semmering and the railroad station was entirely deserted. I had been told that someone would meet me so I poked around the station awhile reading the posters. Finally a taxi arrived but the driver did not speak English. He made me understand that he would take me to a pension or small hotel where someone did speak English. So off we went on the snowy roads curving upward into the village where we stopped in front of the Pension Belvedere.

229

PENSION RESTAURANT BELVEDERE, Semmering

I will never forget Magda Engelschall. She and her husband are the innkeepers at the Belvedere. From her I received the most heartwarming introduction to Austrian country hospitality that anyone desired. The first thing she did was to bring me inside, seat me in a booth and get me a cup of marvelous hot chocolate. She even paid the taxi driver and told me not to worry for we could settle it later. We sat for some time in front of a big picture window overlooking the snow-filled valley with ski tow areas visible on the other side. I explained to her that I was visiting some out-of-the-way places in Austria to put in a book about inn accommodations and then her face lit up immediately with a beautiful smile. "We have heard about you. I know exactly who to call. Everything will be all right."

In the meantime I finished my hot chocolate and she conducted me on a short tour of the pension.

The exterior is of a typical Austrian design with roofs that are made to support considerable amounts of snow and rooms that have balconies so that guests may enjoy the mountain scenery in any season.

"I'm sorry that it is the wrong season for you to see our garden," she said. "Our guests love to sit out there in the warm weather and also on our terrace in the sunshine. We have many flowers."

The Belvedere is a combination restaurant and hotel which is classified as a pension. Magda explained that it is a popular meeting place for all of the people who live in the vicinity and that most of the menu is made up of regional food.

The lodging rooms are similar to those that I subsequently found in other pensions—neat and clean, but with no particular style. Most of them have twin beds with those marvelous eiderdown-filled comforters.

Before my Austrian travels were finished I was to meet many other owners of inns and pensions and hotels. I found them generous, understanding and hospitable. Magda really extended herself to make me feel comfortable. She aptly represents all of the good things about Austrian hospitality. I'm sure that visitors expectant of an enjoyable experience in Austria will find their Magda's everywhere.

PENSION BELVEDERE, 2680 Semmering. Telephone: 02664-270. A very cordial restaurant and pension. Breakfast, lunch, and dinner served daily. Rates: 135-180 schillings (includes breakfast).

GARTENPENSION ALPENHEIM, Semmering

With 38 rooms, this was one of the largest of the hotels and pensions in the Semmering area which I visited. It is actually two buildings in one with the dining rooms and guest rooms in the old building being furnished in a more traditional Austrian manner, and with guest lounges and lodging rooms in the second building furnished in more modern styles.

One of the features of this place is an indoor swimming pool where big sliding glass windows create the effect of being outside. There were four or five people in swimming including some children. The garden, which accounts for the "Garten" portion of the name of this inn, was under the snow but I could see through the windows that it extended some distance into the fields and forests.

It was Mr. Steiner who explained to me that Semmering is indeed a year-round resort with skiing during the winter and a great number of summertime activities taking over in the warmer weather including tennis, golf, bowling, horseback riding, the ever present hiking of which all Europeans seem to be very fond, and many other recreations.

GARTENPENSION ALPENHEIM, 2680 Semmering. Telephone: 0 26 64/322. A bustling, family-operated inn. Rates: 330-370 schillings (includes 3 meals).

Baden

Baden is a small city of 25,000 people which can be reached from Vienna by a number of ways including streetcars. I immediately liked its small town feeling and its many gardens and parks.

From the beginning of the 19th century Baden was a center of social and intellectual life. From 1803 to 1834 it was the summer residence of the Hapsburg Court.

The Spa Park and the Doblhoff "rosarium" are filled with thousands of roses during the summer. Walking paths lead from the city up into the hills and out to nearby castle ruins. The famous Vienna Woods are not far away.

My afternoon of wandering in Baden took me to the pedestrian zone located in the center of the town where no automobiles are allowed. There is a feeling of space and freedom for the stroller. Around this zone are several attractive buildings, many with historical implications. One is the Beethoven House where the Ninth Symphony was begun, and also the Civic Theatre.

For entertainment in Baden there are regular concerts by a symphony orchestra and operettas in the open air all summer. The Baden theatre plays throughout the winter.

In the center of the pedestrian zone there is a three-story statue which was erected by the people of the town to commemorate the fact that Baden was not besieged by the infamous plagues during the Middle Ages.

PENSION WEILBURG, Baden

As I understand it only a technicality of the regulations concerning accommodations places this handsome small hotel in the pension category. It has had a connection with the Bakers' Congress for centuries and the outside of the building has murals showing bakers at work kneading dough and removing bread from the oven.

Inside, the rooms are much larger than the average pension, and on the top floor there are a group of rooms furnished in Austrian country antiques.

PENSION WEILBURG, Weilburgstrasse 37, Baden. Telephone: (02252) 3011. Rates: 225-245 schillings (including wc, bath, and breakfast).

HAUS TURK (FERDINANDSHOF), Baden

Frau Turk's immaculate pension was my first stop in Baden. It is located in the center of town within walking distance of parks, concerts, theatres, etc.

Frau Turk doesn't speak English but she can communicate rather vividly to let guests know that there are some rooms without baths and that baths do cost extra.

Haus Turk is built around an open square which has many beautiful flowers and tables. One wall has a painting of a cross-legged Turk which, of course, refers to the name of the establishment.

There is a homey living room with handsomely carved pieces of furniture. Lodgings rooms are clean and furnished with contemporary furniture.

HAUS TURK (FERDINANDSHOF), Rainer-Ring 17, Baden. Telephone: (02252) 2810. Rates: 125-135 schillings (includes breakfast).

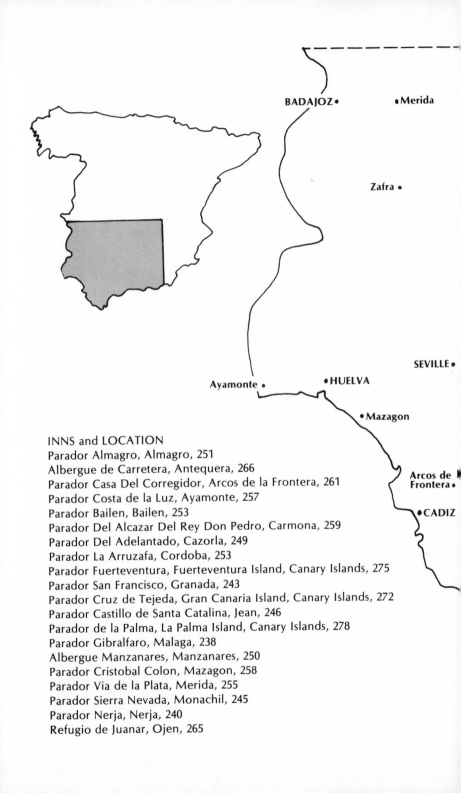

BADAJOZ•　　•Merida

Zafra •

SEVILLE•

Ayamonte •　　•HUELVA

•Mazagon

Arcos de
Frontera•

•CADIZ

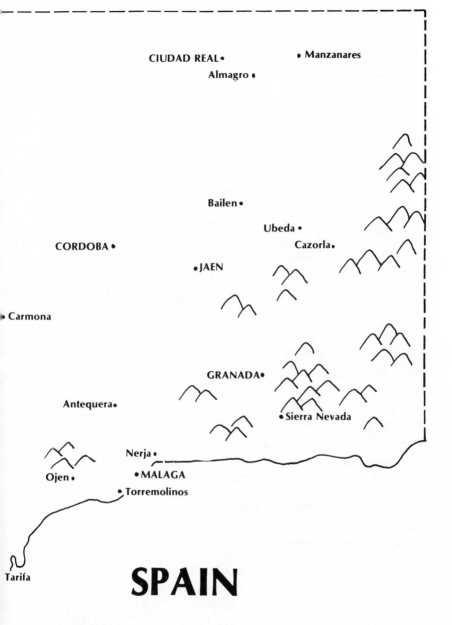

SPAIN

TRAVEL SUGGESTIONS FOR SPAIN

How to Get There

Iberia Airlines provide excellent service from the United States directly to Madrid. From there, domestic airlines fly to all points in Spain. Your Eurailpass is good in Spain.

Country Inns in Spain

All but one of the inns mentioned in this book are owned and operated by the Spanish Ministry of Information and Tourism. For the most part, these are known as "paradores," where it is possible to stay up to ten days; and "albergues" (wayside inns) for stays of no more than three nights on one visit.

Paradores have been established in old palaces, stately homes, castles, convents, and monasteries which have been carefully restored with maximum respect for their heritage, and, propitiously enough, fitted with modern conveniences.

Reservations

These must be made directly by telephone and letter with each individual parador.

Dining in Spain

Each of the paradores offers regional dishes featuring local specialties, and their menus consist almost entirely of Spanish food. For example, paradores on the Costa del Sol offer a great variety of delectable fish dishes including pickled tuna and bonito, shellfish cocktails, and sardines which are cooked both on a spit and in a frying pan. Fried fish is an art in Andalusia. This region is also well-known for gazpacho in many varieties. Other possibilities on the menu could be octopus served in many forms, ham and beans, or the famous Sacromonte omelets from Granada. There are cookies from Antequera and egg-yolk candies from Ronda.

Each parador has two menus, a table d'hote and an a la carte. On the table d'hote, for one price there are several choices within each of the four courses. The first course usually has a choice of hors d'oeuvres or soup; the second course might include poached eggs, noodles, or other light dishes; the third is the main course and offers dishes such as hake, (a Spanish fish,) tuna, roast chicken, stewed oxtails, or York ham and salad. The last course is dessert.

The a la carte menu allows the guest to choose at random, when eating all four courses seems too heavy.

Car Rentals

Iberia has many Fly-Drive Plans that include automobiles. The travelers for whom Spain is part of a Continent-wide itinerary should see the section near the front of this book, "Renting a Car for Europe."

Driving Tips

Seat belts are mandatory in Spain and the Spanish police are very zealous. The roads south of Spain are in good condition and well-marked. Some of the mountain roads are spectacular in their engineering. International road signs which are detailed in the Michelin Green Guide are used.

My Itinerary for Spain

I made a circle tour of southwest Spain, starting from Malaga in a counter-clockwise direction, visiting Granada, Cordoba, Seville, Cadiz, and Algeciras. There were side trips to Ciudad Real, Zafra, Merida, and Huelva. To obtain road maps and guides for Spain, see the section at the back of the book.

PARADOR GIBRALFARO, Malaga

In retrospect I realize that Parador Gibralfaro was a most fortunate choice as my first country inn in Spain. It is located a few steps below the Moorish fortress through which I had been wandering during the late afternoon.

Originally the building was a most impressive home which has been carefully restored and enlarged to accommodate travelers. The most memorable thing about it, of course, is the view of the harbor and the city below. However, even in another less spectacular location it would still be an outstanding experience.

The setting, so high above the tumult of the city creates a total atmosphere of peace and tranquility. In re-designing the building to meet the needs of travelers, the architects made every possible use of the magnificent view; hence, most of the lodging rooms share the spectacle as well as the second floor outdoor terrace. I found that many of the Malaguenans were very fond of having their midday meal or dinner at this parador.

As in all paradores there was a very comfortably furnished parlor with a fireplace where guests frequently gathered at the end of the day. Lots of books and magazines made the place more homelike.

At most paradores the bedrooms and sitting rooms follow a carefully chosen individual decorating theme. At Gibralfaro the colors and textures were in harmony with the closeness of sea, sky and sun, with many beige tones as well as brown and accenting touches of green. The room was basically designed around the large double doors leading to the balcony.

That evening, after dinner, I walked out on the veranda to look at the lights of Malaga below. The balcony apartments of the city were small pools of yellow light in an otherwise velvety blackness. The moon over the Mediterranean created silvery paths along the crescent shores. The boulevard which circles the waterfront had quite a few automobiles. The lights of the cruise ships anchored for the night continued to intrigue me. My eyes kept going back to them and wondering what activity was taking place within these floating palaces which reminded me of the cruise ships in the harbor in St. Thomas, Virgin Islands.

PARADOR GIBRALFARO, Malaga (Malaga). At 556 Km. from Madrid. Telephone: Malaga 22-19-02 RR., airport. Rates: $13.70

The Road to Nerja

Malaga, one of Spain's major cities, is blessed with a very even year-round climate, as is most of the Costa del Sol, which stretches from Algeciras to Almeria, and this section of the coast is one of the most popular summer resorts in Europe. Therefore, April and May might well be excellent months for a visit to southern Spain.

After a short tour of Malaga, Miguel Gutierrez, my driver, and I headed east along the seacoast, passing through resort communities, fishing villages, and by modern condominiums, apartment complexes, and towns — what a fascinating combination of the old and the new. As we left the city far behind, I made my first acquaintance with the "white villages" of Spain with their red-tiled roofs (unchanged for 500 years); many with small flower gardens and women cleaning their front steps.

239

On this seacoast road to Nerja, I first saw a Moorish tower, one of a network of such towers throughout southern Spain, built as lookout points and communication centers to warn of threatened raids from North Africa. Almost every sizable village in Andalusia has some type of Moorish fortification or castle, many in surprisingly good repair even though many were built before 1000 A.D. There are also the well-preserved remains of Roman viaducts.

The road became even more exciting as we approached Nerja, climbing into rugged mountainous terrain, with marvellous overlooks above the ocean, and then dropping down almost next to the sea for a few kilometers, only to twist back up to the cliffs again.

PARADOR NERJA, Nerja (Malaga)

"In the popular summer months it is necessary to have reservations here for at least a year in advance." I was sitting on the terrace of this beautiful seaside parador in Nerja talking with the director, Senor Alphonso. We could see the beach stretching out in both directions and I could well understand why guests from so many countries find this inn an attractive place for a vacation. "We accept reservations for no more than ten days at a time," he said. "But I'm sure that many people would like to stay here for a month."

The village of Nerja is one of the jewels of the Costa del Sol. It is a picturesque town on a cliff in the foothills of southern Spain's mountains and is famous for sea and mountain views. Besides being a resort community, it is also a fishing district and sometimes bathers share the beach with fishermen and their nets. There is sailing, motor boating and sport fishing here as well.

Senor Alphonso had already given me an excellent tour of this inn which is contemporary in architecture. It is built around a hollow square with a modest swimming pool and a beautiful reflecting pool. The gardens, which were already beginning to bloom, are exquisite.

The inn, situated on a cliff, 75 feet above the seashore, provides an elevator to transport inn guests to and from the beach. "Of course the beach is one of our great features," he said. "Many of our guests have been returning year after year to get a beautiful Costa del Sol tan."

Since Miguel and I would have to be in Granada by at least 9 o'clock that evening, I regretfully took leave of this idyllic seaside inn. As we walked through the living room into the open courtyard I noticed that all of the rooms had their own private balconies. The main living room had handsome exposed beams and red tile floors relieved by Moorish rugs.

Miguel told me, as we began our journey to Granada, that because of its nearness to the sea and the great beauty of the flowers, the Parador Nerja is one of the most popular in all of Spain.

PARADOR NERJA, Nerja (Malaga). At 51 Km. from Malaga, 559 from Madrid. Telephone: Nerja 52-00-50. Aquatic sports, beach, swimming pool. Rates: $19.75

On to Granada

Leaving the sea behind us at Motril, about an hour and a half out of Nerja, we turned north toward Granada, and in the twilight hours enjoyed seeing the social gatherings in town squares that is repeated throughout Spain before the customary dinner hour of 8 or 8:30 p.m.

As we approached the mountains of Granada, the valleys grew steeper, the road narrowed considerably in places, and I caught my first glimpse of snow-capped peaks dramatically lit by the setting sun.

We finally reached a place where we could see the lights of Granada reflected in the sky, and although my watch said 9:15, Miguel assured me we would be in Granada well in time for dinner.

Granada

Over the entrance gate of the Watch Tower in the Alcazaba, there is a famous poem by Francisco de Icaza:

Give him alms, woman
For there is nothing in life, nothing
So sad as to be blind in Granada.

Granada is the home of the Alhambra, the palatial city of the Moors spread grandly across the hill bearing its name and protected by a network of walls and towers. Volumes have been written about it. Washington Irving immortalized it in his Tales of The Alhambra and Columbus must have spent quite a few days there waiting anxiously for an audience with Queen Isabella. It's been photographed from every angle, and the gardens and palaces are one of the most exquisite experiences in the world. Incidentally, I found that the best time to visit it is after three in the afternoon, when most of the tours have been completed, and the Alhambra can be enjoyed for all of its beauty and tranquility.

I have heard it said that Granada, rather than being a product of the culture of the Moorish civilization of Spain, was the shaper and builder of that culture. When the Moors came to Spain, they had spent centuries on the desert and were essentially warlike, nomadic people. Seven hundred years later when Ferdinand and Isabella reconquered the city they found a sensual, refined, dreaming race whose chief delights were in art and nature.

PARADOR SAN FRANCISCO, Granada

"Sometimes when people ask whether it's noisy in the morning I tell them that when they wake up they will hear the beautiful singing of birds." I was seeing this beautiful parador, located on the grounds of the Alhambra, through the eyes of the assistant director, Senor Luis Avila. I have never met anyone who enjoyed his job as much as this happy man. I am sure that he has been happy every morning since he found his place in life here 24 years ago. "Everyday is a new experience for me here," he said, as we moved from hallway to courtyard to gardens to patios. "The one thing I love to do is to take guests on tours of my beloved inn so that they will see it as I do."

This parador is one of the most famous in all of Spain. Originally an Arab palace, it was used as a Franciscan monastery under Ferdinand and Isabella, and has been a parador since 1945. The original buildings have been preserved and new additions have been made to provide 26 lodging rooms all in the style of the original architecture. Great care has been taken to be sure that the texture and the color of the brick used is as close to the original as possible.

"Queen Isabella was entombed in this monastery from the time of her death in Granada in 1504 until 1521," Luis explained. We were in a secluded courtyard looking at a marker which indicated her burial place and I, too, felt a sense of quiet respect for this woman who played such an important role in the history of the world.

This parador, which is on the grounds of the Alhambra, is enhanced with many fountains. It was from Luis that I learned that each of the fountains in the Alhambra has a different musical tone. "The Moors," he said, "developed a feeling for peace and tranquility and believed that fountains were one way to achieve it. We have many fountains in the parador." At this particular moment we were standing in a courtyard that had

243

four fountains, each with a different musical pitch. There were tall cypress trees swaying in the wind and birds flitting from tree to tree.

"This is one of the most popular paradores in all of Spain," he said. "Reservations are to be made only by letter and not by telephone or cable. The letter must be sent well in advance. Most people stay for the maximum time allowed in a parador— ten days. I think that it takes at least ten days to experience everything that is here in Granada and to learn about our beautiful, leisurely way of life.

We concluded our tour at the terrace where we walked to a point overlooking the Alhambra which is just a few steps away. We could see the old quarter of the city and the Generalife Gardens which are across the river. The roses, which would be in such profusion in a few weeks, were just beginning to bud, and in the distance I could see the always snowcapped Sierra Nevada Mountains.

PARADOR SAN FRANCISCO, Granada (Granada). At 429 Km. from Madrid. Telephone: Granada 22-14-62. RR., airport. Rates: $19.75

PARADOR SIERRA NEVADA, Monachil (Granada)

Spain is a land of contrasts. Just twenty-four hours ago I had been in a parador on the seacoast at Nerja where it was necessary to reserve a year in advance during the months of July and August. Here, perhaps no more than 90 kilometers distant, I was in a parador above the snow line where reservations for December through March have to be made three or four months in advance. I could, if I wanted to, ski here in the morning and drive to Motril for a swim in the Mediterranean in the afternoon.

This is one of the newer paradores and the design has been created to conform with the contour of the mountains. The dining rooms and parlors have white plaster walls with natural wood ceilings with a high glossy finish. Lodging rooms, many in duplex style, overlook the snow-filled valley in front and the mountains in back.

I walked through the impressive dining room up to a balcony where there was a small fire laid in an open fireplace. As I settled back in one of the comfortable chairs and put my feet up on the hearth, a group of school children in ski outfits trouped in with a look of hunger on their well-tanned faces.

"Oh, it's excellent. We think it is the best skiing in Europe," said one. "We're on a holiday and our parents bring us back here every year. One year we couldn't get reservations here at the parador so we stayed at the ski village just below."

I asked them how the weather had been and they told me it had been sunny all week and that the conditions for spring skiing were perfect.

"It's pretty fast in the morning but along about noon when the sun warms up the snow it slows down and that's when we generally stop and come back here for lunch."

I couldn't resist the opportunity to ask them about the food. "Terrific," one of them said, "we always try to stay in a parador whenever we can because it's real Spanish food." I asked them what they liked at this parador and some of them replied that they liked the Sacromonte omelets and the Andalusian meatballs. I decided to ask all of them where they lived and where they went to school and I had a chorus of answers in many languages and locations. They said they were going to ski the next day and asked me if I could join them. Regretfully I said no. Tomorrow I would be in Jaen and Ubeda. They asked me why I was in Spain and I explained that I was writing a book about the country inns in Europe and they all thought that was real cool.

I do myself.

PARADOR SIERRA NEVADA, Monachil (Granada). At 35 Km. from Granada, 464 from Madrid. Telephone: Granada 42-02-00. Rates: $13.70.

It was a surprise to find such a sophisticated city as Jaen high in the mountains, with one of the most beautiful cathedrals in Spain—300 years old, and a masterpiece of Gothic, Renaissance, and Baroque architecture. We followed the twisting, winding road out of the city and up the side of the mountain, passing finally through an old archway. We had arrived at the Parador Castillo de Santa Catalina.

PARADOR CASTILLO de SANTA CATALINA, Jaen

I viewed this parador with mixed feelings. My first feeling was complete awe of the building with its massive renaissance interior and tremendous, inspiring, mind-boggling view, but I also felt some frustration because it was still under construction and renovation. I had arrived either a year too late or a year too early to find lodgings there.

The Parador Santa Catalina has been in existence for about ten years but because of its unusual location high in the mountains and its tremendous popularity it was decided to enlarge the inn to accommodate more people. It was difficult to estimate when it would reopen,

The first thing I saw when I walked through the massive doors of the main entrance was a three-story-high hallway. To the left was a great hall with two handsome Spanish fireplaces and there were cathedral windows providing a panoramic view of the mountains and the valley. I had received special permission to tour the building promising to keep out of the path of the workmen, so I walked up the massive stone steps to reach the level where the lodging rooms were located. My

footsteps re-echoed on the stone floors of the hallway that has been used for centuries.

I opened the bedroom door and was immediately compelled to walk out on the balcony. It was like being in an eagle's aerie. I had the most curious feeling that I could actually fly out over the rows of olive trees and the houses of Jaen at the base of the mountain. The cathedral which I had just visited a few moments earlier looked like a miniature from this great height. Overhead the blue skies of morning were being replaced by cloud banks and the wind was beginning to rise, causing thousands of olive trees to sway in the breeze.

Each room will have a balcony and will be furnished in the grand style suited to a castle. I could just imagine what an exciting place this is going to be when it reopens.

PARADOR CASTILLO DE SANTA CATALINA, Jaen (Jaen). At 97 Km. from Granada, 335 from Madrid. Telephone: Jaen 23-22-87. Rates: $19.75 (closed for repairs).

PARADOR CONDESTABLE DAVALOS, Ubeda (Jaen)

I was singing in the shower at a Renaissance palace. The bathroom was princely, to say the least. In remodeling this stately mansion, which would be very much in place in Florence, the architect provided the most comfortable of accommodations for two people. There were even twin washbowls.

I stepped out of the shower and wrapped myself in one of those incredible towels that go twice around. Even the most noble families who had previously lived in this palace were not nearly as well accommodated as the parador guest of today.

The bedroom/sitting room had a two-story ceiling and windows and shutters. The customary twin beds were supplemented with some interesting Spanish antiques, including a handsome carved wardrobe. At the moment the most useful piece of furniture was an unobtrusive small refrigerator from which' I obtained a welcome bottle of lime soda.

About an hour earlier I had been greeted by the director of this parador, Senor Garcia, a most accommodating and effusive man. After being registered by the concierge, he was kind enough to give me a tour of the entire inn.

We began with the winery which was in the cellar of this four-hundred-year-old building and is now used as a dining room for special occasions. We sat for a moment at the tables in this low-ceilinged room and talked about the history of the house whose inhabitants were very important figures in the history of Spain.

We returned to the first floor and I observed that the inn is built around a glass-roofed courtyard with lodging rooms on the second and third floor. There were a great many antiques including suits of armor worn by ancient Spanish knights. Senor Garcia proudly showed me the library of the parador which is not only beautifully furnished and decorated, but has some very good books and magazines for the guests of the house. Like most of the paradors I visited, this one also had a television room.

At dinner that evening I met two retired American ladies, Mrs. Harriet Smith and Mrs. Ann Ulrich both from the state of Washington who were traveling through Spain, driving a car and having a wonderful time. When I learned that they did not speak Spanish, I asked them how they were managing. Mrs. Smith said, "Oh, we are doing wonderfully. With a combination of sign language, maps and lots of laughs, we have been kept on the right track by these wonderful people. I just can't say enough about the generosity and manners of everyone we have met in Spain."

PARADOR CONDESTABLE DAVALOS, Ubeda (Jaen). At 55 Km. from Jaen, 338 from Madrid. Telephone: Ubeda 75-03-45. Rates: $13.70

PARADOR Del ADELANTADO, Cazorla (Jaen)

I was having breakfast high in the Sierra de Cazorla with the Davenports, Jenifer and Clark, and their four children, Sara, Jad, Lisa and Sam. They were Americans who were living in Spain for three years.

"We've been at this parador for three days," said Jenifer, passing a plate of rolls to Sam, "and we've had an absolutely marvelous time."

"And we've seen lots of wild animals including an ibex. Have you ever seen an ibex?" This came from Lisa, who has very blonde hair and blue eyes. I had to confess that I had never seen an ibex, which by definition is a wild goat with large, backward-curving horns.

"Well we saw one," she said proudly, "and we also saw some mountain goats and deer."

This parador is a very cozy hunting lodge. The furnishings and decor reflect the wildlife of the region. There are mounted heads of wild boar, deer, bear and mountain sheep. There are also some excellent black and white and full color photographs of the region showing some of the huge rocky mountains, crags and steep dells.

After breakfast we all walked into the living room where a welcome fire was blazing away in a huge fireplace. We made ourselves comfortable in the deep leather chairs and I asked them if they were enjoying their holiday.

"Oh yes, this is really our kind of place," said Clark Davenport. "And I must say that we never expected to find an intimate little inn like this so high in the mountains."

"Yes, and you should see our rooms," said Sara. "They have a wonderful view of the valley. When I wake up in the morning I can see the sun coming through the trees."

"I hope the rain stops today," said Jad, "because we have one more walking trip we want to make. Dad says that if it doesn't stop raining we'll take the road that leads back up into the mountains and is the source of the river that passes through Cordoba and Seville." Clark later confirmed that that was the Guadalquivir, which rises in the Sierra Cazorla.

Incidentally, I have one memento of the trip to Cazorla which I treasure very much. As I was leaving, Lisa Davenport presented me with a crayon drawing of an ibex.

PARADOR DEL ADELANTADO, Cazorla (Jaen). At 27 Km. from Cazorla, 137 from Jaen, 417 from Madrid. Telephone: Cazorla 295. Mountain scenery, golf, hunting and fishing. Rates: $13.70

Don Quixote's La Mancha

When I ventured north from the province of Jaen into the province of Ciudad Real, I came to the land of "Don Quixote" and his creator, Miguel de Cervantes. I was on the edge of the countryside that is known traditionally as La Mancha. Don Quixote, Cervantes' great book, and the recent musical version of it, The Man of La Mancha, *have brought this touching and moving story into homes all over the world.*

ALBERGUE MANZANARES, Manzanares (Ciudad Real)

This highway inn or albergue was undergoing renovation and expansion when I visited and the number of rooms was being increased from 48 to 100. It is a very popular place to stop for lunch or dinner because it is on the road from Madrid to the Costa del Sol, Granada, Cordoba, Seville, Cadiz and other towns in southern Spain. In the newly-constructed portion each of the rooms will have its own balcony and there will be tennis courts and a swimming pool.

ALBERGUE MANZANARES, Manzanares (Ciudad Real). At 48 Km. from Ciudad Real, 174 from Madrid. Telephone: Manzanares 61-04-00. Rates: $10.20. (Undergoing some repairs—some services not available.)

PARADOR ALMAGRO (Ciudad Real)

While visiting the parador in Cazorla I heard about a new parador still under construction in Almagro. In talking to the director at Manzanares he confirmed the fact that this would be one of the most outstanding paradors in all of Spain. He suggested that even though the hour was late it would be well worth the short drive from Manzanares to Almagro to have a look at it. The road was unusual, because instead of being blacktopped, it was constructed of brick and looked as if it had been there for many, many years. The countryside was flat with many fields of early ripening grain. The houses in the villages looked quite different from what I had become accustomed to in southern Spain—these had a sort of squarish look. The second floor balconies had intricate iron grilles and many had red, green and blue pots filled with flowers hanging from them.

Almagro is a middle-sized village and a short visit to the tourist office proved to be most helpful. Among other things, I learned that there is a 13th century theatre here, the Corral de Comedias, which is the only one of its kind left in Spain.

The parador appeared to be about half completed. It is near the center of the town and was a former monastery. I found at least two tiled courtyards with very graceful arches. There were fountains installed and new fruit trees already planted. Again great care is being taken to blend the old and the new.

It will be at least two years before this parador at Almagro is open, but when it is, I am sure it will be a welcome addition to the beautiful land of La Mancha.

PARADOR ALMAGRO, Almagro (Ciudad Real). Under construction.

Cordoba

Cordoba is a city of flowers—the plazas, the bridges, the squares, windows, and balconies all spill over with the riotous colors and scents of flowers.

Cordoba has a lengthy history dating back to the Romans, with a bridge that was probably built during the reign of Julius Caesar. However, most of the 16 arches now supporting the bridge were built by the Moors. Conversely, the impressive mosque, with its series of repeated arches seeming to stretch out of sight, houses a Christian church.

Miguel de Cervantes lived near the engaging Plaza del Potro, where there is an inn which existed before the 14th century. Cervantes mentions the inn several times in his writings; however, today it is a private home.

PARADOR BAILEN, Bailen (Jaen)

This parador is very close to being a middle-size Spanish motel. It is located on the busy highway that leads south from Madrid to the Costa del Sol. At this important junction the traveler may proceed south to Jaen, Granada and Almeria, or he may go to Cordoba, Seville, Huelva, Cadiz or Malaga. The distance from Madrid is 296 kilometers which makes it a comfortable drive from the capital in time to stay overnight. All of the rooms are furnished in modern style and there is an unusually large dining room because many people stop off enroute for the excellent food.

The leisurely-minded traveler remaining for more than one night will enjoy the nearby city of Jaen and the mountainous olive-clad countryside. I'm sure the swimming pool would be welcome during the summer months.

PARADOR BAILEN, Bailen (Jaen). At 39 Km. from Jaen, 296 from Madrid. Telephone: Jaen 372. RR., swimming pool. Rates: $19.75

PARADOR LA ARRUZAFA, Cordoba

I will always remember the Parador La Arruzafa as the place where I had my first experience with Spanish hors d'oeuvres. It was at the midday meal (comida). We had arrived late the previous evening, and I had slept beyond my usual hour in the morning. Miguel had dropped me off at the Mosque and I also took the opportunity to walk through the Old Quarter and up into the main square and shopping district.

I returned to the parador and was taken on a complete tour by the courteous parador director. We visited rooms on every floor and toured the kitchen, the gardens and the recreation area with a swimming pool. We stopped to enjoy the sunshine and some refreshments on the terrace. It had been a very busy morning and I felt unusually hungry, so I ordered the hors d'oeuvres for my first course.

Well, the dishes began to arrive. There were at least 15 and they included delicious small clams and many varieties of small fish, very salty and extremely tasty. There were small dishes containing varieties of vegetables, small chunks of liver and quite a few other items which were from the barnyard and truck farm, which I was unable to identify. This was only the first course.

After I finished sampling everything I felt that I had had sufficient luncheon! But I did try the spinach omelet which is one of the favorite dishes in Spain, and had a light carmel custard for dessert.

The Parador La Arruzafa has all the conveniences that I had experienced in a four-star hotel in Spain except that the general atmosphere is far more relaxed. It is six or seven stories high and all of the rooms have balconies facing the broad plain on which Cordoba is located. The gardens, hedges, flowers, lemon and orange trees add to the atmosphere. There is even a play area for children. Quite a few suites are available and some of them have parlors and dressing rooms.

PARADOR LA ARRUZAFA, Cordoba (Cordoba). At 402 Km. from Madrid. Telephone: Cordoba 27-59-00. RR., airport, swimming, tennis. Rates: $19.75

Land of the Skyline

I call this the land of the skyline because in this section of Spain there is always an interesting or beautiful silhouette on the horizon: rows of trees along a hilltop, saw-toothed mountains, or a castle towering over the crest of a hill. On this particular route, we often saw two or three villages in the distance nestling against a hillside.

PARADOR HERNAN CORTES, Zafra (Badajoz)

In Spain even the expected can be unexpected. Miguel told me that the parador in Zafra was located in a castle, but even with this knowledge I was positively bowled over by the Parador Hernan Cortes.

Unlike most fortresses in Spain, this was not built by the Moors but by the Christian rulers of the region. It has been named for the New World Spanish explorer, Hernan Cortes, who was a protege of the original owners of the castle.

The adaptation of this old world castle to meet the needs of today's travelers has been most subtle. Additions have been constructed in the same architectural style to increase the number of accommodations. Many of the rooms look out over courtyards or gardens and, of course, they are equipped with the modern conveniences including heating and air conditioning. The parador even has its own restored chapel.

Furniture for the public rooms and bedrooms was chosen to harmonize with the dignified formality of the castle. There are quite a few large carved tables and chairs and numerous tapestries and oil paintings. Guests enjoy walking up to the tower above the third floor to enjoy the view.

This is a very popular parador and as in all cases reservations should be made well in advance. There was a line of people at 9 p.m. on the night that we arrived, hoping that some guests would not be there in time to claim their reservation.

Hernan Cortes was famous for his conquest to Mexico, but to a growing number of aficionados his name is now synonymous with a most beautiful parador in Spain.

PARADOR HERNAN CORTES, Zafra (Badajoz). At 85 Km. from Badajoz, 403 from Madrid. Telephone: Zafra 55-00-60. RR., swimming pool. Rates: $19.75

PARADOR VIA DE LA PLATA, Merida (Badajoz)

When we drove into the little square at Merida, one of the first things that I noticed were the storks nesting in the chimneys of the inn. (There is something very comforting about birds nesting in or near a home.) The entrance to the inn was through a garden-like plaza filled with countless blooming flowers whose colors were dramatically heightened by the

255

austere white walls of the parador. Although the building had been put to a variety of uses through the years (at one time it was a prison), the most recent and longest use was as a convent. It was modified and enlarged about 10 years ago and I was told that the furniture and decor in the lounges, parlors and lodging rooms were typical of this region of Spain.

In spite of the many centuries of Moorish occupation and subsequent reconquest by the Christians, the city has retained strong Roman influences. It was established during the height of the Roman Empire. The name of the parador, Via de la Plata, is a combination of Latin and Spanish—it was the name of an old Roman road in Merida.

Reflecting the various cultural and architectural influences, the interior of the parador has quiet corners with single Roman columns and a profusion of intricate Moorish iron work and decoration. The chairs, tables and other furnishings suggested the later Christian influence.

Because of the location of this parador in Merida, it is very popular with travelers enroute to and from Portugal. There is a three-night limit in effect.

A special surprise awaits the traveler stopping here. Besides the appealing plaza at the entrance, the inn has its own private gardens in the rear with carefully trained hedges about 12 feet high that form a series of Moorish arches around a fountain bedecked with pots of carnations.

PARADOR VIA DE LA PLATA, Merida (Badajoz). At 61 Km. from Badajoz, 343 from Madrid. Telephone: Merida 30-15-40. RR. Rates: $19.75

PARADOR COSTA DE LA LUZ, Ayamonte (Huelva)

"Right now we are looking down on a place where history has been made for thousands of years." I was standing on the terrace of a beautiful parador which is located at the estuary of the Guadiana River which separates southern Spain and Portugal. My host, Senor Garcia, director of the parador, was discussing the history of the region.

"First the Phoenicians came here and then the Romans," Senor Garcia continued. "This area was taken over by the Kings of Portugal who then gave it to the Spanish knightly Order of Santiago. On two occasions it was the dowry of Spanish princesses who were to become the Queens of Portugal. In fact, we might say that Ayamonte is a link between the two nations of the Iberian Peninsula.

"For a short time it was the capital of Spain during the Napoleonic Wars," he added. "But with all of the conflicts in Europe, this particular place has never known the ravages of an invading army."

We watched the ferry boat crossing the river to Portugal. We were within sight of about three small villages on the other side of the river and I could see the long rows of olive trees and rich green fields.

We went back inside and passed through the lobby where there was an art exhibition featuring the work of local painters. Senor Garcia explained that the combination of bright sunlight plus water and landscapes made this a very popular location for artists. The long hallway was accented with huge pots of ivy whose green tendrils reached to the floor. Senor Garcia explained that the parador, which is a newer one, was especially designed for this site, and each room overlooks either the town or the estuary. It is a single-story building designed to blend with the skyline.

As we turned toward the dining room the parador director explained that because of the proximity to the sea the typical Ayamonte cuisine tends to center around fish and crustaceans. "We have a continual change of specialties," he said. "Sometimes we have marine stews and now and then we have fresh sardines which are caught at dawn. There are lobsters, prawns, crayfish and clams available, and we try to keep our menu exciting by having as many of these regional specialties as possible."

The village of Ayamonte has received numerous national and provincial prizes in recent years for the beauty and cleanliness of its streets, gardens and parks. After visiting this attractive fishing port, I can certainly see why.

PARADOR COSTA DE LA LUZ, Ayamonte (Huelva). At 60 Km. from Huelva, 696 from Madrid. Telephone: Huelva 32-07-00. RR., swimming pool. Rates: $19.75

PARADOR CRISTOBAL COLON, Mazagon (Huelva)

I visited this parador on a stormy day and it still looked beautiful. It is located on the Costa de la Luz, south of the city of Huelva, overlooking the Gulf of Cadiz.

I toured the grounds after borrowing an umbrella from the concierge. From the cliffs, where the parador is located, I could see the whitecaps tossing about in the Gulf. This is one of the older paradores which was especially constructed by the Ministry of Tourism for the purpose of accommodating travelers and holiday-seekers. There is a swimming pool and a beach, both of which are very popular during the summer months. In fact, the concierge informed me that reservations for the warm weather months must be made a year in advance.

The interior design reflected the colors of the landscape and sea, with a great many yellows, light greens, blues and light browns. The dining room had picture windows with a fantastic view of the gardens, cliffs, and the ocean beyond. As far as I could see every room had its own patio, either overlooking the garden or the ocean.

As we were leaving this parador, the sun was breaking through and the afternoon promised to answer the wishes of all of those children and their parents who were hoping for the good weather. I, too, would have liked to remain for two or three days at this delightful parador on the Costa de la Luz.

PARADOR CRISTOBAL COLON, Mazagon-Moguer (Huelva). At 42 Km. from Huelva, 639 from Madrid. Telephone: Huelva 303. Beach, swimming pool. Rates: $19.75

PARADOR DEL ALCAZAR DEL REY DON PEDRO, Carmona, (Seville)

We were on the road from Seville to the mountain village of Carmona, a distance of only 35 kilometers. The torrential rain which had drenched the city and cancelled the Holy Week procession the night before was now replaced by brilliant Andalusian sunshine. Even from some distance we could see the white village and the Alcazar located on top of a precipitous hill.

Upon our arrival we stopped for a few moments to do some shopping and then proceeded through a huge stone gate to another world—the world of Don Pedro the Cruel, for this magnificent parador was once his castle.

The completely walled courtyard was big enough for six football fields. In one corner, the unrestored crumbling remnants of the castle still stood as mute reminders of another epoch. Before going through the front door of the inn we turned aside and walked through a colonnade of Moorish arches to a precipice overlooking the countryside. The vista was idyllic. It was Spain in springtime. Stretched out farther than the eye could see was a series of small farms whose tilled grounds were bursting forth into life in the warm sun. It was a panorama of countless shades of green gathering new strength every day.

We passed through a large two-story living room with walls decorated with armor and swords. These bellicose artifacts were balanced by the serenity of the open courtyard, where the fountains sent melodious sounds into the atmosphere. The sun was now shining directly overhead into this gentle haven and I appreciated once again the Moorish affinity for the musical sounds of water.

We walked through still another handsome living room and out onto a terraza, which I understand is the correct term for the outside larger balcony. Here we had another view of the countryside including the swimming pool of the parador, a blue oval shape directly below us.

We were joined briefly by the assistant director of the parador, who had some interesting news for us. "Our King, Juan Carlos, was here just two weeks ago," he announced. "We are the newest of all paradores, that was really our official opening day."

Since we had a short wait, he suggested that we might enjoy a tour of some of the lodging rooms of the inn. We walked through a courtyard with a fountain and up two flights of stairs to the top floor. An elevator was also available.

He ushered us into an attractively designed bedroom and explained that all of the rooms had balconies. As is true in most of the paradores, the bedspreads, curtains and rugs have designs that are identified with the local region.

"It took six years to build this parador," he explained. As I stepped out onto the balcony I leaned over to look at the walls below, and I could see that restoration of this magnificent building was an engineering feat. Some of the skilled workmen must have been able to fly.

Other interior touches were handsome carved doors and carefully designed windows with multicolored panes.

As we returned to the main floor, I asked him about the swords hanging on the walls and he explained that these were copies of weapons belonging to Don Pedro and his brother Henrique. "They had a duel," he said. "Henrique killed Don Pedro and became king. That was long ago."

PARADOR DEL ALCAZAR DEL REY DON PEDRO, Carmona (Seville). At 35 km. from Seville. Telephone: 25-32-60. Rates: $19.75.

PARADOR CASA DEL CORREGIDOR, Arcos de la Frontera (Cadiz)

Arcos de la Frontera is one of the white villages of Spain. This particular group of villages is located in the peninsula with the Costa de la Luz on one side and the Costa del Sol on the other. Some of these highly picturesque villages are on one of the coasts, and others like Arcos de la Frontera are in the highlands that lie midway between the two coasts. The "de la Frontera" portion of the name was bestowed on the town by a Spanish king as the result of noble achievements by the townspeople. "Frontera" refers to the Spanish-Moorish frontier of the 14th century.

Arcos de la Frontera is a community that commands the traveler's attention. Sitting high on a promontory above the Guadelete River, the white walls of its houses and the gay colors of its patios have been likened to a staircase of light which compels the visitor to scale the height. Many of the houses hang precariously over the edge of a ravine.

The road through the village to the plaza at the top led through narrow streets where there seemed to be barely enough room for a single car.

However, the crest is a prize well worth the effort of negotiating the narrow streets because the beautiful church, the exceptional parador and the plaza all share a vista that reminded me of the beautiful panorama at Carmona.

The parador is built in a restored stately home with all of

261

the bedrooms and dining rooms sharing the impressive view. The comparative austerity of the white-walled exterior calls attention to the Gothic facade of the church.

Each of the twin-bedded rooms has attractive furniture and the entire atmosphere would encourage me to remain the full ten days which is the maximum stay permitted.

The director of the parador was a most pleasant and accommodating man. I learned to my surprise that he had been in the hotel business in Mexico before coming to this parador about twenty years ago. We sat on the terraza and talked of innkeeping in Spain and America. "One of the things I enjoy most about being here is that many people return each year because they find it such a restful and inspiring experience," he said.

Even as we were talking on this very subject, a schoolteacher from Connecticut who was on a year's sabbatical in Spain, approached and introduced himself and said that he had visited this parador three times during the past two years. "I have been to many," he said, "but this is by far my favorite."

PARADOR CASA DEL CORREGIDOR, Arcos De La Frontera (Cadiz). At 85 Km. from Cadiz, 666 from Madrid. Telephone: Arcos 362. Rates: $19.75

HOTEL DOS MARES, Tarifa (Cadiz)

This is the only Spanish inn included in this edition of this book that is privately owned. All the remaining paradores are owned and operated by the Spanish government.

Miguel and I were on the road from Cadiz to Algeciras driving along next to the ocean when I saw a sign that said "Hotel dos Mares." It directed us through a grove of trees to a group of buildings on the beach.

That's how I met Robbert Jan Van Looy, the innkeeper and owner of the Hotel of the Two Seas. Robbert (two b's are correct) and I hit it off immediately. He is a Dutchman and although he is in his mid-thirties he has had wide experience in the hotel business in various parts of Europe. We settled down for a chat in the lounge of the inn which enjoys a most, impressive view of the ocean.

"We call this the Hotel dos Mares because we are at the point where the Atlantic Ocean and the Mediterranean Sea almost come together," he said.

Robbert suggested a tour of the inn so we started out by walking downstairs using a circular staircase that sweeps its way into a dining room which overlooks the sea. The atmosphere was bright and gay with blue tablecloths and nautical decorations. We walked out through the adjoining terrace with its stone arches to a grassy part of the beach and I looked at some of the little bungalows in which most of the lodgings are located. The cottages are separated by sufficient distance to give a feeling of privacy and all of them overlook the dunes and the rolling surf. The rooms have twin beds and are very clean but somewhat austere.

We returned to the inn and talked about the food. "Our menu is international because our guests come from all over the world. Of course, we always have Spanish dishes as part of the choice but a typical dinner menu has a choice of four first courses and two middle courses. Generally we have a choice of either ice cream or fresh fruit for dessert.

"We have a funny situation here. We don't have any telephones and so all of our reservations and confirmations have to be handled by mail. Many of our guests return year after year and a great many bring their friends with them."

I was very glad to find this intimate little fourteen-room inn on the water. From now on I will always follow my intuition.

HOTEL dos MARES, Apartado 80, Tarifa (Cadiz). Open April 1-November 1. No telephone. Necessary to contact by mail well in advance. Send first night's room charge as deposit. Rates: Room for two with bath, breakfast and dinner, $17.00. Approximately 25 kilometers from Algeciras. Robbert Jan Van Looy, Owner.

Jimena de la Frontera

Miguel wanted to show me one of his favorite villages, and we drove on a back road northeast of Linea heading into the hills. The road followed a small river lined with many trees and springtime flowers. After a stop at a clean little country store, we continued our journey and soon came to this ancient fortified village built on the side of a steep hill and topped by a great, round tower. The houses, built centuries ago, were all huddled together near the base of the fortress. At the top of the village, the ancient crumbling walls still loomed overhead. I walked to the top through an arch which must have been part of a wall around the village, but now had grass and nesting birds in its crevices. Crumbling blocks of stone were all that remained, however, the threatening presence of the tower which commanded the valley in three directions still dominated the entire hilltop. Just below, a caretaker serenely tended an orchard and a small vegetable and flower garden.

REFUGIO DE JUANAR, Ojen-Sierra Blanca (Malaga)

Snow on the Costa del Sol! Miguel said it was most unusual, especially in April. We had turned off the main highway and were headed into the mist-shrouded mountains. Even while we were still in sight of the fashionable high rise condominiums of Marbella, the road started to twist and double back through the foothills as we shifted into low gear to make the ascent. In the distance was an upland meadow covered with goldenrod-like flowers softly covered, for just a few hours, with lightly fallen snow.

The road swung around the shoulder of a mountain and we now had our first look at the village of Ojen. Like many other "white villages" it clings to the side of a hill among orange and lemon trees. Some of the houses have terraces on the roofs where there is a view of the sea which is just twenty kilometers away.

I realized later that part of the fun in visiting this inn is the adventure of reaching it. We did not notice any directional signs in the village but since there was only one road we continued to press on.

We approached a valley and found our first directional sign to the refugio since Marbella. It directed us to the left fork in the road and although it was blacktopped it was still quite rough.

The road was making a wide ascending semicircle around the mountains, and to our right we could look down on the olive groves. In the distance were indications of a mining operation. Just when I began to think that we had arrived at the crest of the mountains, we would see another rise ahead of us. There was a jagged saw-tooth peak with a sprinkling of snow and a dry creek bed which I am sure fills up after the rains. We dropped down into a protected valley with many trees and there a sign told us that we had arrived at our inn.

We stepped inside the rather simple white building and found the atmosphere rustic and informal. There was a combination living room and lobby furnished with rough mountain lodge furniture. On the walls there were some hunting prints including one of a Belgian hare. There were mounted horns of an ibex and a deer.

After a lunch which included scrambled eggs cooked with tomatoes and a mixed salad, I took a short tour of the refugio.

There are only eight double rooms in this inn and it was obvious that reservations for the weekends must be made considerably in advance. I wouldn't advise a casual drive up the road anticipating a night's lodging without reservations. It is wise to phone ahead even for meals. Afterwards, when we went outside, children were making snowballs out of season and the sun was rapidly melting the inch or so of the white stuff on the ground. It made a pretty scene with the sparkling snow and the many fruit trees in the vicinity in bloom. I hoped that the frost would not nip their buds.

REFUGIO DE JUANAR, Ojen-Sierra Blanca (Malaga). At 10 Km. from Ojen, 20 from Marbella and 621 from Madrid. Telephone: Malaga 88-10-00 Rates: $13.70

ALBERGUE DE CARRETERA, Antequera (Malaga)

This inn is an example of a typical albergue or wayside inn. It was built a number of years ago when the parador program was in its infancy. Today it is very popular, being ideally located 54 miles north of the city of Malaga on a road between Seville and Granada.

As usual, this albergue is very busy at lunch and dinner since it serves the Spanish food of the region. Overnight stays are limited to three nights.

ALBERGUE DE CARRETERA, Antequera (Malaga). At 54 Km. from Malaga, 530 from Madrid. Telephone: Antequera 84-17-40. RR. Rates: $9.15

Ronda, the Delightful and Unexpected

The road from San Pedro on the coast to Ronda in the mountains is unbelievable. It is one of the most twisting, turning, exciting scenic roads I have ever been on in my life. It is a steady climb for 40 of the 54 kilometers with views of the mountains whose beauty is in their starkness. There is a moonscape quality about everything with different strata of rock revealing surprisingly brilliant streaks of color. Sometimes on the distant ridges, I could see a cluster of houses clinging precariously to the sides of the mountains.

There were sweeping views of valleys and range after range of mountains, some of them snowcapped. As we neared the end

of the trip, the terrain softened somewhat, and there were pine and oak trees and flocks of sheep and goats being tended by a lone shepherd.

I never expected to find a town of such dimensions at the end of this narrow, twisty road. The biggest surprise about Ronda is that this small city has an extraordinary setting of almost unequaled grandeur on the lip of a gorge which the guidebook says is 1000 feet deep. Ronda makes a wonderful side trip.

PARADOR DEL GOLF, Torremolinos (Malaga)

My back swing was controlled. My grip was firm, but not clenched. My weight shifted as I started my downswing and my head stayed down as my hand swung through the ball. It was a picturebook golf shot—except that my ball hooked into the Mediterranean.

I must confess that when I left New York I never expected to be playing golf at a country inn in Spain, but here I was at the Parador Del Golf in Torremolinos playing nine holes.

I had heard about the Parador Del Golf from Marilyn and Dan Sullivan, who live almost next door to me in the Berkshires.

Many of my readers and most of the innkeepers mentioned in *Country Inns and Back Roads* know Marilyn because for at least eight years she was my administrative assistant. She and Dan are enthusiastic golfers and travelers, and it so happened that they went to Spain about three weeks ahead of me. They stayed ten days at this parador, which by the way is the maximum stay permitted. In her letter to me from Spain, these are some of the things she had to say about her stay at this inn in Torremolinos:

"I know you will like it here. The beach is only about 100 steps away. We spend most of our time walking on the beach or on the golf course or enjoying the swimming pool built in the center of a three-sided square that is formed by the buildings of the inn. Our room is lovely with walls of pine board and drapes and bedspreads of a finished burlap material with a Spanish design. And I have never seen such beautiful, enormous bathrooms.

"Be sure you get a chance to meet Julian, the assistant parador director. He speaks three languages and is a great help to all the guests. He's just a marvelous person.

"The golf course was great. You know how Dan is—it has to be just right to please him, and he is ready to come back to Spain anytime. One thing we couldn't get over was the food. I think we would have put on ten pounds apiece if we hadn't been careful.

"Be sure you visit Marbella, it's an attractive seacoast town—there are many Americans who have condominiums

there. I am enclosing a postcard showing all of the sailboats. I have to go now because Dan says that we are teeing off in about three minutes. By the way you can rent golf clubs here, so don't bother to bring yours."

Well Marilyn, thank you so much. I think we have seen the Parador Del Golf from your eyes. The only thing you didn't send me were instructions on how to correct my American hook while in Spain.

PARADOR DEL GOLF, Torremolinos (Malaga). At 14 Km: from Malaga, 580 from Madrid. Telephone: Malaga 38-11-20. RR., airport, beach nearby, swimming pool and golf. Rates: $19.75

THE CANARY ISLANDS

What and Where Are the Canary Islands?

The Canary Archipelago, actually a part of Spain, is composed of seven islands and various islets. It is in the Atlantic off the coast of Africa just four degrees north of the Tropic of Cancer, on the same parallel as Havana. The Canaries are subtropical in appearance, but have a spring climate all year round. Their position in the Atlantic makes them a port of call on almost all sea routes between Europe, the Middle East, Africa, and the Americas.

Each of the islands has its own peculiar and distinctive beauty—volcanic in nature, they present every kind of scene from towering, even snowcapped, peaks, and lofty ranges to out-of-the-way secluded valleys, sandy deserts, rugged crags, perfect craters, and lovely woodlands. Each island is a true continent in miniature with scenes recalling, in some way, beauty-spots from every corner of the globe. Pine, palm, and chestnut trees are as likely to be found on the various islands as that ubiquitous desert plant, the cactus.

The Canaries, incidentally named after wild dogs that formerly overran them, have large sophisticated cities such as Santa Cruz de Tenerife, Puerto de la Cruz and Las Palmas, as well as dozens of small towns and villages that are very natural and appealing. The warm sunshine, beautiful beaches, and easy accessibility by jet from Europe have made the islands very popular as vacation and holiday objectives. The result is an abundance of high-rise buildings in some cities near the beaches.

How to Get There
From North America, Iberia Airlines has flights directly to Madrid from whence there are several two-hour flights daily to Tenerife and Las Palmas International Airports. Fuerteventura, Lanzarote and La Palma have domestic airports. Travel among these and other islands is also possible by ship.

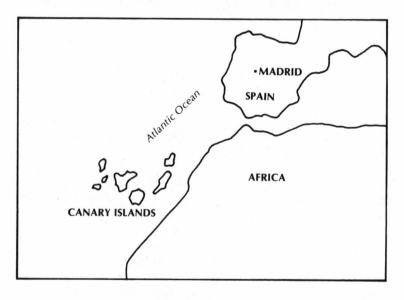

Country Inns in the Canary Islands
I visited four different islands and stayed at the four paradores which are maintained by the Spanish Ministry of Information and Tourism. Just as on mainland Spain, these quiet country inns are definitely Spanish in character and cuisine, and differ greatly from the towering hotels in the larger cities.

Reservations
Reservations should be made directly with each of the four paradores. When telephoning, ask for the Director of the parador.

Dining in the Canary Islands

The traveler will have an ample opportunity to enjoy typical Canary Islands cuisine at the paradores, and also at the many, many small restaurants in villages throughout the islands. The fish is marvelous. It is generally served with the celebrated "wrinkled" potatoes and an especially piquant sauce called "mojo picon." Other Canary Island dishes are "potage de berros" which is a soup made from watercress and herbs, "sancocho canario," a salt fish, also with a special sauce. Bananas and tomatoes, as well as alligator-pear and papaws, appear on island menus, also "gofio"—flour made from wheat, corn, or barley, toasted before milling, and eaten in the form of gruel or dumplings instead of bread. Some islands have their own specialties. By all means, eat at these small village restaurants. They are unlike anything we have in the United States and they are a new experience in good food.

Renting a Car

It's possible to arrange a car rental in advance from AutoEurope in New York. (See section in front of book.) In addition, buses run almost everywhere and are an excellent way to get around within each island. They are usually plainly marked and even without much Spanish, I was able to inquire about how long the bus would remain or what time it would return.

Maps and Guides

The best maps and guides are available through each of the paradores. An overall brochure of the islands is available from any Spanish National Tourist Office, but the more specific folders are obtainable only on each individual island.

My Itinerary in the Canary Islands

From Madrid I flew to Las Palmas Airport on Gran Canaria Island where I remained for a few days. Then I took a plane to Fuerteventura for a 24-hour visit. Another flight took me to the Island of Tenerife for a two-day stay, and still another, to the Island of La Palma. I returned to Madrid by way of Las Palmas Airport on Gran Canaria. I rented cars on Gran Canaria and Tenerife and used taxis and buses on Fuerteventura and La Palma.

PARADOR CRUZ de TEJEDA, Tejeda, Gran Canaria Island

I was seated on the terrace at this parador enjoying the sunshine. Behind me I could hear the singing of the girls as they washed the floors and prepared the dining room for the noon meal. The concierge was whistling as he sorted out the mail and took care of the accounts.

For the moment, I was content to think back on my adventures the previous two days and enjoy them in retrospect.

My two Iberia flights—New York to Madrid and Madrid to Las Palmas were on time and most pleasant. Since this was my third time in the Madrid Airport, I found no difficulty in distinguishing between the international and domestic sections. After my arrival in Las Palmas I picked up my rented car and drove north straight up into the mountains to Tejeda. It wasn't necessary to go into the city of Las Palmas. I was greeted by the manager of the parador who spoke excellent English and immediately conducted me on a tour of the lodgings. They were all very light and airy with wooden beds and wardrobes, good lamps for bedside reading, and rather large bathrooms. I asked to be shown several different rooms and finally chose a room with a view of a sensationally gorgeous valley and the mountains beyond. The manager pointed out a terrycloth bathrobe which I later found very comfortable to slip into after a hot shower. Speaking of the hot water, in this parador it is necessary to inform the concierge of the intention to bathe and then to wait five minutes. There is ample hot water, but the pressure must be built up in advance.

I walked out on the terrace and immediately made the acquaintance of Elizabeth and Walter Lillie from England, and spent the best part of the day with them touring the mountains. More about that later.

The parador is a white building with a traditional red tile roof and an informal garden in the front. Many pine trees grow on and near the grounds, and there are flowers in pots and in beds everywhere.

The village of Tejeda is in the heart of the island. Nearby the majestic Roque Nublo, a jagged spike of basalt reaches to the sky, and almond groves, truck gardens, and rugged peaks look out over the splendid panorama.

After the Lillies and I spent a day of sightseeing, we returned for dinner and we all sampled each others' courses. I had some of

the famous salted fish with the Canary Island sauce which is hot and tasty. For dessert there was a combination of fruits served in an almond sauce with ice cream.

Most visitors to Gran Canaria stay at hotels in the city of Las Palmas, and do not really experience the heart of the island. For this, it is necessary to drive up into the mountains into the "green belt" where the country people live and where it is not tourist-oriented. Here I found people walking on the road wearing straw hats and gathering flowers and herbs from the roadside. They are polite, and happy to be living in such mountainous splendor. The air is clean and clear and everything is green and fresh, a marked change from the seashore. This is the soul of Gran Canaria, and the Parador Cruz de Tejeda is right in the middle of these mountains with a marvelous view across the straits to the high mountains on Tenerife Island.

PARADOR CRUZ DE TEJEDA, Tejeda, Gran Canaria, Canary Islands. Telephone: 65-80-50. A 19-room mountaintop inn approximately one hour to the city of Las Palmas and one hour to Las Palmas Airport. Within one hour of the Gran Canaria beaches, and very short drives to unbelievable mountain scenery and villages. Breakfast, lunch, and dinner served daily to travelers. Rates: $10.20 for 2.

Directions: Rent a car at the Las Palmas Airport and proceed, following the map, through the towns of Telde and San Mateo to Tejeda.

An Afternoon with Walter and Elizabeth Lillie

The Lillies were ideal sightseeing companions. They were wonderfully informed about the flora of the island and kept exclaiming joyfully at new discoveries. There was a lovely purple flower along the road which Walter told me was called a "wallflower." He identified quite a few varieties of small field daisies and red and purple poppies.

We stopped off at the village of Artenara to have tea at the Restaurant La Silla which is reached through an ancient arched cave which emerges onto a terrace carved out of the rock overlooking a splendid valley. Below us were groups of villages and we could see the roads twisting around among the terraces. It was a moody kind of day with moving clouds and bars of sunshine alternately highlighting the trees on the skyline that looked like horsemen climbing to the top of the hill. We were at 6000 feet altitude enthralled by a panorama of differing textures

and shades. As Elizabeth remarked, "This is a land of fore-grounds and backgrounds."

Walter ordered tea, which we enjoyed in the glass-enclosed section of the terrace as the wind was getting a bit chilly.

Continuing on, we stopped for some photographs at one of the village laundromats—Canary Island style. This is an open wash-house with water rushing through a trough in the middle; there the women, wearing straw and knitted hats, stand on both sides pounding away on their clothes and carrying on animated conversations. I'm sure the village gossip was quickly going the rounds.

Drying takes place very quickly as the clothing is spread out on the ground. There were a great many jeans and brown panty-hose.

I drove the Lillies to a beachside hotel in the city of Las Palmas where they were going to spend a few more days, because "we enjoy the constant supply of warm air which is so wonderful after a chilly English winter." The view from their room offered a continual cinema-like parade of visitors at all hours of the day and night, with streams of young people from all over Europe who were in search of sun in the daytime and swinging fun at night.

I bade them farewell, and look forward to seeing them at their home in England within the next year. I left the city and the beaches and drove back up to the top of the mountain, glad to be back to the peace and quiet of the parador.

PARADOR DE FUERTEVENTURA, Puerto del Rosario, Fuerteventura Island

I slipped between the sheets of my sleigh bed—yes, that's right, a sleigh bed in this Canary Islands parador on the Island of Fuerteventura.

I had arrived by Iberia in mid-afternoon and was most gratified to find such a modern and attractive parador located on the ocean with a very welcome swimming pool. From the air, Puerto del Rosario, the principal city of the island, seemed quite small in comparison with Las Palmas. It was on this flight that I made the acquaintance of Senor Sergio Bareria who gave me a clue to future activities on the island. Sergio, it developed, was a man in charge of making loans at a Las Palmas bank and he was flying to Fuerteventura to meet a gentleman who was going to go into the ice cream manufacturing business. Sergio explained to me that his bank believed in the future of the island, and they felt this was an excellent investment.

It was through Sergio that I arranged for a taxicab ride of about 60 kilometers through some of the more mountainous sections of the island. The terrain was rocky and arid, and the mountains were not high enough to have the green vegetation of Gran Canaria. This is the island with the longest shoreline, the widest plains, and the gentlest streams. The beaches are immense. My driver explained that the fishing was exceptional with sardines, tuna, and swordfish racing back and forth through the straits which separate the island from Africa.

I enjoyed dinner that evening with two Dutch businessmen who gave me an indication of things to come. They were interested in buying land for future development and told me that a great many Dutch people feel that this island is very suitable for vacations in the sun. They told me about the broad, white sand beaches on the north end, and beautiful beaches in some places where there were as yet no roads. "However, we would put in the roads, if necessary."

Dinner with my two acquaintances from the Netherlands was marked by my first taste of fried squid which was one of the parador specialties as well as grouper fish which is caught on the waters off the island and served in various ways. The waitresses were in island costumes.

The parador was relatively new and furnished with the same taste that I had seen in many of the paradores on the mainland of Spain. One wall of my lodging room was of sliding glass overlooking the sea. The bathroom with its big parador towels was a joy.

The other furnishings and decorations included some excellent reproductions of full-color prints done in an art-nouveau style depicting Greek legends.

Still another interesting indication of the island's future unfolded as I waited at the airport. I made the acquaintance of a young Spanish couple planning to set up a law practice on the island after they moved from Seville. They spoke glowingly of the future of the island, although at the moment they were "in the early stages of development."

In many ways I felt that I had discovered something quite special on this rather remote island. The people were friendly; it was not crowded as yet; and I saw enough to feel glad that I had gotten there among the first. It may be relatively undiscovered now, but it is only a matter of time.

PARADOR FUERTEVENTURA, Puerto del Rosario, Fuerteventura, Canary Islands. Telephone: (928) 85-1150. A 24-room seaside parador on a quiet Canary Island. Swimming pool and beach within a few steps. Rates: $13.70 for 2.

Directions: The best way is to take a taxi from the airport, about 2 km. It is another 3 km. into the small city of Puerto del Rosario.

PARADOR DE LAS CANADAS del TEIDE, Las Canadas, Tenerife Island

I have found country inns in many different places but I never expected to find one in the crater of a volcano! This parador is completely removed from the sights and sounds of the remainder of the highly touristic island of Tenerife. It is over 6000 feet in altitude and sits in the middle of the crater of the now-extinct volcano of del Teide, the cone of which at 12,250 feet is the highest in Spain. The area immediately adjacent to the inn reminded me a great deal of Arizona and New Mexico, although the vegetation is much more varied and in some cases heavier. It consists of bushes with long pine needles, and sometimes when the sun is right it looks like acres and acres of porcupines!

Immediately in front of the parador are pinnacle rocks which appear to be precariously balanced on uncertain feet getting weak at the ankles. Footpaths have been carved into some of them and it is great fun to climb to the top.

Fortunately, just a few years ago a good blacktop road was completed to the mountain, bringing beaches of Tenerife and the tourist areas within an hour's drive. It is possible to lodge at this parador and drive to the beaches or wander around the island and be back well in time for the evening meal which is served at 8:30. The wonderful, fresh, cool mountain air is most conducive to good sleeping. While I was there, there were no clouds at all at this height, although each day, driving down to the beaches, I had to drive through an encircling blanket to reach the seashore.

The parador is delightful. I became acquainted easily with the concierge, the staff, and the director who has excellent English. The building is constructed of white plaster, and inside there are columns of green granite with additional decorative wood panels. My bedroom overlooked the uppermost section of the volcano's cone, which is always snowcapped. The twin beds were attractively carved, and there was the usual superb parador bathroom.

An interesting quirk here is that all the lights go out at 12 o'clock midnight and the electricity is not turned on again until 6 a.m.—that's when I learned the purpose of the candle placed at my bedside table. This is done to help preserve energy.

I understand this parador is very popular with the inhabitants of the island who frequently come here for dinner as well as short vacations.

Most of the visitors to Tenerife find the beaches and large seaside cities a great attraction. As in Gran Canaria, a very few find their way up the imposing slopes of del Teide to the dry, desert country—the entirely different world—up above.

PARADOR DE LAS CANADAS del TEIDE, Tenerife, Canary Islands, La Orotava, Telephone: Tenerife 222. A 27-room inn 6000 feet high in the crater of a volcano. Swimming pool. Nature walks. Approximately one hour's drive to most beaches. Breakfast, lunch, and dinner served daily. Rates: $13.70 for 2.

Directions: Rent a car at the Tenerife Airport (you'll need it). Parador is 1 hour from airport on a road straight up the mountain. Follow the signs that say Las Canadas. The trip from sea level to the parador includes some positively gorgeous pine forests and the scenic vistas are remarkable.

PARADOR DE LA PALMA, Santa Cruz de la Palma, La Palma Island

"In this part of the world," said Harry Evermann, "the idea is to find an island that is at least comparatively undiscovered. I think we've done it." Harry and his wife Anne and I were enjoying breakfast at the Parador de la Palma which overlooks the sea in this beautiful city.

This was a farewell meal. The final chapter of an adventure that had started more than 36 hours earlier when I deplaned at La Palma Airport and Harry retrieved my wide-brimmed coconut straw hat. When he handed it to me I discovered that he spoke English.

In the short time while we were awaiting a taxi at the airport I learned that Harry was a purser for Lufthansa Airlines; that he and Anne were looking for property for a vacation home in La Palma, and that they were not acquainted with the parador where I would be stopping.

I persuaded them to come and see it for themselves and everything worked out beautifully. There was a double room available for them, and they were kind enough to invite me to share the cost of a rented car to see the sights of the island.

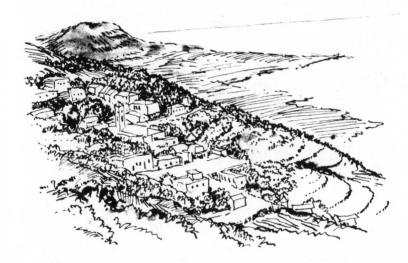

We started early the next morning, driving across the island for a visit to one of the most amazing national parks anywhere in the world—Caldera de Taburiente. Inside a volcanic crater, there is an observation point in the park where the peaks seem close enough to touch on every side. It has exceptional beauty and awesome scenery.

We continued across the island, enjoying lunch at a Spanish sidewalk restaurant in a small town, and then drove north amidst views of the ocean and mountains that were really beyond description.

La Palma with its 457 square miles and only 76,000 inhabitants is an ideal green island. It has the greatest altitude in the world relative to its circumference. Most of it is covered by beautiful green vegetation and there are many farms and orchards.

After some rather exciting adventures on narrow back roads, we returned to the parador for dinner at approximately ten o'clock. Among the specialties were chicken soup, fried octopus, delicious gazpacho, rabbit, and a goat cheese, native to the island, which I liked very much.

The parador is one of the oldest in Spain and the furnishings are all in the traditional style. The very attractive main lounge has an attractive television room and a library where there were magazines and newspapers in several different languages. Almost all of the bedrooms face the sea and have their own balconies and terraces. Perhaps this parador's most beguiling feature is the fact that it is located on the main road around the harbor where modern buildings are next to old mansions with great wooden balconies and terraces.

I awakened at daybreak and sat on my terrace overlooking the semicircular expanse of the broad harbor and watched the sun come up out of the sea. The warm prevailing wind was delightful.

During our final meal together, the Evermanns and I were exchanging notes and addresses and promising to contact each other. We agreed that La Palma, the island, and Santa Cruz de la Palma, the city, had exceptional qualities of sunshine, tranquility, and marvelous scenery. As Anne said, "I wouldn't be at all surprised if we find our little house here, and if so, you must come visit us."

PARADOR DE LA PALMA, Santa Cruz de La Palma, La Palma, Canary Islands. P.O. Apartado 48, Tel. 41-23-40. A 28-room inn located on the Avenue Maritime overlooking the sea in downtown Santa Cruz de La Palma. Breakfast, lunch, dinner served daily to travelers. About 5 km. from nearest beach. Rates: $13.70 for 2.

Directions: Take taxi from airport.

NOTES

SWEDEN

GOTHENBU

TRAVEL SUGGESTIONS FOR SWEDEN

How to Get There

SAS (Scandinavian Airlines) maintains flights from the United States to all Scandinavian countries. There are flights to Stockholm and Gothenburg in Sweden. Numerous ferries provide service to Sweden from other parts of Europe. The Eurailpass is good in Scandinavia.

Country Inns in Sweden

Country inn hospitality in Sweden falls into two categories: there are lovely old manor houses and small castles, and there are the more traditional country inns in southern Sweden, in the province of Skane, which are similar to their Danish cousins. The latter I have described more extensively in the section on Denmark.

Those inns to be found in manor houses and castles often have historical or literary connections, with an ambience in which their gardens play a special role. Decorated in harmonizing Scandinavian fabrics and furnished with both traditional and modern furniture, most have lodging rooms with private baths. The food is always excellent, usually prepared and served by members of the owner's family which make up the modest staffs.

Dining in Sweden

Everything I've ever heard about Swedish smorgasbord is true: it is fabulous. Served as a noon meal, and all day on Sundays and holidays, smorgasbord has many varieties of fish, as well as the famous Swedish meatballs which are served with lingonberry sauce. Also included are salads, cheese, marinated meats, breads, and relishes. I found that each chef was proud of his smorgasbord, which involves many hours of preparation.

I had my first taste of small, fresh raw herring for breakfast in Sweden and found them delicious. Evening meals in many Swedish manor houses and restaurants are served in the Continental style with a great deal of emphasis on French dishes.

Car Rentals in Scandinavia

SAS has many different "Fly-Drive" plans that include automobiles. Travelers for whom Scandinavia is part of a continent-wide itinerary, or those who are not on a "Fly-Drive" plan, will find more information in the section "Renting a Car for Europe," in the front of the book.

My Itinerary in Sweden

Because I entered Sweden from Norway, the account in this edition starts in the western part of Sweden called Varmland, and proceeds eastward through the Dalarna region, and thence to Stockholm and south, past Lake Vattern to Skane, the resort area of southern Sweden. To obtain Sweden road maps, see the section at the back of the book.

Varmland, My Introduction To Sweden

I crossed the border into Sweden at Eda, and was now in the rich Varmland country in western Sweden, north of Karlstadt. This was an area blessed with most of the good things that Sweden has to offer—great forests, lakes numbering in the thousands, hiking trails, canals, folklore festivals, crafts of all descriptions, and rivers which are not only famous for their natural beauty but also avenues of commerce with many floating logs.

This is a region replete with the opportunities for active outdoor sports. These include tennis and golf, swimming, canoeing and boating. In winter there is downhill and cross-country skiing.

The town of Sunne, where I remained overnight, is deep in Selma Lagerlof country. It is on the straits connecting the upper and middle Fryken Lakes. In August there are nine days of Fryksdal festivities based on Selma Lagerlof stories.

The fairs and festivals in this area, I am told, are most enjoyable. For further information about Varmland write: The Varmland Tourist Association, Kungsgatan 4, B S 65224 Karlstad, Sweden.

LANSMANSGARDEN, Sunne

I was completely entranced by this lovely manor house. It is located on the banks of Lake Fryken in Sunne, which is the center of Sweden's famous Varmland area. For one thing it re-acquainted me with the Swedish Nobel Prize winning author, Selma Lagerlof. She had used this inn as a locale for one of her books, and her home Marbacka, just a few kilometers to the south.

I arrived about 9 p.m., driving from Norway. My first experience was heartening, indeed. I had arrived long past the dinner hour, but the girl at the desk said that the cook could prepare something for me if I were willing to wait a few minutes. I was. Then an accommodating waiter with a good sense of humor showed me to a table in a most attractive dining room. After a very tasty bowl of soup, he brought me a warm plate with five delicious seafood-filled crepes. This was accompanied by an excellent tossed salad and some homemade Swedish bread.

The dining room, like the remainder of this inn, is a tribute to Swedish furnishing and decorating. It was a tasteful blend of painted furniture and natural wood. There were flowers on each table, and the knives, forks and plates were Swedish Modern.

After dinner, I went out on the terrace and met a Swedish couple and their English friends who had been coming to Lansmansgarden for many years. We talked about traveling and promised to meet the next morning for breakfast.

My room in this manor house could be a model for country inns anywhere. It had a lacy bedspread, Swedish designs on the wallpaper, a blue carpet, and painted furniture. Erik Biorklund, the innkeeper, later explained to me that these were the "romantic" rooms which, whenever possible, were reserved for honeymoon couples. The rooms in this building were named

after characters in Selma Lagerlof's novels.

The next morning, breakfast with my four new friends was great fun because they took delight in introducing me to several typically Swedish dishes, of which there were several. For one thing, I had my first taste of fresh, raw herring. I'll never be satisfied with pickled herring again. I was also introduced to a breakfast porridge made from rye grain to which I was instructed to add applesauce and a small amount of sugar and milk. Delicious. There were many other dishes including meats and cheeses.

LANSMANSGARDEN, Sunne, Sweden, S-686 00, Sunne. Telephone: 0565-10301. 29-room manor house in a garden setting in the Varmland section of Sweden. Summer sports include swimming, rowing, badminton, tennis, golf, fishing, walking, hiking. Winter sports include several different ski lifts within a short distance. Rates: SKr 60-130.

Marbacka and Rottneros

The fact that novelist Selma Lagerlof was born in this part of the Varmland in 1858, and subsequently made her home here from 1907 until 1940, has asserted a tremendous influence on the area. Her home, Marbacka which is open to the public, has been preserved exactly as she left it at the time of her passing. It is visited by thousands of people every year.

Rottneros is identified as the "Ekeby" in Selma Lagerlof's novels. It was probably the residence of an important country squire as early as the 13th century. It is the former garden of an important iron foundry. It covers almost 100 acres which in themselves are surrounded by both natural and formal park land. In the gardens are more than 100 sculptures representing a large part of what Swedish sculptors have created during the past century. These marvelous pieces of sculpture are carefully placed within the natural atmosphere of gardens and trees, and are one of Sweden's foremost tourist attractions.

Marbacka and Rottneros are open from May 15th to September 15th. There is a coffee room at Marbacka and a restaurant and cafeteria at Rottneros.

STOLLETS GASTGIVAREGARD, Stollet

A great deal of Sweden's appeal lies in its great stretches of forest and beautiful rivers. I found this place while driving from Sunne to Tallberg through the forest next to the Klavalven River. Stollets is a bit too large to be called a pension and probably could not qualify as a hotel according to Scandinavian standards because it lacks certain facilities. However, I found it to be a typical resort accommodation and for the short time that I was there I was the only English-speaking guest.

Stollet is a very small town located on the important Klaralven River, which serves as a waterway for the logging business. There is a swimming pool overlooking the river and a very pleasant terrace. The river scene and the countryside are most attractive. There were many flowers in bloom on the river banks including tulips and lilacs. Oddly enough there were a few seagulls swooping over the river.

The lodging rooms in the older section of the inn have been modernized, and there are quite a few rooms in a newer section.

The Stollets Gastgivaregard is not at all pretentious. I found it to have a great deal of natural country hotel charm.

STOLLETS GASTGIVAREGARD, 680 51 Stollet. Telephone: 0563/811 50. Rates: SKr 85.

Dalarna

Dalarna is comprised of a considerable area to the north-west of Stockholm. The word means "the valleys between the

east and west Dal Rivers."

From my talks with Signe Keyes in Siljansgarden, I learned that the entire area is rich in folklore, history, handcrafts and the preservation of old Swedish ways. It is also the home of the famous Dala paintings, which are decorative paintings by self-taught artists who lived between 1780 and 1870. The famous Dala horses, which are occasionally found in imported craft shops in the United States, come from a small village near Leksand.

The Leksand area itself is comprised of 90 villages and the resort towns of Tallberg, Siljansnas and Insjon. They are all located on the shores of beautiful lake Siljan which is a most attractive natural area.

For further information about Dalarna write the Dalarna Tourist Association, Bergslagsgrand 1, S-791 00 Falun, Sweden.

SILJANSGAARDEN GUEST HOME, Tallberg

I just happened to be walking down a lane toward the shore of Lake Siljan when I saw a group of several old, sod-roofed houses. The sign said, "Siljansgaarden Gasthem." This was the beginning of a most wonderful adventure which included meeting Signe and Kenneth Keys, the proprietors, and several of the guests at this unusual country inn.

This inn, which is really the inspiration of Signe's mother and, later, her father, not only preserves the Sweden of the past, but actually makes it useful and viable today. Many of the living rooms and bedrooms are furnished with antiques. However, there are some lodgings with modern furniture. Perhaps the best description of the inn is found in Signe's words:

"The first question we tend to get here is 'How old is this place?' When you arrive here it seems so settled in its environment and so peaceful that people think it must be an old farmstead. But it isn't. I used to answer that 'the house is much older than the place as you see it.' The oldest house in the group is from the 16th century and that house also has guest rooms in it.

We don't know the age of some of the houses. Many of them have dates engraved on them or you can tell from the way they are built.

"When my mother arrived in 1916 there was nothing here—just meadows, forests and stone heaps. She was born and grew up north of here. She had been married in Stockholm, and for a woman of that time she was very unusual. She was well-trained in many subjects and wanted to work among people as well as have a family.

"In those days it was uncommon to buy a house. You usually tried to find an old one—old houses were of timber. It was common to move houses. The first house she bought had been a mill at the foot of the mountain across the lake here. The millstone we have on the front lawn was one of the millstones inside the house—and it's now used as a coffee table. The house became much bigger than she had intended. She couldn't build the cellar deep enough so the house became higher. That was in 1917. She was well known for her taste in furnishings and art, and the big room is today as it was then. In the old days people slept, worked, and ate in the one room, therefore it was named the 'Big Room.' (Stor Stuga.) In one corner you had the fireplace, in the other corner you had the beds, similar to what are now known as bunk beds. The bottom was a double bed for the older people and the top for the younger folk. The big drawers were pushed in during the day, and at night were used for the very young children.

"In 1925 my father came here. They found that they had similar interests, and in 1927 they opened this as a guest home where you could come for rest and recreation, and to meet people. They began to offer summer courses in music, singing, dancing, and literature. When this was started it was very unusual—a pioneer movement."

The above paragraphs are for the most part exactly the way Signe Keys explained this unusual inn which is really a preserved environment which has been put to good use today. If possible, a guest should try to stay here at least three days, which is usually the minimum length of stay suggested by Signe and Kenneth. It truly is a unique experience.

SILJANSGAARDEN GUEST HOME, S 793 03 Tallberg (Dalarna). Telephone: Leksand 0247/50040. A wide range of rooms, some with private bath. In addition to the preserved Swedish environment, guests can enjoy sauna, tennis, rowboating, table tennis, croquet, badminton, and many walks and hikes throughout the remarkable scenic Dalarna area. Closed from the end of September to Christmas. Open for Christmas. Rates: SKr 75-130 per person (includes breakfast and dinner).

THE LIDINGOBRO WARDSHUS, Stockholm

My host and hostess for the evening in Stockholm were Ake and Margaret Gille. Ake, a very gentle man, had been connected with the Swedish tourist information center for some time, and for eight years was located in New York City.

Our first visit was to a lovely restaurant on the water, the

Lidingobro Wardshus, just a few miles from downtown Stockholm (Centrum).

Apparently it was located in a former manor house, as are many Swedish inns. My first impressions were most favorable. As soon as we stepped inside the old gates which are now permanently opened, I saw three old-fashioned Swedish sleighs loaded with flowers. There were flowers everywhere—in formal gardens, in large tubs placed all around the terrace, and in hanging baskets. The rather formal buildings are wooden, painted in a muted yellow color with white trim, with red tile roofs.

On one of the terraces a cook was barbecuing some meat on a charcoal brazier, and the aroma did amazing things to my already substantial appetite. There were many chairs and tables placed around the terrace which were not being used on that evening, but were very popular during lunchtime and in the afternoon because of the beautiful view of the pleasure boats and the shore beyond.

Inside this old restaurant, there was a series of small connected dining rooms, each with a view of the terrace and the water. Apparently the buildings were in existence before the 1700's and the decorations have been done in the old-fashioned Swedish way.

We walked through the kitchen and had a conversation with a few of the chefs who were getting ready for the considerable number of people who were already seated in the dining rooms. I was allowed to sample four or five dishes including some delicious fish. Because we were going on to dinner, I was not able to eat an entire meal; it took all of my will power to keep from devouring each portion.

LIDINGOBRO WARDSHUS, Kaknas, Djurgarden 62, Stockholm. Telephone: 08-62 06 94. A country restaurant overlooking the water, just a few miles from central Stockholm. Luncheon and dinner served daily. No lodgings available.

ULRIKSDALS WARDSHUS, Stockholm

Margaret and Ake Gille and I arrived at the gardens at the Ulriksdals Wardshus just as the Swedish flag was being lowered at approximately 9 p.m. It was a lovely moment because the guests in the restaurant had assembled on the terrace to join in singing the Swedish National Anthem. I understand that, weather permitting, this is the custom almost every evening.

Ulriksdals Wardshus has the really fine extra touches, many of which are supplied by the hostess and owner, Kerstin Bergendahl. She is an extremely handsome lady of great energy, ability and graciousness. I was delighted when she and her husband and a friend from Canada decided to join our table. A little earlier she had introduced herself and said that she was going to sing for a wedding party which was being held on the porch upstairs. She invited us to come along.

Walking as softly as possible we went up the stairs of this unusual manor house which was built in 1868. Apparently it has changed very little since then, and the romanticism which is associated with the reign of King Karl XV, still persists. The wedding party with all of the ladies in their beautiful gowns and handsome gentlemen in their white ties and tails indeed seemed to belong to another day and time.

We stood quietly, while Kerstin sang a lovely little peasant song in Swedish. Then all the guests rose and shouted "good luck" to the happy couple and drank a toast.

The dinner was a complement to the ambiance. My main course was red trout served in a special sauce with brown potatoes and dessert was grapes and figs with small balls of ice

cream all topped with delicious freshly whipped cream. Cream is one thing that the Scandinavians have in great quantities and it is usually served with dessert.

ULRIKSDALS WARDSHUS, S-171 71 Solna/Stockholm. Telephone: 08-85 08 15. A striking restaurant just a few miles from downtown Stockholm. Luncheon and dinner served daily (on my last visit). No lodgings available.

HOTELL REISEN, Stockholm

When I find myself in large cities I definitely prefer the conservative type of hotel: the Algonquin in New York, the Cheshire Inn in St. Louis, and the Huntington in San Francisco, for example. In Stockholm, where large hotels are a way of life, the Reisen fits right into my personal preference. Although it is somewhat sophisticated and definitely European in style, this rather small hotel has a very personal air about it, and I found it quite easy to feel at home almost immediately. This was partially because of the friendliness and informality of the staff members who, by the way, are fluent in many languages including English.

The hotel is housed in three beautiful 17th century residences in the Old Town section with narrow cobblestone streets and several attractive shops.

The Reisen has other amenities as well, including music in one dining room that has been designed to resemble the elegant saloon of a 19th Century ship. There is also a very welcome sauna and an indoor swimming pool.

HOTELL REISEN, Skeppsbron 12-14, S-111 30 Stockholm. Telephone: 08-22 32 60. Rates: SKr 235-345.

GRIPSHOLMS VARDSHUS, Mariefred

My reason for visiting Mariefred was to see Sweden's oldest inn and possibly to look in on the famous Gripsholms Castle. After just one inquiry, I found myself walking through the garden of the inn, which faces the quay and the Castle.

I easily located the enthusiastic innkeepers, Bengt and Inger Erikson, who said that I could tag along with them while they took care of the last minute preparations for the Sunday smorgasbord which would be served in just a few minutes.

Inger assured me that the Gripsholms Vardshus was indeed

the oldest inn in Sweden dating back to 1623. "But," she added, "the Castle over there is much older, by at least 300 years."

I followed her into the kitchen where a dozen people were busily preparing special dishes for the smorgasbord. In one corner, fish was being sliced and boned and in another, cheeses were being prepared. There was a table where all of the many salads were being put together, an elaborate bread tray with at least eight kinds of bread, and there were at least three people working on some delectable homemade cakes and tarts.

The dining room was furnished with beautiful native antiques and there were many oil paintings and prints on the walls. In the corner of one of the blue and white dining rooms there is a very handsome old-fashioned white stove which served as the principal means of heating the rooms during past centuries and is now decorated with blue figures and gay flowers. Each of the dining rooms has a different color scheme and theme.

In the center of the main dining room were the tables set with the delectable choices for the smorgasbord. Bengt Erikson was on hand with a few of the last-minute touches and in a matter of moments the doors would be open. It was like waiting for the curtain to go up on the first act of a play.

Subsequently I did have time to visit the old castle and to walk about the town, where I found a little Sunday flea market in progress with many handcrafted items displayed on little tables placed around the square.

There are 10 rooms in the inn, most of them modernized and many of them with a view of the castle.

The inn, the castle, and the town make visiting Mariefred a very happy experience.

GRIPSHOLMS VARDSHUS, Mariefred, Sweden. Telephone: 0159-100 40. Rates Skr 95.

I was breezing along on Highway E-4 from Stockholm to southern Sweden, admiring a lake on the left side of the road, when I spied a stately white house and some formal gardens on my right. I was almost positive that I had seen the word "Vardshus" as well. Impatiently I sought out an exit on my right so that I could turn back for a second look. (E-4 is a divided highway at this point so there were no left turns.) I drove on for about 6 kilometers, although in my impatience it seemed like 26. Finally I turned off and learned from a friendly gas station man that what I had seen was indeed a "Vardshus" or inn. Following careful directions I returned and the result was one of my most memorable adventures in Sweden.

VARDSHUSET STENKULLEN, Aby

The grounds of this inn were a tribute to the art of gardening. Everywhere I looked there were plants and flowers, well-trimmed hedges and carefully pruned trees. In mid-June the colors were kaleidoscopic. There were gardens on all four sides and on the second floor balconies there were great hanging begonias and containers and tubs of other cascading flowers. There were three or four fountains, some with water lilies in bloom.

While I stood there for a few minutes contemplating camera angles I discovered I had a companion. A gigantic St. Bernard nuzzled me, nearly knocking me into a rose bush. For a moment I thought he was going to stand on his hind legs and put his paws on my shoulders, which surely would have been a disaster for me. Just at this crucial point, I heard a voice call something in Swedish and the dog disappeared. A young woman then came out on the rear veranda of the inn and said, "Good afternoon, may I help you."

The young lady, as it developed, was Maria Svensson and her family owns the inn. After I had explained that I was writing a book about country inns in Sweden and that this inn looked like something quite special, she gave me permission to wander around and promised to give me a few minutes later on.

"We are serving a special party right now," she said, "but please make yourself at home."

As soon as I walked into the reception area, I realized that I was supposed to remove my shoes and choose a pair of sandals from a neat collection just inside the door. After I saw the handsome Oriental rugs on the floors of every room I knew why.

My next impression was that almost every square inch of wall in the hallways and living rooms was covered with some type of wall hanging, portrait, reproduction or print. There were also notices of exhibitions of paintings and concerts, past, present and future. Every room also had many pieces of sculpture placed on the wide windowsills, tables, and among the books on bookshelfs that ran from ceiling to floor.

It was obvious that the owners and guests of this lovely inn took delight in music, art, history, and literature.

I could hear the guests in the dining room singing Swedish songs. Between courses, Maria managed to come out and explain a few things to me. My principal regret was that I simply could not take the time to remain there overnight.

The Vardshuset Stenkullen is a family operation with Maria and her mother and father doing most of the work themselves. Maria explained that nearby Lake Brovikien provided water sports and recreation and that there were lovely walks and drives in the countryside. "Many of our guests," she said, "some of whom have been returning for quite a few years, prefer to just walk in the gardens and sit on the terraces and perhaps read. And, of course, we have music available at anytime. Everyone seems to be content."

I certainly had no trouble believing that.

VARDSHUSET STENKULLEN, Aby, Sweden. Telephone: 011/690 19. Closed Christmas, New Year until Jan. 15. Rates: SKr 70-160.

LOFSTAD SLOTT, Norrkoping

I imagine that everyone has reveries about owning a castle or a palace. It does, however, present a few difficulties. The upkeep is terrific. Just keeping the grounds presentable and the walls in repair is a fulltime job. Imagine repairing a leaky roof on a castle! In many places in Europe, palaces and castles are maintained by government grants and by offering conducted tours. Quite a few of them offer accommodations and some have restaurants in them.

The latter is the case at the Lofstad Castle or slott as it is known in Sweden. This particular castle was recommended by Ake Gille who said that if I felt like having a meal or a cup of coffee in a castle then I should by all means stop at this place which is on Route E-4 just south of Norrkoping. The sign for it is on the right-hand side of the road and it sits on a wooded hill overlooking a field and brook.

I walked into a courtyard and joined a handful of people walking around the area. I peeked in on one of the many dining rooms on the first floor where there were busy preparations for a wedding. Tables were also set on the outer porches which have an excellent view of the orchard and countryside.

I wandered through some of the dining rooms which had painted ceilings and painted furniture, and in the corner of one I saw electronic equipment that could only mean that a rock band plays here. I could also see that one of the other uses for old palaces and castles is to present musical and theatrical programs. Here at Lofstad Slott this is true almost every weekend. Bach, Beethoven and Gershwin were on the program for the coming Sunday afternoon. There were also notices of several small chamber groups as well.

I walked down to the stable area where a very pleasant outdoor dining area had been created. There were quite a few people enjoying themselves in a Forge Room which had been converted into the restaurant.

As nearly as I am able to understand the brochure from this castle, it apparently dates back to the 1600's. It looks as if it has had a long, peaceful and productive life and now continues on as a reminder of some of Sweden's opulent past.

LOFSTAD SLOTT, Norrkoping, Sweden. Telephone: 011 351 65. A castle restaurant serving from 11 AM to 8 PM. No lodgings.

HOTELL RIBBAGARDEN, Granna

"And this is the room occupied many times by Greta Garbo." I was being conducted through the Ribbagarden in the very orderly village of Granna which is located on the shores of Lake Vattern.

The Ribbagarden is located two squares from the main street on one of the town roads leading down to the lake. The innkeeper's daughter, who had just completed her "middle schooling," took me through the entire inn explaining that its history dates back to 1569. The building has been increased in size many times over the years so that the interior has many different levels on the same floor. On the top floor of the main building she showed me to a large room with windows on three sides. One of them offers a view of Lake Vattern. It was a much larger room than the others that I saw. "This was the room that Greta Garbo occupied many times" she said. The other rooms were more or less conventional in size and for the most part had been modernized.

The living rooms had arrangements of old-fashioned Swedish furniture with many landscapes and prints on the walls. Its furnishings are more in keeping with the exterior of the inn which has many little balconies and windows overlooking a large park-like area with fruit and pine trees and quite a few tables and chairs for outdoor relaxation. Just outside the main entrance the path into this secluded woodland passes through an old grape arbor.

Because the Ribbagarden is a very popular place to dine attracting many people from the nearby cities of Jonkoping and Norrkoping, the two dining rooms are most spacious. I happened to be there on a Sunday which is one of the favorite dining-out days for Swedish smorgasbord. I understand that there were many specialties connected with the area which has excellent vegetables and fruits, as well as fish from the lake. Almost every town in Sweden has a different specialty for the smorgasbord.

Just for the record, I don't think that Greta Garbo has visited the Ribbagarden in many years.

HOTELL RIBBAGARDEN, 56030 Granna, Sweden. Telephone: 0390/10820. This is an old hotel still keeping some of the traditional Swedish ways. Rates: SKr 83-125.

HOTELL VASTANA SLOTT, Granna

I always thought of castles as having moats, drawbridges and crenelated battlements where men-at-arms in chain mail poured down a rain of arrows from their crossbows at besieging armies. Here, however, was a gentle castle filled with luxurious antiques, paintings and sculptures and just a low decorative wall on the front, erected no doubt to complete the setting.

I entered, crossing a stone threshold over 300 years old and found myself in a large reception area with a huge fireplace at one end. Originally the "working rooms" of the castle were found on either side—the scullery, pantry, storehouses and servants' rooms. The owners and their guests occupied the spacious second floor. This is reached by a set of stone steps that have been well-worn by many generations. Imagine 300 years of castle visitors all using these steps to present petitions, or perhaps pay respect to the nobility.

Halfway up the twisting passage a formidable figure in medieval armor with a battle-axe in its fist confronts and scrutinizes all visitors. When I saw that no one was watching I lifted the visor to see if there was a man inside. There wasn't.

The living rooms, dining rooms, library and lodging rooms are all lavishly furnished and decorated in the florid castle style that represents 300 years of adding more furniture and seldom removing any. Carved chairs, benches, tables, beds, armoires, and the rooms themselves, are all on a larger-than-life scale. Naturally with so much wall space many of the paintings, which are all in the classical style, are tremendous in size and scope.

Today, in these more modest times, the castle is open only in June, July and August and the only meal offered is breakfast, although large dinner parties may be arranged.

Most of the bedrooms are very large and many have casement windows that open out to a generous view of the lake. I did see a few smaller bedrooms. No doubt they were reserved in the old days for guests of lesser rank.

HOTELL VASTANA SLOTT, 560 30, Granna, Sweden. Telephone: 0390/107 00. Rates: SKr 110-125 (does not include breakfast).

HOOK MANOR HOUSE, Hok

I teed-up my ball, took a long look down the first fairway and stopped to speak to my hostess at Hook, Gunilla Hogbom. "This looks like an excellent cross-country skiing area," I said. "Do your winter guests enjoy outdoor sports here?"

"Oh, yes," she replied, "winters are really fun here. We Scandinavians enjoy being outdoors then just as much as we do in the summer. Besides skiing, we have skating on the lake, tobogganing and curling. Everybody enjoys walking in the snow and our woods are particularly beautiful after a fresh snowfall!"

We then decided that one of the best ways for me to get acquainted with this old manor house/modern resort inn, was to play a few holes of golf and enjoy the countryside. It was a most entertaining few hours. In addition to the golf course (there were 11 holes when I visited although 7 more were under construction), the resort offers tennis, badminton, swimming (in the pool and in the lake), bocci, sailing, boating and fishing. There was also a rather elegant billiard room.

In fact, elegant is a good word to describe much of the Hook Manor House. In addition to the main building which was built in the 1700's, several other buildings have been added, providing rather luxurious accommodations for approximately 120 guests. The inn is well known as a conference center as well as a sports-minded resort.

When I commented that there seemed to be quite a few guests in the "young married" category, Gunilla said, "Yes, and many of them bring their children. I think that we have guests that enjoy both the old-fashioned and the modern things that they find in Hook. The setting is romantic, but the facilities are very much up to date."

We played three holes and I lost three balls and then Gunilla suggested that it would be fun to go for a sail on the lake before lunch. "I would like you to see Hook from that side," she said. "We all think it's the best view." It was.

RELAIS CHATEAU 256, HOOK MANOR HOUSE, 56013 Hok. Telephone: 0393/21080. An 80-room resort-inn and conference center in an old Swedish manor house. 370 kilometers from Stockholm, 230 kilometers from Halsingborg, and 180 kilometers from Gothenburg. All summer and winter sports. Rates: SKr 90-135 per person.

SUNDS HERRGARD, Sunds

There are a few interesting little notes about this inn. For one thing it is an unusual family arrangement. Two Swedish sisters inherited this property, each married a German fellow a few years ago, and now they all live in harmony keeping this lakeside inn.

It has prospered and grown in many respects starting with the main house which has conference rooms, kitchen and dining rooms. After a few years additional lodgings were created in some small adjacent buildings which helped to form a type of open square. More recently a number of lakeside cottages with all conveniences have been added. It is now an active resort with its own lake recreation and the advantages of being just a short drive from Lake Vattern and Granna.

One of the reasons that it is popular with families is that the proprietors have left the surrounding woods and fields in their natural state with many trails for pleasant walks. Children especially like it because there is a large fenced-in area where deer and wild boar are kept, (some of these eventually appear on the menu.) This is where I had my first glimpse of a live wild boar. Although they weren't very big, I must say they did resemble all of the old prints I had ever seen with those formidable curved tusks. This inn has a very informal air and most of the guests had been there for a one or two week holiday. It is located on the beautiful rolling farming country and from the sports car badges displayed at the front entrance it is quite popular with the motoring crowd.

SUNDS HERRGARD, 560 28 Lekeryd, Sweden. Telephone: 036/82006. Rates: SKr 150 (includes three meals).

Skane

Skane, like Varmland, Dalarna and Granna is one of Sweden's enticing playgrounds.

Skane is assuredly unique. It has great cultivated fields, beautiful wooded areas and miles and miles of beaches. Here in Skane it is possible to take eight different auto tours and never repeat a single place. For example, there is the Gold Coast Tour which includes the 700-year-old city of Malmo and is in the area which immediately adjoins Denmark. There is also a tour of the great golden farmlands, a tour of the white sand coast, an apple blossom tour through the extensive orchard section, a green forest tour through the wooded areas, and perhaps one of the most enticing of all, the red castle tour which directs the traveler to at least 18 different castles in Skane, most of which are more than 300 years old.

For additional direct information about Skane write: The Skane Skanes Turisttriafikforbund, Box 4277, 203 14 Malmo 4, Sweden.

MARGRETETORPS GASTGIFVAREGARD, Hjarnarp, Skane

History, intrigue, beauty—the Margretetorps Gastgifvare-gard has them all. It also has the most difficult name for an American to twist his tongue around. When asking directions to reach it I finally gave up on the second word and took the easier first word. Even that took some adjustment.

The first thing that impressed me was a brightly painted old farm cart outside the entrance piled high with flowers. All Scandinavians love flowers and this section of Sweden is blessed with warm sun and fertile soil so every farm has a generous flower garden.

The word "farm" is appropriate here because this inn, certainly one of the oldest in Sweden, dating back to the 1200's, was also a farm for many centuries. The buildings form a hollow-square shape, a pattern which I saw repeatedly among the Swedish farms.

I arrived well past the dinner hour and found my way to the reception desk which was located in the kitchen. I also found this arrangement in several Danish inns.

There's a very practical reason for the reception desk being located in the kitchen: this is the center of most of the activity, especially for inns on a more modest scale.

Modest is also a good word for describing this inn because there are only ten rooms, and as I learned, just one bath. It is necessary to ask for the key to the bathroom. (The w.c.'s are always open.)

Even though the kitchen had been closed for sometime, I was given a large jug of milk and great quantities of ham, cheese and bread—so I had a satisfying late-night snack.

In the morning I was roaming around the inn when I made the acquaintance of a man who works there. He explained that he was from Holland. I was surprised to learn that he had done the very impressive mural on the walls in one of the dining rooms. He supplied me with a great deal of extremely valuable and interesting information.

The inn has been the host to much of Swedish royalty during the 700 years of its existence, and also to many Swedish writers, artists and musicians. There are several large dining rooms and the smorgasbord which is served daily is one of the most famous in all of southern Sweden.

As I left this lovely little inn later that morning a little drama unfolded in the fields immediately adjacent. A sturdy Swedish farmer was having trouble getting a young bull under control and he went into his farmhouse and returned with his equally sturdy wife and the two of them finally herded him into the next field.

MARGRETETORPS GASTGIFVAREGARD, 260 84 Hjarnarp, Skane. Telephone: 0431/540 08. 10 kilometers from Helsingborg. Rates: SKr 75 (without bath).

RAA WARDHAUS, Raa

This little inn, typical of others in Skane, has an interesting nautical theme explained by the fact, I am sure, that Raa is a seaside village. There are many ship models on display throughout the dining rooms as well as dozens of photographs and prints of old steam and sailing ships. Brass name plates, old bells, telescopes, pulleys, anchors and many other nautical items are tastefully placed throughout all of the public rooms.

There are just 12 lodging rooms in this rather modest hostelry, mostly furnished in modern Scandinavian style. Some look out over a park. Raa is a very picturesque little town and it is possible to rent sailboats and enjoy excursions from its waterfront. I had a definite feeling that both the town and the inn had not been discovered by tourists as yet.

RAA WARDHAUS, Raa, Helsingborg, Sweden. Telephone: 042-260000. Rates: SKr 70.

Sweden in Retrospect

I felt I was fortunate to have visited both Varmland and Dalarna, two sections of Sweden rich in historic and cultural backgrounds—Dalarna means "The Valley." In almost every little village, people still practice their traditional handicrafts like pottery, metal work, and woodcarving. Every parrish has its own folk costumes which also vary at specific times in the church year. The countryside ranges from gentle woods, fields, and lakes to the mountains in the north, where bears still roam.

Varmland is Europe's number one canoe center, and this area is the scene of the annual Vasa ski-race which has as many as 10,000 entrants. It takes place on the first Sunday of March, and is world's longest ski-race.

The coast of Sweden, itself, is longer than the coast of Africa, because of the innumerable islands and islets ... there are 100,000 lakes, and many opportunites for swimming, sailing, and camping. Some of these lakes are as large as inland seas. Sweden has more than 135 golf courses, and in the north country, there is skiing in midsummer by the light of the midnight sun. Other interesting Swedish sports are gliding, parachuting, riding, pony-trekking, water skiing, hunting, bird watching, tennis, bowling, and ice hockey. There are music festivals, folk-dancing, and open-air theatre, country fiddlers' teams, pop music—just about everything in the summertime.

The city of Stockholm is built on 13 of the 24,000 islands surrounding it, and there is a network of tunnels and bridges that connect the islands. Some of the cellars in the Old Town date back to the Middle Ages.

One word of caution: please don't, when in Stockholm or in any other town, cross the street when the little man in the traffic light is red—you may be fined.

DENMARK

INNS and LOCATION
Kongensbro Kro, Ans, 327
Plaza Hotel, Copenhagen, 312
Falsled Kro, Falsled, 318
Store Kro, Fredensborg, 311
Svostrup Kro, Grauballe, 326
Hovborg Kro, Hovborg, 325
Steensgaard Herregaardspension, Millinge, 319
Schackenborg Slotskro, Mogeltonder, 321
Weis Stue, Ribe, 323
Sortebro Kro, Sejrskovvjej, 315
Sollerod Kro, Sollerod, 213
Tranekjaer Guest House, Tranekaer, 317

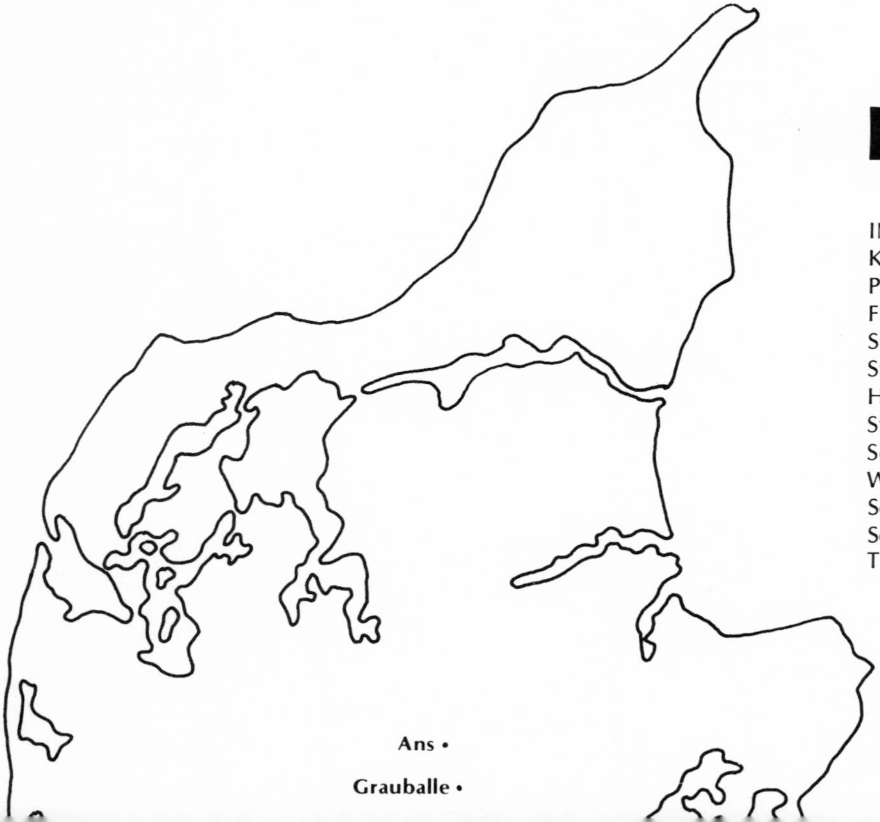

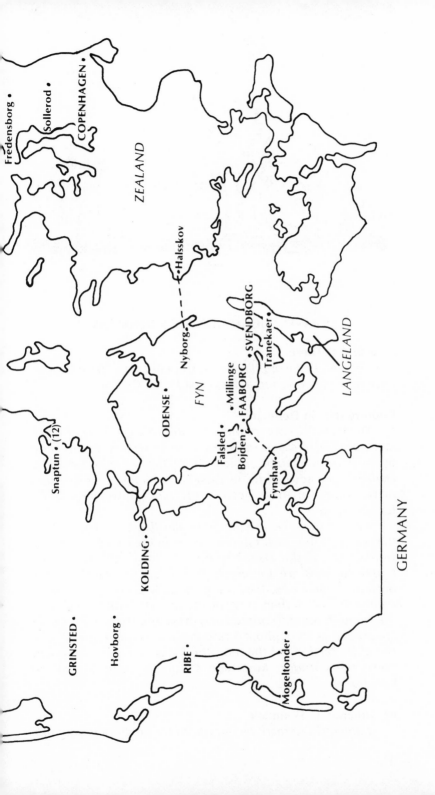

TRAVEL SUGGESTIONS FOR DENMARK

How to Get There

The SAS flights go directly to Copenhagen. There is a car-ferry from Norway, and a direct road from Germany.

Country Inns in Denmark

Denmark is a country with a tradition of inns, some of which date back 300 to 400 years. A few were designated as royal inns by reigning monarchs, which meant that a bedroom and a change of horses had to be available at all times for the royal party. Some inns have been in the same innkeeping family for generations.

I found these Danish inns in small villages and towns, with the name of the town often included in their own name. The word "Kro" is the Danish word for "inn." Although these traditional inns are frequently sought out by travelers from outside of Denmark, they are principally used by the Danes themselves. All of them serve hearty and wholesome food, with the menus frequently printed only in Danish. The lodging rooms are always, as throughout Scandinavia, clean and practical. In the older sections of the inns, the baths and wc's are usually down the corridor. Reservations can be made by mail or telephone.

My Itinerary in Denmark

I entered Denmark by ferry from Helsingborg in southern

Sweden. From north of Copenhagen I continued through Zealand, proceeding by ferry to Fyn Island and then south to Denmark's summer resort area called Langeland. Again a ferry took me to Jutland, that portion of Denmark which is located on the European mainland adjacent to Germany. From here the road leads north and I could have continued on to Norway by ferry from northern Jutland. To obtain Denmark road maps, see the section in the back of the book.

STORE KRO, Fredensborg

"Oh yes, the King and Queen are dining here tonight." I stopped short and turned to learn whether I had heard correctly. Ronald Larsen, the innkeeper at Store Kro went on: "Well, the castle is nearby," he said, "and there are strong links between the castle and the inn.

"In 1723, King Frederik IV constructed Fredensborg Castle and at the same time he had an inn built nearby which was named Store Kro and consisted of two separate buildings. For a number of years the King, himself, was the keeper of this inn. One of the original buildings is still in use and its exterior has not changed during the many years. It serves as an annex and the interior is equipped with beautiful, modern guest rooms."

The proximity to Fredensborg Castle accounts for the fact that the inn has been the scene of royal receptions and royal weddings. There is one dining room which is known as the King's Room with either photographs or paintings of every Danish king.

Catering to these unusual functions has carried the inn's reputation for good food to places considerably far from Denmark. Mr. Larsen explained that the chef has traveled widely, preparing meals in other countries and bringing some Danish specialties with him such as bread, butter, salmon and fresh herring.

As we moved into another room with many photographs and paintings of what appeared to be the same man on the wall, he explained the decor to me.

"We Danes are very fond of the theatre," he said, "and Olaf Poulsen was probably the most outstanding actor of the Danish stage. He played every major role up to the time of his death in 1923. Some years ago I began to collect photographs, prints and paintings of him playing various theatrical characters. Now we have put them in this room where they are well-preserved and displayed for everyone to enjoy. I think it's better than a museum because they are in an atmosphere that he, himself, would appreciate."

Store Kro is located on one of the quiet streets in Fredensborg. There are spacious grounds and a garden in the rear of the inn.

Although this inn is larger than many of the inns I visited in Denmark and a bit more formal because of the many functions which take place here, it is nonetheless most hospitable. Each of the rooms has highly individual decorations.

Just imagine the King and Queen would be dining here tonight!

ROMANTIK HOTEL, STORE KRO, 3480 Fredensborg. Telephone: (03) 280047. A royal inn immediately adjacent to a royal palace still in use. All of the North Zealand recreational facilities and historic castles are nearby. Rates: DKr 175-260.

PLAZA HOTEL, Copenhagen

I believe that anyone visiting Denmark would want to spend some time in the beautiful city of Copenhagen. My time in Copenhagen on my first visit was somewhat limited.

However, I did look at a small hotel in the central part of town not too far from Town Hall Square—the Plaza Hotel. I found it to be an elegant, conservative hotel in a town that specializes in big hostelries. My first impression of the lobby was one of restraint and calm. For the most part the luncheon guests seemed to be Copenhagen businessmen rather than tourists.

My lunch was excellent and I was very much impressed with the comfort of the dining room as well as the relaxed service.

After lunch I was invited to have my coffee in the Library Room which is an impressive two-and-a-half-story room with a glass dome. It is lined with books from floor to ceiling. There are several arrangements of luxurious leather chairs placed around handsome round tables. It reminds me of the lobby of the Hotel Algonquin in New York.

While I was there I saw several lodging rooms and suites which were all tastefully designed. This hotel has an old section and a new section and appears to be very well run.

PLAZA HOTEL, 6 Bernstorffsgade, 1577 Copenhagen V. Telephone: (01) 149262. A luxurious hotel in central Copenhagen. Double rooms in old part of building start at DKr 220-395.

SOLLEROD KRO, Sollerod

Annette Heuser and I were wandering about the church-yard immediately adjacent to Sollerod Kro. The rain which had been spouting all afternoon had stopped and scudding clouds frequently opened long enough to light the scene with tints of silver.

All of this was a most appropriate postlude to a delightful evening at the inn just across the village road. Actually, it had begun for me just before lunch when I left Store Kro in Fredensborg to drive to Copenhagen. I located the village of Sollerod with just one inquiry and after driving through a Danish Forest of Arden, suddenly came upon a serene and peaceful crossroads with a triangular-shaped flowerbed literally overwhelmed with blossoms. The words "Sollerod Kro" were in large letters stretched across the front of the inn.

The principal entrance was through a cobblestone court-yard which was in the shape of a hollow square formed by the buildings of this ancient inn. In the center there was a tinkling

fountain and around the edges and in sheltered nooks and crannies were tubs of daisies, pansies and cornflowers. Much to my surprise there was a large birdcage with colorful exotic birds.

It was too early for lunch but the innkeeper was happy to explain the history of the inn and invited me to walk through the spacious dining rooms.

It was during this tour that I learned that the church where Annette and I were strolling once owned the inn which dates back to 1677. It has remained unchanged ever since except for certain strengthening of walls and re-thatching of roofs. The building is exquisite, one of the best examples of traditional romantic Danish architecture that I encountered during my trip.

All the rooms are decorated with Danish antiques, and the reception rooms are hung with Professor Aksel Jorgensen's historical paintings and a selection of original manuscripts of the best-known works of Danish workers.

From May to September meals are served in the courtyard, and include dishes from the open grill.

I felt that I would like to see more of this inn so I suggested that afternoon that we might go there for dinner. Incidentally, Annette lived for sometime in Stockbridge, so this was a reunion of old friends.

That brings us to where I started with Annette and I strolling in the churchyard and listening to the organ. To my knowledge, the church does not own the inn any longer. But the tradition remains and many of the inn guests attend the church and enjoy the church gardens. There are no rooms at this inn but luncheon and dinner are served continuously from 11:30 a.m. to 10 p.m.

RELAIS CHATEAU 254, SOLLEROD KRO, Sollerod Vej 35, 2840. Telephone: (01) 802505. A country restaurant just a few kilometers north of Copenhagen. Open from May 1 to September 15. No lodgings.

SORTEBRO KRO, Sejrskovvej

"Welcome to Sortebro Kro." That was Herr Nielsen, the innkeeper and owner of this unique museum-inn. My visit with Innkeeper Nielsen was memorable for several reasons. First, there were prodigious amounts of lunch, which I kept insisting that I didn't want as I kept eating. Then there was the fact that the inn is a museum-inn, adjacent to a very extensive restored farm village which is preserving some of the old ways of Fyn Island. Finally, there was Mr. Nielsen, himself, with his bright red suspenders and leather apron.

Mr. Nielsen is very proud of his inn and of the model farm village and promised me that we would have a short tour as soon as we had completed lunch. When I asked him about the specialty of the house he had a surprising reply. "We take pride in the fact that we can prepare almost any dish for which a guest may ask. We do have specialties but we are always pleased when one of our guests asks for a Danish dish that is not on the menu so that we can cook to order.

My luncheon began with a large portion of delicious pickled Danish herring and four small white potatoes. I insisted that that would be enough.

Meanwhile, the waiter brought some sausage and red cabbage with bread and butter. I watched Mr. Nielsen as he cut a piece of sausage and combined it with a sliver of bread on his

315

fork and ate with his left hand in the continental style, something that I simply haven't mastered as yet.

"There are hundreds of thousands of people passing through the Funen model village every year," he said, "and of course this means that the inn is very popular. We open at 10 o'clock in the morning to serve a light breakfast, and then continue to serve our regular menu from about 11 a.m. to 9 p.m. We do not have any rooms."

The main dining room at the Sortebro Kro, which has been constructed in the same architectural style as the farm village, has low ceilings with varnished beams and a large collection of antique Danish tools and memorabilia. The floors are rough scrubbed boards and the dining room furniture is heavy and sturdy in the Danish country style. There were fresh flowers on every table and many old wooden trays on which cold Danish plates are carried. These, as Mr. Nielsen explained, are known as "trougs," a wooden platter which is only used for cold dishes.

True to his word, after lunch we toured the Funen Village, starting in the gift shop where there were all kinds of Danish ceramics and wooden crafts including spoons, forks, and miniature trougs all hand carved. We ventured out into the village and the first thing I saw was a pond with baby ducks just

across a country road from a beautiful meadow where some baby chicks were being herded by their mother.

This restored village is an important link with the agricultural past of Denmark and old farm implements, tools, and carts have been collected from every point in Fyn to form what is still today a working farm.

One interesting feature was a natural arena where dramatizations of Hans Christian Andersen's stories are given during the summer months. I was particularly intrigued with the large collection of old Danish sleighs. I found the kitchen with its great big iron stove where stones were heated to put into the beds quite fascinating. Incidentally the inn also has two or three rooms that are set aside with small artifacts and old utensils.

SORTEBRO KRO, 5260 Hjallese, Sejrskovvej, Denmark. Telephone: (09) 132826. 4 Km. from Odense. Open from 10 a.m. to 9 p.m. No lodgings available. This inn is a part of the well-known "Funen Village," a restored agricultural environment.

TRANEKJAER GJAESTGIVERGAARD, Tranekaer

Herr Carl Gammelholm, the innkeeper at the Tranekjaer Gjaestgivergaard supplied me with some excellent information about Langeland Island, which is located just off the southern tip of Fyn Island.

"We are one of the great vacation places in Denmark," he said. "We have a delightful holiday atmosphere along with good beaches, swimming, sailing and fishing, hunting, tennis, horseback riding and many other sports. I mention hunting, because there are many people who come to the inn to enjoy the game and deer that we have on the menu. They are in abundance in the forests nearby."

A great deal of our conversation took place in the dining room of the inn which had a red brick fireplace at one end. There were beamed ceilings, flowered wallpaper, leather chairs and a plate rack with dishes of old Danish design. The atmosphere was old-fashioned and quite comfortable.

There were two styles of bedrooms. Some were rooms that had been here for a great many years and had beds with wicker headboards and old paintings on the walls. There were also motel-type rooms, each with its own terrace and flower boxes. To the rear and on the sides there was quite a bit of land around the inn and many, many flowering bushes.

Herr Gammelholm explained that in addition to the deer and game, other menu specialties were fish and eel. "You're seldom far from water here in Denmark," he said. "We Danes love the products of our seas."

Before I left the Tranekjaer Gjaestgivergaard I took advantage of the opportunity to ask the innkeeper about the sign I had seen on my journey from Odense to Langeland. One of the roads was called "Elvira Madigan's Way." "Oh, many people ask us about that. The locale was the southern part of Fyn and some of the film was shot in this region," he said.

"By the way, it is possible to come directly to Langeland Island from North Zealand Island by taking the ferry to Lohals and bypassing Fyn Island entirely."

TRANEKJAER GJAESTGIVERGAARD, DK 5953 Tranekaer, Langeland, Denmark. Telephone: (09) 59 12 04. Rates: DKr 115-196 (includes breakfast).

FALSLED KRO, Falsled

The Falsled Kro is not a conventional Danish country inn. I think it would be outstanding in any country. Like the Solerod Kro, just north of Copenhagen, it is included in "Les Relais de Campagne," a directory of rather elegant and exclusive European restaurants.

The owners of this inn are Sven and Lene Gronlykke. Unfortunately Sven was not at the inn during my visit, but Lene and I had an opportunity to get acquainted. It was from her that I learned that although the inn was a farm during the 16th century it became a "privileged inn" which means there would always be room for the King and his horses.

I am certain that it is Lene's experiences in the fields of film and fashion which account for the fact that this inn is so exquisitely furnished. For example, my lodging room had Danish tables and leather-covered stools which were complemented by the white-washed walls. There were several original paintings as well. I had the opportunity to look at several other rooms during my stay and one of them in particular was most attractive, with the bedroom on the second floor reached by old stone stairs.

318

Outside my door was a broad lawn, and it was just a few steps to a very pleasant harbor. There were birds, flowers, flowering bushes and beautiful trees everywhere.

The main sitting room had a beautiful center fireplace with comfortable low leather seats which invite everyone to stretch out and enjoy coffee after dinner. There are groupings of wicker furniture in various corners and many arrangements of freshly-cut flowers. It is the kind of atmosphere that draws people together in conversation.

The cuisine at Falsled Kro is basically French, prepared by a team of chefs. My mixed salad followed by salmon souffle would have been equally at home in Paris. The dessert table had at least eight different types of pastries including a delicious chocolate mousse.

I had been hearing about Falsled Kro since my arrival in Scandinavia and I was told that it would be a beautiful and idyllic place and, indeed, it was. I could only add one further word—sophisticated.

RELAIS CHATEAU 252, FALSLED KRO, 5642 Millinge, Falsled. Telephone: 0968 1111. Rates: DKr 175-275.

STEENSGAARD HERREGARDSPENSION, Millinge

The clock over the stable sounded twelve times, just as it has been doing for hundreds of years. I paused in my walking tour of this elegant manor house located just a few minutes from the sunny beaches of South Fyn Island, to watch two colts hardly more than two months old chase each other across the meadow.

The hostess at Steensgaard, Inge Seidel enthusiastically explained that the manor probably belonged to Hartvig Steen, a man most likely of noble means, and that it was apparently mortgaged by him to another family in 1310. This makes it date back considerably before Columbus discovered America.

After a brief account of owners and mortgagees, I was amazed at how well the manor house-cum-castle appeared today.

"Oh yes," she agreed. "The original sections were built to last and the other buildings, which were added to form three sides of the square, are quite in harmony. Don't you agree?"

Indeed I did. All of the buildings are made of rough stone and half timbers.

Steensgaard is in one of Denmark's most beautiful sections. It offers a magnificent view of fields and forests which extends onward to high hills.

"We call it 'smiling countryside,'" said Mrs. Seidel. "Our guests love to walk in the manor park which extends through the woods down to the beach. There are fourteen other forests nearby if they really like longer excursions.

"There are also tennis and croquet. By the way, you have never played croquet until you have played with enthusiastic Danes."

The interior of this manor house is quite exciting. I passed from one room to another with original oil paintings, beautiful furniture, and rich rugs. The library has a chess board in one

corner and comfortable chairs drawn close together to invite conversation.

Lodging rooms are unusually large, since they were built for private occupancy hundreds of years ago. Many of them have canopy beds.

In a country where there are dozens and dozens of beautiful old country inns, I found Steensgaard Herregards-pension a most interesting contrast. It offers the opportunity to spend a few days in a luxurious manor house.

STEENSGAARD HERREGARDSPENSION, 5642 Millinge, Fyn, Denmark. Telephone: (09) 61 12 90. An elegant 15-room manor house serving three meals a day. Five rooms have private baths. All types of outdoor recreation available. Rates: DKr 125-195.

SCHACKENBORG SLOTSKRO, Mogeltønder

So far I had visited inns on two principal Danish islands: North Zealand which is close to Sweden, and Fyn which comprises Denmark's geographical center.

Now I was in Jutland which is that part of Denmark connected directly to the European continent. It is also closest geographically to North America.

I had crossed by ferry from Bojden to Fynshav on a brilliant sunny day and, after taking back roads to avoid some industrial districts in southern Jutland, arrived in Mogeltonder just south of Tonder to visit Schackenborg Slotskro.

At the outset let me say that it takes more than a few hours of casual visiting to appreciate and participate in all of the natural beauty and cultural influences in this part of Jutland. That's why Schackenborg Slotskro, a modest country inn on a most fascinating village street, is a good place to stay.

"Slot" is the Danish word for castle, and Jutland has quite a few. Schackenborg castle is just a few paces from the kro or inn, hence the natural use of the term "Slotskro" or castle inn.

When I arrived in the village after driving from the larger community of Tonder I drove on a bone-cracking cobble street lined on each side with lime trees—a real surprise.

Schackenborg Slotskro proved to be a pleasant two-and-a-half-story red-roofed inn with bright white walls. The first thing I noticed was a delightful arrangement of rough benches and

tables in front of this inn where guests could enjoy refreshments while sitting in the sun.

While this inn is typical in many respects of old Danish inns it has quite a few extra touches. Most of the available lodging rooms are located across the street in one of the Friesland houses. The rooms are quite modern with telephones and radios as well as a small refrigerator. There is a beautiful view of the garden.

I spent some time in the kitchen while a young chef explained that everything is homemade. The freshly baked Danish coffee cake looked delicious. "We have what I believe is a very complete French menu," he explained, "but there are also some Danish country specialties such as pickled herring and country ham, both of which are quite famous in this region. We also have trout, eel and pike."

It was from the chef that I learned that the inn which is over 300 years old is owned by the proprietor of the nearby castle, Count Hans Schack.

As I was leaving, a young bridal couple came across the threshold of the front door. The innkeeper explained that this was a region for marriages. "People come from all over the world to Tonder to be married," he said. "It is mostly a civil ceremony, and the formalities can be completed in a couple of days. However, I think that the romantic atmosphere has a great deal to do with their choice."

So do I.

SCHACKENBORG SLOTSKRO, Møgeltønder, 6270 Tønder. Telephone: (047) 4 83 84. Rates: DKr 120-210.

Ribe

I could have spent a month in Ribe (Ree-ba). To me it is the penultimate medieval town. It has fascinating 16th century houses which are actually lived in today, intriguing alleyways, unexpected courtyards and cobbled streets everywhere.

Dominating the center of town, just across a small square from Weis' Stue, an ancient village inn, is the Cathedral. It is partly constructed of stone carried to Ribe from the Rhineland in Germany. One tower has loop holes, evidence of the war with Sweden. The bells of the Cathedral play two songs, each twice a day—a hymn at 8 a.m. and 6 p.m., and folk song at noon and 3 p.m.

Ribe's port area, the Skibbroen, is the oldest harbor in Denmark. The storm flood column marks the height the waters have reached during some of the worst floods down through the ages. Here is a lovely town richly endowed with areas of outstanding beauty and many charming bridges across, and paths along, the river. There are gardens, museums, castles, fenlands, churches, and a fascinating little island off the coast called Mando which is reachable by the "postal nan."

WEIS' STUE, Ribe

"Yes, the village watchman starts out from here every night during the summer. He drops in around 9 p.m. and sits here in this room, in fact, in your chair, and enjoys conversing with his friends. At 10 p.m. he picks up that long pole there in the corner and walks out to the street singing."

I, too, was enjoying myself immensely at Weis' Stue. The building and the atmosphere picked me up almost bodily and carried me back to medieval times. The very personable young innkeeper, Knud Nielsen, was telling me what great fun it is to be the keeper of an ancient inn.

"The watchman is an example of the good times we have here," he said. "He is a great storyteller and also has an extensive knowledge of the town. People follow him all around the town just like he was the Pied Piper of Hamlin. He tells them about the old buildings and stories about the town. Everyone eventually ends up here again. The night watchman is a well-

323

established Ribe tradition."

Knud invited me to join him on a tour of this modest inn. To go up to the second floor I had to duck under a very low doorway and climb steep stairs with the aid of a rope bannister. At the top of the stairs were just four double rooms and one single. The running water for all rooms was available in a wash bowl in the hallway. That's where guests would brush their teeth and do their shaving. There were no private bathrooms and all shared a w.c. "in the corridor."

When I asked him about his guests' reaction to this old-fashioned mode of innkeeping, he replied, "They love it. Many come back quite often. Actually we're quite luxurious compared to two or three hundred years ago."

As we returned to the first floor I became aware of a great number of students who were lounging in one small dining room, playing chess, arguing and even studying. "This has always been a students' favorite," he said. "For centuries they have been meeting here just as you see them today."

The food being prepared for the evening meal looked sumptuous. There were many Danish dishes as well as a few German and French. We passed through an open courtyard and into the Danish Marine Room which was very imaginatively decorated with old ship's models, marine sabres, guns, pictures of ships, ships' wheels, old brass, maps. He explained that it is given over the Marine Club about six times a year to members who wish to come and have dinner.

The town of Ribe and the Weis' Stue proved to be a most pleasant Jutland experience. It is hard to imagine one without the other.

WEIS' STUE, Torvet 2, 6760 Ribe, Denmark. Telephone: (05) 42 07 00. DKr 65-90.

HOVBORG KRO, Hovborg

The thing I remember about this inn is that the innkeeper and staff were hosting dinner for a number of people in wheelchairs. One entire dining room had been set aside that evening, and vans and small buses carrying guests were arriving every few minutes. They were all having a marvelous time and I understand that the inn provides this entertainment for this group at least once a year.

I mention this because Hovborg Kro is typical of the spirit of Danish innkeeping. For example, this inn has been in the same innkeeping family since 1836 and the members have played an important role in community affairs throughout these years.

I found it very easy to identify with many of these traditional country inns in Denmark because they are quite similar to many American inns that I have visited. This inn was built in 1790 and for centuries was used by drovers on their way to and from the market.

I made the acquaintance of some Danish guests at dinner and amidst some really great laughs at my attempts to understand them, they explained that they had stayed for four days of fishing and boating on the river and horseback riding in the woods. English is spoken by the key staff people of this inn and occasionally the head waiter gave me a hand in understanding my dinner companions.

The oldest part of the inn has lodgings of the more traditional nature and a recent addition has rooms that are furnished in modern Danish fabrics and furniture. All of these have their own baths.

I felt very much at home at the Hovborg Kro.

Incidentally, there are ferries to Norway in the northern part of Jutland and this and other inns in central and northern Jutland could be a place for a convenient overnight stay for anyone en route.

HOVBORG KRO, Hovborg, Jutland, Denmark, P.O. 6682 Hovborg. Telephone: (05) 39 60 33. A 29-room inn in central Jutland. Lunch and dinner served daily. Angling, riding, backroading, walking and boating. Rates: DKr 77-125.

SVOSTRUP KRO, Grauballe

By now I had traveled some distance into Jutland, and I found that the farther I went from Copenhagen, the towns where English was spoken became fewer and fewer. Such was the case at the Svostrup Kro. This was more of a fun challenge than a problem. I always find it a thrill to be some place where English is a rarity rather than commonplace.

Finding this inn took some persistence, and I am sorry that I cannot be more detailed. I advise the traveler to ask the Tourist Office in Silkeborg for exact directions.

At first I felt that it was hopeless. After 30 minutes of circling, I stopped the car at a stone bridge to look at the water and realized that I was looking squarely at the inn!

The entrance was through a low arch formed by some old stone barns. I was in a lovely country courtyard with four or five large trees at one end in front of the inn. There were many flowers everywhere.

The lady at the reception desk and I tried to communicate, but she gave up and brought in the owner. He and I did somewhat better. He showed me all around the inn and answered my many questions as well as he was able. He even arranged for me to make a long distance telephone call!

This inn, so close to the river, was once used by bargees, the men who use the river as a highway for transporting goods by barges. One of the dates on the buildings was 1286. Herr Lauesen, the innkeeper showed me a collection of Stone Age artifacts found in the vicinity. There were many arrowheads and primitive spearheads as well as knives.

All of the rooms overlook the orchard and the river. As in many cases, there were a few rooms furnished in older, more traditional furniture, and some in a more modern style. Only a few had private baths.

I was not able to be at Svostrup Kro for any meals, but from the look of the kitchen where eels fresh from the river were being prepared for the evening meal, I was certain that it would be wholesome and hearty!

SVOSTRUP KRO, P.O. 8642 Grauballe, Jutland, Denmark. Telephone: (06) 87 70 04. A 10-room inn, 10 kilometers from Silkeborg. Rates: DKr 125.

KONGENSBRO KRO, Ans

Mr. Hans Andersen, innkeeper at Kongensbro Kro, made it quite clear during the first few minutes of our meeting that his middle name was not "Christian." He was one of the more sophisticated innkeepers that I met in Jutland and the inn reflected the fact that he and his wife had tastes and preferences that would be appropriate in many other settings as well.

We got acquainted in the Residents' Lounge of the inn,

which had a small fire going at one end and overlooked the river. We soon found that innkeeping joys and tribulations are much the same in Denmark as they are in the U.S.

"It is a 24-hour-a-day job, he said, "especially when one wishes to hold a good reputation."

A good reputation is something that Herr Andersen possesses in abundance. I had tried to reserve a room for just one night, six weeks in advance but it was impossible. "We take bookings this year for next year," he said. I asked him if there was an explanation for this popularity.

"This is a good place to stay for anyone who wants to take his ease in a time of hurry, and feel in close contact with the peaceful rhythm of nature.

"It is a good place for nature lovers and bird enthusiasts and it is a paradise for anglers." He confirmed: "Many a lovely hour can be spent fishing and watching the animal life and nature at large.

"The staff at the inn can supply good tips about short or long trips and several of these trips will bring to mind days gone by. One of them is on the old tow path at the bank of the river which is now able to be used for a distance of 25 miles. Incidentally we also rent canoes for use in the river."

Later on I had a chance to talk to Mrs. Andersen whom I met in the garden. She invited me to walk over to a little building next door on the banks of the river where a special party was being held and a man who lived in Argentina was cooking barbecued spare ribs.

All across Denmark, I kept hearing from other travelers about how much I would enjoy Kongensbro Kro. "You'll especially enjoy Mrs. Andersen," I was told. "Besides, she has written a cookbook."

During my stay I had a long talk with Mrs. Andersen, and she presented me with a copy of her book entitled *Inn Food*.

Mr. Andersen's middle name may not be Christian but the Kongensbro is a real Danish fairy tale come true.

KONGENSBRO KRO, P.O. 8643 Ans By, Jutland, Denmark. Telephone: (06) 87 01 77. A 27-room inn in Danish farm country, 25 kilometers from Viborg, 18 kilometers from Silkeborg. Golf, fishing, walking nearby. Rates: DKr 65-180.

Random Reflections on Scandinavia

Although there are many language similarities, the three countries, Norway, Sweden, and Denmark, are highly individualistic. Each year they are becoming increasingly popular with visitors from North America.

Scandinavia is the home of some of the world's famous artisans and craftsmen. Glassware, ceramics, rugs, tableware, handicrafts, and jewelry are to be found everywhere. The performing arts are a great tradition in all three countries, and there is a wide choice among lawn concerts, dramatic presentations, opera, symphony, and folk dancing.

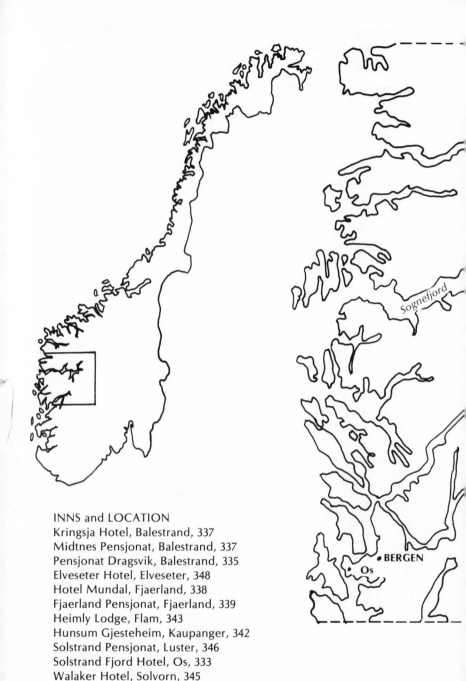

Sognefjord

• BERGEN

Os

INNS and LOCATION

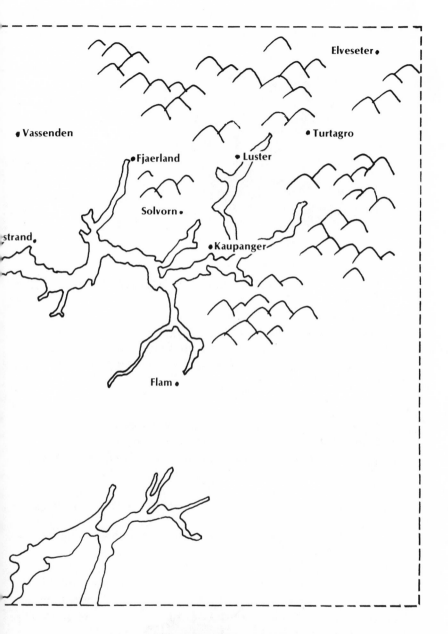

Elveseter•

•Vassenden

•Turtagro

•Fjaerland   •Luster

Solvorn•

strand•

•Kaupanger

Flam•

NORWAY

TRAVEL SUGGESTIONS FOR NORWAY

How to Get There

SAS has direct flights to Oslo, as well as Bergen and Stavanger, both of which are in the fjord country. Norway can also be reached directly by car from Sweden and by car-ferry from Denmark.

Country Inns in Norway

My visit to Norway was confined for the most part to the Sognefjord district where I found hotels and pensions. In Norway, a hotel is legally classified as having enough bedrooms and reception rooms to adequately house at least 20 guests, and is required also to have a certain number of available wc's. Some Norwegian hotels have many resort facilities on the grounds or nearby.

The pensions share a number of common virtues: most of their rooms have twin beds with down comforters covered by a washable sheeting. Almost all have running water in each room, and sometimes there is only one wc and one bathroom for seven or eight rooms. All serve three meals a day, and often offer between-meal snacks of delicious homemade cakes with coffee or tea.

All have living rooms where guests can relax before and after meals. Both pensions and hotels have plans that include three meals a day and special rates for three days or more.

Reservations can be made by mail or telephone.

Dining in Norway

Every hotel and pension has a single-price meal, as well as an a la carte menu. The evening meal consists of three courses: soup, usually homemade, a main dish — a large platter with meat or fish and a vegetable, as well as lettuce and tomato or other salad vegetables — and dessert, which is usually fresh or frozen fruit served with whipped cream.

Breakfast, Norwegian-style, is a real eating adventure. This is where I found the many varieties of cold fish, cheese (including delicious goat cheese), breads, crackers, and jams.

Driving Tips

Public transportation in Norway is excellent, and in a great many cases it would be advisable to leave the car in Oslo or Bergen and travel by train, bus, or ferry to a central point such as Balestrand, and then make a series of daily or overnight excursions into the fjord country using the carefully coordinated schedules of both ferries and buses. That's what I did. I had to grow accustomed to the long daylight hours and the occasional rain and mist which are part of the fjord country ambience. I was glad that I brought a raincoat. There was, however, plenty of sunshine. Incidentally, gasoline stations and supermarkets close early, usually at five o'clock.

My Itinerary in Norway

I flew to Bergen and, before proceeding into the Sogne-fjord country, I spent one night south of Bergen in Os. Then I took the car-ferry to Balestrand and used this as a base of operations for several days, after which I proceeded to the end of the Sognefjord, up and over the mountains, and down the other side into Sweden.

To obtain Norway road maps, see the section in the back of the book.

THE SOLSTRAND FJORD HOTEL, Os, Bergen

My table in the dining room had a perfect view of the Bjornaford. I could look across the green lawn, past the tennis courts and out into this water wonderland. The Norwegian flag stirred lightly as breezes from across the water picked up its elegant long tail and made it look like a kite in the sky. The Hardanger mountains across the fjord had patches of snow, and, in the distance, the peaks of higher mountains were almost

333

completely covered with snow.

After an afternoon of learning more about the fascinating city of Bergen, I set out on the road to Os, Route 14, and now was enjoying my first evening meal in Norway.

It began with a delicious vegetable soup served in a big bowl. The table was laid with old-fashioned silverware. The main course was fresh trout served with a tartar sauce and white potatoes. The dessert was tasty fresh fruit including oranges,

grapes, and peaches, topped with freshly-whipped cream. A young man played the piano throughout the entire meal, alternating his selections between such old favorites as Errol Garner's "Misty" and Chopin's "Minute Waltz."

All of the guests in the dining room seemed to be Norwegian. As far as I could tell I was the only non-Scandinavian present. However, the entire staff of this resort-inn spoke English and I was made to feel at home at once.

One of the outstanding features of this waterside hotel is a large heated indoor swimming pool, a sauna, and some extensive exercise equipment.

Lodging rooms at this hotel are typical of what I found everywhere in Scandinavia. There are older rooms with traditional furniture and decor, typical of many American and British country inns. Then there is a newer wing of modernized rooms with furniture reflecting modern Scandinavian design with greater simplicity and austerity of line. The tables, chairs, lamps, and beds are not as decorative as they are functional. I found this functional style most everywhere that I went, for more and more pensions and small hotels have been redecorated and refurnished.

THE SOLSTRAND FJORD HOTEL, N-5200 Os, Norway. Telephone: Bergen 27-70-55. 17 mi. from Bergen Airport, 18 mi. from Bergen. Accessible by bus from Bergen. Located in scenic fjord area. Indoor heated swimming pool, sauna, private beach, rowboats, speedboats, waterskiing, fishing, horseback riding, walking, tennis, mini-golf. Rates: NKr 135-180.

Balestrand

On the map showing the Sognefjord area I have indicated the location of the town of Balestrand. Balestrand is the principal stop on the ferries which leave from Bergen each day. There is a car ferry that leaves at 9:30 in the morning and arrives at 6:30 at night, and another ferry leaves at 8:30 a.m., arriving at noon, but does not permit automobiles. Balestrand is approximately a 5-hour drive from Bergen and can also be reached conveniently by bus.

I found that I could use Balestrand as a base for traveling anywhere in this particular fjord system and the nearby mountains. There are ferry, bus, and automobile connections in all directions. The local tourist office which, by the way, is typical of similar offices everywhere in Norway, is most accommodating. It is open from 9:30 until 6:30 every day with two hours off for lunch. It is possible to arrive in Balestrand and get assistance at the tourist office in planning either a one-day or a two-week stay in the area. This includes making reservations at various hotels and pensions. Travelers are also invited to contact the Balestrand tourist office in the off-season for information about the area which can be studied in advance of arrival. The mailing address is: Balestrand Tourist Office, N-5850, Balestrand, Norway. It can also be reached by telephone: Balestrand 80.

PENSJONAT DRAGSVIK, Balestrand, Sognefjord

This was my first stay in a Norwegian pension. It is located in a very pretty village just across the Esefjord from the village of Balestrand. It is within walking distance of the Dragsvik ferry stop which means that guests here have the entire Sognefjord area

335

accessible by water. My room which was furnished in a modern Scandinavian fashion overlooked Balestrand and the main fjord.

I'll take a few moments to describe the dinner served here because it was typical of pension fare that I enjoyed during my trip. The first course was a piquant homemade asparagus soup. The main course for two was served on a large platter. This consisted of sliced roast beef, cauliflower, pickles and prunes, and generous amounts of lettuce, arranged most artistically. There was a separate dish of boiled white potatoes which I found was a staple in the Norwegian diet and a bowl of tasty gravy prepared from the juices of the meat. Dessert was freshly-whipped cream and peaches.

The view from the dining room was lovely, overlooking the fjord and the mountains. In the foreground there were fruit trees in blossom. Overhead the sky cleared for a short time and a bar or two of sunshine dramatically lighted the fjord.

PENSJONAT DRAGSVIK, N-5850 Balestrand, Norway. Telephone: Balestrand 100 A. Dragsvik is a hamlet across the Esefjord from Balestrand. All of the fjord outdoor recreation and excursion advantages are available. Rates: NKr 60-80. Rates with meals available.

MIDTNES PENSJONAT, Balestrand, Sognefjord

I stayed one night in this pension in a modest single room that overlooked the flowering hillside. There was running water in the room as usual but both the w.c. and bath were "in the corridor" as they say in Scandinavia.

This family-owned pension has a beautiful dining room overlooking the fjord and an outdoor terrace which is very popular on clement evenings. A few steps away it has its own dock and facilities for hiring sailboats, rowboats and water skis. The owners were most accommodating and I noticed that they spent a great deal of time sitting in the salons talking with their guests.

I particularly remember the dozens of yellow tulips that were in bloom on the terrace and in the yard of the inn during my stay. It is immediately adjacent to St. Olav's English church.

MIDTNES PENSJONAT, N-5850 Balestrand, Norway. Telephone: Balestrand 17. Rates: NKr 60-113.

KRINGSJA HOTEL, Balestrand

This is a good example of the difference between a pension and a small hotel in Norway. In this case there were much larger living rooms and salons. The furnishings were more modern and the decor was tastefully harmonized. The bedrooms were a bit larger and more imaginatively furnished.

In one of the lounges there were modern reproductions of Norwegian runic writings on the walls. There is usually entertainment during the weekend—dancing or perhaps folk singing. Although this is a bit more formal than a pension it still has a very homey feeling. It has a view of the fjord and sits in a small orchard of fruit trees and lilac bushes which were in bloom during my visit.

KRINGSJA HOTEL, N5850 Balestrand 8, Norway. Telephone: Balestrand 8. Rates: NKr 70-75.

The Fjaerland Fjord

A trip by ferry on the Fjaerland Fjord is an exciting way to spend a day, or even a longer visit with an overnight stay at the Hotel Mundal or the Fjaerland Pensjonat. I made the trip for the day and was entranced with this strange and marvellous corner of Norway. The Fjaerland Fjord is one of the most famous and unusual in Norway with its everchanging shoreline, from serene pastoral meadows to steep cliffs and snow-topped mountains on both sides rising to 3,000 feet. And at the end of the line, there is a bus trip up to the Jostedal glacier and its spectacular waterfalls.

HOTEL MUNDAL, Fjaerland

I had a feeling that I had been at this beautiful inn before. Perhaps it was because it was like so many country inns that I had visited in both Britain and North America. As a matter of fact it had a distinctly British atmosphere. When I mentioned this to Marit Mauritzen, who is the daughter of the owner, she said that it was quite possible because they have had so many guests from the British Isles even as far back as the late 19th century.

"The British are great walkers," she said. "And I think that our proximity to the Jostedal Glacier which is the largest ice field on the European continent, makes the prospect of mountain walks and climbing even more attractive. With this in mind, we have always offered courses in glaciology and geology. We're very popular here with botanists and ornithologists as well.

I could feel the innkeeping tradition radiating from this old building and its owners. It was obvious that this hotel had been well cared for by its owners, and loved by guests for many years. In the main living room, a fireplace with intricate hand-painted designs of Norwegian flowers was surrounded by deep leather chairs which invited both reverie and conversation. While I was walking through the hotel I could hear someone playing the piano in the background and there was one particularly interesting room with a circular seat in a beautiful bay window. I also found a billiard room with a wood-paneled ceiling.

In the dining room there were some large painted panels depicting the fairy tale of the three princes who were turned into bears and could only be turned back into princes if they could find princesses who would be willing to take them into their bedchamber. There is one panel showing the three princesses with their hair literally standing on end upon being confronted by the bears. The happy ending is that somehow or other the bears did turn into princes the next morning.

The lodging rooms on the two upper floors were most comfortable with some rooms overlooking the fjord and the garden below. Perhaps most interesting of all is the fact that the Hotel Mundal and the Fjaerland Pensjonat are reached only by ferry from both Hela or Balestrand. However I understand that a road has been approved and will be under construction shortly.

HOTEL MUNDAL, N-5855 Fjaerland, Norway. Telephone: Balestrand 3101. A country hotel in a beautiful Norwegian village with capacity for 80 guests. Many bedrooms modernized. Boating, badminton, fishing, walking, hiking, and glacier excursions. Rates: NKr 120-160.

FJAERLAND PENSJONAT, Fjaerland

Mr. Ansgar Mundal was my guide through this pension with a friendly atmosphere located on the fjord side in Fjaerland. He explained that his family has owned this property for many years and that he, in fact, grew up here. There were photographs of his father and mother and grandparents in the reception rooms. Both the main salon and the dining room overlooked this enchanting fjord and there is a wonderful view of several waterfalls cascading from the mountains.

There were a number of people seated in the salon on this particular day because there was a slight drizzle. Ordinarily they might have been walking in the mountains or venturing on to the great glacier, but today they were inside drinking coffee and carrying on enthusiastic conversations. Ansgar explained that the pension was very popular with Dutch, English and Norwegians, many of whom return year after year.

I looked at several of the lodging rooms on the second floor and found them clean and comfortable. Some of them have their own baths and w.c.'s. The dining room had paintings of fjord scenes, a sparkling floor, white tablecloths, and flowers on each of the tables.

It certainly looked like a delightful place to me.

FJAERLAND PENSJONAT, N-5855 Fjaerland, Sognefjord, Norway. Telephone: Balestrand 3150. A 25-room pension at the end of the Fjaerland fjord within 7 mi. of the glaciers. Bathing, rowing, badminton, fishing, walking, hiking and glacier excursions. Rates: NKr 90-135.

A Day Trip from Balestrand

My drive into the mountains north of Balestrand on Route 5 turned out to be a very scenic one with prosperous farmlands, mountains with rushing brooks and streams and waterfalls coursing down their sides carrying melting snow to ponds and lakes below. The frequent bus signs reminded me this beautiful trip can be made by bus in a day, or with an overnight stay at the pension in Vassenden. A bus schedule can be obtained at the Balestrand Tourist Office.

VASSENDEN TURISTPENSJONAT, Vassenden, Jolster

This interesting pensjonat might well be considered a hotel. The road led through some spectacular mountain and lake country and quite a bit of it was well above the snow line. One could really appreciate why it was closed during the winter.

The community of Vassenden proved to have many surprises. The inn was one of the biggest. I wasn't expecting anything quite as complete. It is located at the southern end of Lake Jolster with mountain and lake recreation readily available.

A girl behind the desk offered to take me on a tour of the dining rooms, salons, and some of the lodging rooms. The first thing we looked at was the main salon which had a very cozy fireplace, numerous chairs and tables for conversation and games, and a view of the lake.

When we went upstairs I realized that the inn was actually in two sections—the original main building and a new wing recently built. In this new section each room has its own bath and is furnished with rather simple furniture and bright wallpaper.

The old section has an entirely different atmosphere. Some of the rooms have walls made out of painted boards. There is old furniture including some carved headboards, tables and chairs and a very warm, homelike feeling. Some of these rooms have also recently been remodeled, and while there is a bathroom and a w.c. on the corridor, all that I looked at had running water in the rooms.

She explained that the area is very popular with vacationers because there are many excursions in the mountains for which Vassenden can be the starting point. She explained that it was possible to take a plane ride over the famous Jostel Glacier, which is nearby. This glacier, by the way, covers quite a bit of the mountains in this section and extends south into the Sognefjord area.

While we were talking, I happened to notice a book that included full-color reproductions of paintings by a Norwegian artist. She explained that these were the works of Nicolai Astrup who lived nearby until his death in 1928. As I leafed through the book I remembered seeing copies of Astrup's work in other inns in Norway. They are characterized by bold strokes in somewhat somber tones and depict Norway's mountains and fjords.

Before I left Vassenden I drove to the top of a high hill nearby so that I could get a good look at the town, the inn, the lakes, the mountains and even the glacier. It was easy to see why this section of Norway provided inspiration for artists and writers.

VASSENDEN TURISTPENSJONAT, N6840, Vassenden i Jolster, Norway. Telephone: (057) 27192 Vassenden. A very comfortable hotel with many modern features combined with a homey atmosphere. Folk singing weekly. Rowboats, trout fishing, swimming, many excursions can be arranged by bus or ferry and also excellent walking and hiking nearby. Rates: NKr 70-110. Rates with meals available.

HUSUM GJESTEHEIM, Kaupanger, Sognefjord

This place was another pleasant surprise for me. I was enroute from Balestrand to Flam, catching the 9 p.m. ferry through the fjord system from Kaupanger. Near the ferry landing there was a small sign that indicated that the Husum Gjesteheim was just a few kilometers away. I would have time to visit it before catching the ferry.

Although it was about 8 p.m., the sun was still well above the horizon since it was just a few days before the longest day of the year. The waters of the fjord were the deepest blue. It couldn't have been more than three minutes when the road, which led around a secluded harbor went up an orchard-covered hillside, and I could see this inn peeking out from the apple trees.

It was immediately obvious that there were two sections to the inn. The main building which had the dining room, a number of guest rooms as well as the reception rooms and salons. The other section had been added in recent years and looked more modern.

I liked the older section immediately. There was homey furniture similar to American Victorian and the bedrooms were a generous size with windows overlooking the bay. Some of them had the old-fashioned Norwegian stoves in them.

Mr. Husum explained that Kaupanger was an important ferry terminal with bus connections to many points in the Sognefjord district. He said that many guests make their first stop just overnight, but come back again in later years to spend a longer time.

"I hope you will have a chance to visit our folk museum which you passed coming up here. It has the most notable collection of rural arts and crafts, tools and implements here in the Sogne district."

The traditional Norwegian breakfast is the only meal served here.

HUSUM GJESTEHEIM, 5880 Kaupanger, Sognefjord. Telephone: Sogndal 3101. Open from May 20 to Sept. 10. Rates: NKr 44-70.

HEIMLY LODGE, Flam, Sogn

The twilight ferry trip through the Aurland fjord was such a beautiful and tranquil experience that I would have been disappointed if there hadn't been an inn in this little town at the far end of the fjord which breathed the same kind of atmosphere. Fortunately there was — the Heimly Lodge.

It seemed that my head had just touched the pillow when the alarm went off. I wanted to get an early start on the day as there was really so much to see and do in Flam. I took a quick shower in the bathroom down the hall and joined the other guests for breakfast in a sunny and delightful dining room.

The breakfast was indeed unbelievable. There was a large table in the center of the dining room laden with a wide assortment of fish, and many different varieties of cheese including some delicious cheese made from goats' milk. There were six varieties of Norwegian bread, sliced ham, liverwurst and other meat. There were all kinds of fresh fruit jam and several varieties of hot and cold cereal. I filled my plate with as many of the breakfast offerings as possible, and took a seat by the window. I was immediately drawn into conversation with people around me who were pointing out the fact that the morning ferry boat, which was down the fjord, seemed to be floating in space because of the illusion created by the brilliant sunshine,

343

the steep sides of the fjord, and the absence of wind.

As we watched, far down the fjord a huge cruise ship came into view and it was explained that occasionally these luxury liners, which can go almost anywhere on the fjord system because of the deep water, frequently make calls at Flam, and the passengers ride the Flam railway up the mountain to Myrdal.

It was an absolutely gorgeous morning, and the sunshine on the garden of the inn found ready reception from the fruit trees in blossom as well as the geraniums decorating the terrace and bordering the walk down to the road. I started counting the waterfalls that could be seen from the dining room and finally gave up at 18.

Heimly Lodge has the same type of atmosphere that I found at the Hotel Mundal in Fjaerland and the Hotel Walaker in Solvorn. There were many original touches in the salon and quite a few photographs of Norwegian craftsmen and crafts.

After breakfast a group of us went out on the terrace to enjoy the really magnificent presence of the high mountains in this valley and to try to store up some of the incredible serenity. Then, one by one, we all separated to do whatever pleased us for the day. Some were going to go hiking, others bicycling, and some were going boating on the fjord. A great many were going to take a good book into the mountains and disappear for awhile. I was going to take the Flam Railway to Myrdal. We would all be together at dinner for what I knew would be an outstanding experience.

HEIMLY LODGE, N-5743 Flam, Sogn, Norway. Telephone: Flam 1. A 40-room inn located at the end of the Aurland Fjord in the beautiful Flam valley. All types of outdoor recreation available. Open May 1-Oct. 30. Rates: NKr 73-90. Half-pension rates for 3-to-5-day stays.

WALAKER HOTEL, Solvorn, Sogn

The sign off the main road pointed to the right, saying, "Walaker Hotel." A dirt road took me past some upland meadows with cows grazing and I headed for the fjord at the bottom of the mountains. The road looked well traveled and I later found out it was the main road into this village. I passed through some orchards and soon the church spires of the village came into view. It was also lilac time in Solvorn. Norway is captivating in June with all the fruit trees in blossom.

The Walaker Hotel deserves this setting. One thing I learned is that the house is 325 years old and the old portion of it is called the "Tingstova," which is the Norwegian word for courtroom, and is so called because at one time this is where a judge held trials.

The Walaker Hotel has been owned by the same family for centuries. The present owners, Hermod and Oddlaug Walaker were married in peasant costume here in the village just a few years ago, and their photographs were taken in these costumes on the front porch of the hotel. Fortunately they were in color and I was delighted when Oddlaug presented me with a copy.

I was pleased to see these two young people, along with Hermod's mother, keeping this country inn in a captivating village amidst awe-inspiring scenery. (I continually find myself running short of adjectives to describe the fjord country of Norway.)

It has a real country inn atmosphere with some beautiful old Norwegian antiques, some of them from the "old church" in the town which dates back to the 11th century. Open fireplaces, beamed ceilings, a collection of family photographs, and winding staircases add to the comfortable homelike feeling.

There is also a section which contains new rooms furnished in the modern mode.

Across the fjord from the village is one of the old stave churches of Norway and there is frequent ferry service to the opposite shore. Incidentally, Solvorn is also on the express boat schedule from Bergen, and has direct bus connections with principal Sognefjord points.

The Walaker Hotel is one of the beautiful country inns in Norway.

WALAKER HOTEL, N-5815 Solvorn, Sogn, Norway. Telephone: Hafslo 107. A delightful hotel in a secluded fjordside village. Hiking, walking, glacier trips, fjord fishing, rowboats, saddle horses, swimming, frequent entertainment. Boat, bus and ferry connections to all points. Rates (including breakfast): NKr 63-85.

SOLSTRAND PENSJONAT, Luster, Sognefjord

My stop here was unexpected. I saw a little sign on the side of the road indicating that there were accommodations and I went in to ask information about the road ahead. What I found was a rather substantial pension.

I arrived right at the height of breakfast and was invited to join some Americans at their table. We introduced ourselves and exchanged some travel notes.

The breakfast was typically Norwegian, with just about as many dishes crowded on one table as was possible. The guests were talking about the cable railway immediately next to the pension which ascends the mountain, and they spoke of the fantastic view of the Sognefjord and its neighboring mountain ranges.

"The rooms here are very clean and comfortable," said one lady. "We have decided to stay an extra night for this is an excellent location for trips up in the mountains to see the Jostedalsbreen, the largest glacier in northern Europe."

The pension, located on the banks of Lusterfjord, is entirely surrounded by fruit trees which were in full bloom. The aroma was most enticing.

I might have missed this place except for the fact that all of the accommodations in Norway have a roadside sign with a symbol of a bed. The places for eating have a knife and fork.

SOLSTRAND PENSJONAT, Post Boks 9, N-5830 Luster, Sogne-fjord. Telephone: 50. Rates: NKr 90.

Through The Mountains Towards Sweden

My short time in Norway was drawing to a close. I was driving east on the main highway which leads from the fjord country high through the great mountains and snow fields to Lom, which is on the other side of the mountain. This road, closed for the winter, had been open only four days when I ventured upon it. In some places the snow plows had carved through drifts twice the height of the car, and only continual sanding and filling prevented the cars from being mired down in the spring thaw.

Between Luster on the Sognefjord and Lom, I passed a few small hotels and pensions, most of which were closed. Here are my impressions of two that were open.

TURTAGRO HOTEL, Turtagro, Sogn

Here I discovered a great mountain experience—a rustic hotel with a spectacular view of mountains in all directions. I arrived after a series of hairpin turns with constantly spectacular vistas which brought me up from the fjord floor to approximately 2700 feet into the Jotunheimen mountains in about 45 minutes. Untamed is the one word that keeps returning to me when I think back on the region.

As might be expected, the inn is the center of rock-climbing expeditions and glacial tours. There is much of the paraphernalia of this type in many corners of the inn. These include special ropes, picks, and rock-climbing shoes and clothing. I understand that courses are given in these activities on request by experts at the inn.

This hotel has been here for many years and is furnished in the traditional Norwegian style. The exterior of the inn is of weathered wood which has been painted brown with white trim and is attractively set off by the green backdrop of the mountains. The views of the Skagastol mountain peaks are spectacular to say the least.

TURTAGRO HOTEL, N-5834 Forton, Turtagro, Sogn, Norway. Telephone: Skjolden 6616. A mountain inn specializing in rock and glacier excursions. Salmon and trout fishing. Approximately 109 miles from Balestrand. Rates: 70 NKr.

ELVESETER HOTEL, Elveseter, Norge
This hotel which is 2100 feet up in the great Norwegian mountains was originally a manor farm that was converted into what are for the most part modern accommodations. A considerable number of new buildings have been added in recent years. A great deal of effort has been made to create the atmosphere reminiscent of an old Norse "Home of the Gods" and every room has a name derived from Norse mythology.

The buildings are grouped together around a square and are linked by heated corridors and an elevator. Each room has a private bath. There is an indoor swimming pool, a gymnasium and several facilities for meetings.

I was quite surprised to find an accommodation so large and so luxurious in this part of Norway. I wouldn't describe it as a country inn but it is certainly most impressive.

ELVESETER HOTEL, 2689 Elveseter, Norge, Norway. Telephone: Lom 9811. Rates: NKr 140.

It was all downhill from here to Lom. As I descended from the alpine heights, the wild terrain was replaced by farming country and quite a few fields had sprinkling systems which were now in use because the rain in Norway stays on the west side of the great mountains.

The Norwegian portion of my trip was, for all practical purposes, completed. There remained only to drive to Lillehammer and cross the border into Sweden.

NETHERLANDS

OVERIJSSEL

FRIESLAND

• Harlingen

• Piaam

• Bolsward

• Giethoorn

• Vollenhove

• Kampen

• Zwolle

Afsluitdijk

Zuider Zee

Monnickendam•

AMSTERDAM•

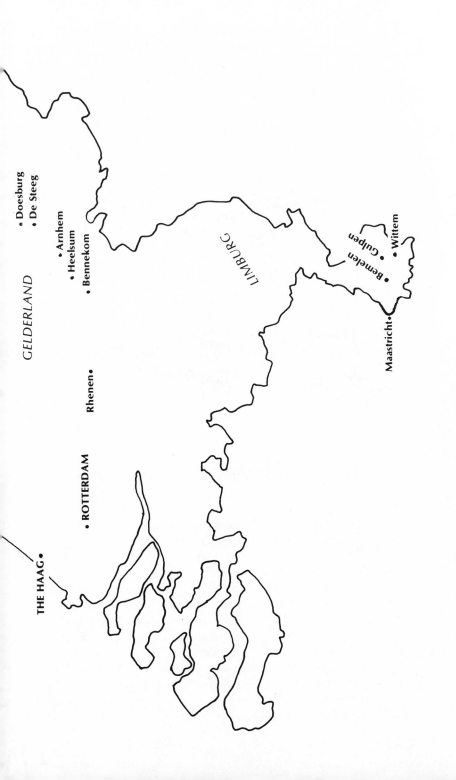

TRAVEL SUGGESTIONS FOR THE NETHERLANDS

How to Get There
Pan American Airlines and KLM provide service to Amsterdam from the U.S. A Eurailpass is good in the Netherlands.

Country Inns in The Netherlands
I saw very few accommodations that precisely resemble American country inns. Many places that I visited were small and middle-size hotels offering bed and breakfast as well as other meals. Many had rooms with private baths and wc's, but there were also other rooms with conveniences "in the corridor."

These hotels had parlors and lounges where guests could get acquainted. Many were owned and managed by families who frequently did the cooking, serving, and housekeeping. I also stayed at three or four star hotels including castle hotels.

Reservations

Hotel reservations in the Netherlands can be made through the NRC, the National Reservation Center, P.O. Box 3387, Amsterdam, Tel. (020) 211-211; Telex T 15754.

Tourist offices called VVV are located in every community to provide help in finding local accommodations.

The VVV has jointly set up a nationwide hotel reservation system known as the VVV Logies Service which is to assist travelers who have arrived in the Netherlands and wish to make hotel reservations for the same day or the next few days. Go to a VVV office to make these reservations. No telephone or written reservations. There is a nominal charge. Reservations for accommodations mentioned in this book can be made directly by letter or telephone, as well as through the NRC and the VVV.

Dining in The Netherlands

Among the intriguing Dutch dishes are many different species of eels. Other Dutch food are broodjes, which are small rolls stuffed with cheese, shrimp, pork, and ham. These are served in small snack bars called broodjeswinkeles. There are also croquetten, which consists of spiced meat fried in bread crumbs and served with French fried potatoes. Erwtensoep is a Dutch pea soup with slices of sausage. Other dishes are sauerkraut with bacon and sausage, minced beef with fried apples and red cabbage, and hutspot, a stew of onions, potatoes, carrots, and ribs of beef.

In the larger cities of the Netherlands I found quite a few Indonesian restaurants. Pancake restaurants are popular. The Netherlands also has restaurants with Continental menus and service. These meals are often served in sumptuous surroundings and in great style.

Driving Tips

Backroading in the Netherlands is one of the great sports. I will certainly remember to bring a compass on my next trip because even with the very best road map I still needed help. I was forever getting turned around and on days when the sun was behind the clouds the best Boy Scout would have had a hard time.

My Itinerary in The Netherlands

I started in Amsterdam and drove in a clockwise direction around the Zuider Zee into Friesland and then down the other side through Overijssel through Arnhem into Maastricht.

To obtain Netherlands road maps, see the section at the back of the book.

Amsterdam Reflections

I was not prepared for the great number of canals in Amsterdam, even though I'd been told of their importance to the city. They are everywhere, intertwined, crossing and re-crossing.

Driving from the airport, Amsterdam looked like one giant traffic jam of cars, while the swarms of bicycles and the triple streetcars rolled by silently amid the squeals of brakes and the roar of traffic. Parking, as might be expected, is a problem; however, I easily found space in front of my hotel, the Pulitzer.

Most of the Centrum shops are closed on Saturday afternoon. Those catering to tourists are always open. Earlier, driving from the airport, I saw many open-air markets, obviously not aimed at tourist trade. Walking is a fine pastime in Amsterdam, seeing all the interesting and intricate architectural styles with the mansard and traditional Dutch "step" roofs, and buildings with little penthouse studios and windows with flowers in them.

Amsterdam is one of the several principal gateways to Europe. I stayed just long enough to be intrigued by all its many possibilities for sightseeing, amusement, and culture.

HOTEL PULITZER, Amsterdam

The brochure for this hotel says that it provides comfortable, contemporary accommodations in Old World surroundings, and I think that is a fair evaluation. Amsterdam has 218 hotels of which 18 are towers of Continental-style hostelry. The other 200 are more modest in both size and intent. The Pulitzer, which certainly is not one of the grand palaces, did very nicely for my one-night stay. My room overlooked the Prinsengracht Canal and some most fascinating centuries-old town houses on the other side. One of them had the date of 1733 in ornate scroll.

The Pulitzer was rather busy since it was the height of the tourist season and there was at least one tour booked into it. It is within walking distance of all of the downtown Amsterdam attractions (Centrum). It was reasonably quiet, and the carillon bells of the Westekerk Tower were happy and welcome sounds.

The hotel is made up of a series of old Amsterdam town houses that have been modernized and interconnected. It stretches for a block between two canals and there are many hidden gardens and courtyards within the complex.

One of its most appealing features is the very pleasant breakfast room which overlooks the canal.

HOTEL PULITZER, Prinsengracht 315, Amsterdam. Telephone: 202-228333. A 176-room canal-side hotel where all the rooms have baths, w.c.'s, radios, telephones, TV, and mini-bars. Well within walking distance of all Amsterdam attractions. From Dfl 150.

DE DEYSELHOF RESTAURANT, Landsmeer

Christl de Boer was telling me about some of the early beginnings of the De Deyselhof.

"My husband John worked in the kitchen when we first opened here ten years ago. I was waitress, hostess, cashier and everything else. It had been a working farm up until one year before we purchased it and then we rebuilt it, thatched roof and all, into a restaurant. We have retained the lovely old red brick walls and added to the collection of farm implements.

"You'll notice that over some of the tables we have put farm baskets turned upside down with a light bulb mounted inside. The old beams and uprights are from the original farm and I

hope we have kept the cozy feeling. Of course, we have put in air conditioning. We serve two meals a day and in the summer we have barbecued specials served outdoors."

In Europe I became increasingly aware that in some restaurants like the one I was visiting, the appearance and service of the food is of equal importance with the taste. In the kitchen the chef prepares a platter with the main course laid out in a most artistic manner. This is brought into the dining room and the waiter proudly shows this platter to the guest for their approval.

In some cases the next step involves a small stove on wheels where the waiter himself may prepare a special sauce or combine a sauce with one of the dishes from the kitchen.

This scene with the small stoves on wheels was going on at many tables throughout the dining room. At some tables a flaming dessert was prepared and at the crucial moment when a match had been applied to the puddings or peaches, the resultant blue flames brought appreciative smiles from everyone. It makes dining so much fun.

Another fun feature here is the menu. They have been placed in little wooden cabinets and when the door on the left is open there are the first courses. When the door on the right is opened there are the main courses and dessert.

The De Deyselhof belongs with other restaurants in the Netherlands, to L'Alliance Gastronomique Neerlandaise, a group of restaurants serving food in the French style. I visited two others during my stay.

It was a most auspicious beginning for a short trip through Holland.

NOTE: *Just before going to press with this edition, we received the sad news from the Netherlands that this beautiful restaurant had been destroyed in a disastrous fire. I'm sure that Mr. and Mrs. de Boer have already started the reconstruction.*

North of Amsterdam along the Zuider Zee (Now known as the Ijsselmeer.)

Poring over the road maps of Holland brought back some of its history; just the names evoked memories: Edam, the home of the great red cheeses; Kampen, the town famous for its foolish wisemen; Nijmegen and Charlemagne's Castle, and Leyden where a sneeze might have changed the course of history for awhile.

The Zuider Zee, once a great inland sea, had important harbors from which Dutchmen sailed the seas of the world, until 1932, when a dam turned it into a large lake. This changed the plant and marine life, and among other phenomena, caused the proliferation of the famous Zuider Zee eels. Many new towns were created on the reclaimed lands (polders).

RESTAURANT STUTTENBURGH, Monnickendam

Honestly, this place is incredible. It is a very pleasant old building sitting back from the busy harbor street in the center of a sizable lawn with quite a few tall trees and many flowers. I had a clue to its uniqueness when I noticed a few exotic birds in cages on the terrace, but it was when I stepped inside the front door that the real nature of the place impressed me.

It was the music boxes. I gave up counting at 45, but later learned that there were at least 150 with that many more at various stages of repair at a workshop. Everyone of the music boxes in the restaurant was in working condition. The natural question is, "What happens if they all play at once?" I was reassured that they only play one at a time. However, most of the time I could hear one tinkling away in the background.

There are small music boxes, large ones, and miniatures. There are music boxes mounted inside of birds, elaborate cabinets, and dancing dolls. There is even an antique machine that plays two discs at the same time with a stereophonic effect!

Even without the music boxes this restaurant is worth a visit. For one thing, almost every table has an unobstructed view of the canal and marina traffic which is gliding by continuously.

I had my first taste of eels here. These were pickled eels served cold with a peach salad. At first I thought the portion would be too big but I enthusiastically consumed every last one. There are many different ways of preparing eels.

The table d'hote menu has traditional Dutch farm food. The a la carte menu has many French dishes.

My visit here was made more enjoyable because of meeting Peter Koster of Rockport, Massachusetts. He was a native of this province but had returned with his family to pay a visit. We discovered mutual friends in Rockport, Fred and Lydia Wemyss, who are innkeepers at the Yankee Clipper.

RESTAURANT STUTTENBURGH, Monnickendam, North Holland. Telephone: 02995-1582. A restaurant overlooking water, serving typical Dutch food and specializing in eels. No lodgings.

To Friesland Via the Afsluitdijk

The Afsluitdijk is the road over the Zuider Zee Dike (29 kilometers to Friesland), and I took it at Ben Oever, after driving back roads through the towns of Edam, Enkhuizen, and Twisk. I was heading for Harlingen in Friesland, situated on the Waddenzee, a channel of the North Sea between the mainland and the offshore islands of Terschelling and Vlieland. A romantic place with many canals, a picturesque town square and many medieval buildings, Harlingen is one of the towns to see in Friesland.

HOTEL HOFSTEE, Harlingen, Friesland

I did have to get directions at least twice to find this hotel which is located a few blocks from the main harbor but directly on one of the major canals.

One of the problems is findings bridges over canals. Mr. Hofstee, himself, answered the bell at the front door and proved to be a very communicative man who has owned this hotel for quite a number of years.

I followed him up a set of winding stairs with a brass railing and looked at several rooms. Those on the front were sunny and overlooked the canal. He also has collected quite a few interesting original paintings for the rooms.

Mr. Hofstee explained that while they had served meals for many years, the hotel now was strictly bed and breakfast, and that he was prepared to recommend several different restaurants to his guests, some of whom come to Harlingen every year and spend one or two weeks at the hotel.

One or two rooms have been modernized but for the most part they were furnished in traditional furniture. I don't think Mr. Hofstee is a man who gives up the habits of many years without a struggle.

HOTEL HOFSTEE, Frankereind 23, Harlingen, Friesland. Telephone: 05178-2762. A 25-room canal-side, modest hotel. Located away from the harbor noises and traffic. Rates: Dfl 40-70 (includes breakfast).

NYNKE PLEATS RESTAURANT, Piaam, Friesland

Piaam is considerably off the main track and one of the problems involved was in finding someone out in the country early in the evening from whom to obtain directions after I got lost. But what matters all this if I am in Friesland where the horizon line is always dotted with the rows of picturebook trees and where the golden sun was dropping into the Zuider Zee and the breeze was bending the fields of golden grain?

Frankly, after my adventures in reaching Piaam I wish I could be of help to my readers. But I am afraid that everyone must take their own chances. What I was prepared to find was the Nynke Pleats Restaurant which I thought was one of the best-kept secrets in the country.

Nothing could have been further from the truth! Even with just 30 minutes before the kitchen would close the parking lot was filled and people were still arriving.

The building was modeled after a traditional Friesland barn. It has a high-pitched thatched roof with walls of light tan brick. The interior emphasized the farm-style construction with sturdy exposed beams, posts and rafters. Old watering troughs were used as planters. Huge windows at one end provided light and allowed an unobstructed view of the Friesland meadows. The floor was board tiling. The walls were lined with paintings by local artists and also an excellent collection of hand-painted tiles. Long wooden tables set with chairs accommodate the large Dutch families who apparently enjoy eating here because of the good food. The menu matches the farm-style design. Food is served on individual large platters. I had sliced fried potatoes, small peas, pork chops with a sauce of apples and a salad. Salads in Holland are quite apt to be elaborate. This one had slices of mushrooms, eggs, fish, all placed very attractively on a bed of lettuce and served with a salad dressing. Dessert was a very tasty apple pie served with ice cream—a dish that was invented in a small upstate New York hotel during the 19th century.

NYNKE PLEATS RESTAURANT, Piaam, Friesland. Telephone: 05158-1707. This is a farm style restaurant near the shores of the Zuider Zee about 12 to 15 kilometers from Bolsward. Closed Mondays. Allow extra time for making wrong turns. No lodgings. Dinner: Dfl 16½.

HOTEL DE WIJNBERG, Bolsward, Friesland

Bolsward is a small town not far from the shores of the Zuider Zee, and would be a good place to stay for two or three days while touring the remainder of Friesland. It is noted for having a very famous town hall and also for one of the oldest churches in Friesland dating back to 1446. This church has ceiling paintings and handcarved choir stalls.

The Hotel De Wijnberg is clean and comfortable and has apparently been modernized recently. My room on the third floor overlooked some of the roofs of the town.

When I returned from having dinner at the Nynke Pleats Restaurant in Piaam I found that everyone was gathered in the main salon watching the soccer match between Czechoslovakia and Germany. There was a big table in the middle of this room with all kinds of magazines and newspapers to be used by guests. The match turned out to be one of the most important and there was a great deal of interest among all of us. The enthusiasm got so hot that two or three of the guests started shouting advice to the players. In one respect some of the hotels that I visited in Holland were quite similar to American country inns. The guests gathered in the main salon or living room to enjoy after-dinner coffee, read the papers and talk among themselves.

Breakfast at this hotel, which was my first overnight stop outside of Amsterdam, was three different kinds of bread served with butter and jam, sliced cheese and ham. It was here also that I first discovered that in Holland soap is not provided for hotel guests although they did thoughtfully give me a bar when I made inquiries.

HOTEL DE WIJNBERG, Bolsward, Friesland. Telephone: (05157) 2220-3120. A pleasant conventional hotel offering all services. Most of the rooms have their own baths and w.c.'s. Rates: Dfl 40-66 (includes breakfast).

SEIDEL RESTAURANT, Vollenhove, Overijssel

The Seidel Restaurant overlooks the harbor. It is in a building that has the classic Dutch step design on the side walls. However, the front of the building and the entrance is through a row of colonnades and arches that reminded me of Italy.

To make things more enigmatic, the other part of the building must have been a church a few centuries ago. Now the two are joined together with a mutual purpose.

Inside is a wonderful collection of the Holland of the past with faded old paintings, maps, and clocks, heavy wooden furniture, and tiled floors.

The menu indicates that it is a French restaurant and I am sorry to say that although lunch was in preparation, I was expected at a pancake restaurant in Giethoorn and could not possibly indulge myself with two lunches. (Ever try to eat half a lunch in two places?)

SEIDEL RESTAURANT, Kerplein 3, Vollenhove, Overijssel, Holland. Telephone: 05274-1262. An attractive restaurant with a French menu overlooking the Vollenhove harbor. Lunch and dinner served daily except Monday. No lodgings. Dinner from Dfl 21.

PANNEKOEKENBOERDERIJ RESTAURANT,
Giethoorn, Overijssel

This is a restaurant that specializes in pancakes. Pancakes with ham, pancakes made with cheese, with apples, with ginger, with mixed fruit, with peaches, with strawberries—pancakes with just about everything. It is located in a thatched-roof barn-type building that was made into a restaurant and is immediately next to a small canal. The decorations include mounted birds of all kinds.

This is a place that Hank Fisher in New York at the Netherlands National Tourist Office had told me about. He said that it was quite an experience. Well, it was.

My pancake was as big as a small pizza, rather thin and covered with slices of candied ginger. I ate about half of it, and then skimmed off the ginger from the uneaten half. A glass of cold milk was welcome. This was really a most enjoyable meal.

After lunch I walked outside and found that there were a number of small excursion boats that were used to take passengers along the tree-arched canals. These are the streets of Giethoorn where punts were used instead of cars, a sort of village Venice. The whole area is in fact one big nature reserve —the Wieden, which consists of 10,000 acres with an unbelievable wealth of flora and fauna.

PANNEKOEKENBOERDERIJ RESTAURANT, Zuiderpad 32, Giethoorn, Overijssel. Telephone: 05216-428. This is a pancake specialty restaurant open from the 1st of April until the 15th of September. No lodgings. Pancake meal: Dfl 6½.

HOTEL VAN DIJK, Kampen, Overijssel

I did not stay overnight at this hotel but I looked at several rooms and the main salon and it seemed very pleasant. Some of the lodging rooms overlook the river. The hotel also has a restaurant a few doors away.

HOTEL VAN DIJK, Ijsselkade 30, Kampen, Overijssel. Telephone: 05202-4925. A 48-room in-town hotel. Most rooms have w.c. and bath in corridor. Within walking distance of the town center. Rates: Dfl 40-60 (with bath).

GOLDEN TULIP HOTEL WIENTJES, Zwolle, Overijssel

In Zwolle, I stayed overnight at the Hotel Wientjes which had several very attractive rooms. Most of them had their own bath and w.c. My room had been modernized and overlooked the tree-lined Stationsweg. The front desk staff were most accommodating and I found the general atmosphere very friendly. I particularly enjoyed sitting on the broad front terrace and, like everyone else, watching the traffic pass by. The dining room was extremely attractive with high ceilings and great French windows. I had an excellent evening meal with John Smulders, and he acquainted me with the charms of Overijssel and made suggestions about places to visit. The hotel also has a restaurant that is typical of the country. The service is more informal.

GOLDEN TULIP HOTEL WIENTJES, Zwolle, Overijssel. Telephone: 05200-11200. A 45-room conventional in-town hotel in a thriving central Holland community. Well within walking distance of the town's attractive center. Breakfast, lunch, and dinner served daily. Rates: Dfl 60-70.

RESTAURANT DE WAAG, Doesburg, Gelderland

My way now led south through Deventer and Zutphen on well traveled main roads, for I had no time for meandering.

I was now in the Arnhem district, most of which is in Gelderland Province. This is an area rich in recreational opportunities and has many hotels, pensions, restaurants, sports and cultural activities. The VVV office at Arnhem is extremely busy at all times. They literally loaded me with pounds of information about all holiday and vacation attractions.

Anticipating my route from Zwolle, Hans Withagen, who is the assistant to the director of the Arnhem VVV, directed me by telephone to two inns on the outer perimeter of Arnhem which he thought I would find intriguing. He was correct.

The first inn was in Doesburg, a comely town with quite a few 16th century Gothic buildings. Here I visited Restaurant De Waag as they were serving afternoon tea and preparing for the evening meal.

To begin I was awed by the facade of the building which is about 5½ stories high, as can be seen from the accompanying drawing. The ground floor dining room is about two stories high with graceful arches supporting the upper stories. (I later discovered that as in Amsterdam, the two top stories were false. This is typical of Dutch classicism.)

The first thing I saw inside was a huge farmer's scale hanging from the high ceiling. It was made in 1640. I was most impressed with this antiquity until I learned from the hesitantly bilingual head waiter that this restaurant has operated since 1449! In some ways the town and restaurant reminded me of Ribe in Denmark.

The interior is rather formal with heavy wooden chairs

and tables which looked quite ancient though sturdy. There were many plants and flowers on various tables.

There was a huge fireplace at one end with a gigantic oil painting hanging over it. Around this fireplace was a grouping of big, comfortable leather chairs that looked perfect for dissertative conversations.

On the front sidewalk there were many chairs and tables which were filling up with townfolk seeking refreshment in the late afternoon.

The menu, as I suspected, was dominated by French cuisine. I could not arrange to eat here, but if the food was just half as good as the decor, it would be a delight.

RESTAURANT DE WAAG, Doesburg, Gelderland, Holland. Luncheon and dinner served daily except Monday. No lodgings. Dinner for two: Dfl 75.

HET WAPEN VAN ATHLONE, De Steeg

Now this one was a dandy. A real American style country inn in Holland. It is on one of the main roads, a few miles from Arnhem, so it has all of the advantages of the activities in the vicinity.

Even before I met the distaff side of the innkeeping team, I could see that lots of tender loving care was being lavished on this old inn. This was verified in a conversation I had with Ale Van Dyk as we sat on the terrace in the late afternoon sunshine.

"We're at least 150 years old," she said. "Part of the building is from 1700 but most of it is from 1824. Last year we had our 150th celebration here.

"At Christmas we always have lots of people who come and stay for about ten days. We have a wonderful party and dinner at Christmas with presents for any of the children who are here.

"Many people who come here enjoy the long walks in the woods which are right next to us. We have 15 beds and serve breakfast only for our guests. Would you like to see some of the lodging rooms?"

I followed her to see five or six of the rooms which looked very comfortable.

We stopped to look at a most unusual Dutch fireplace with two seats conveniently placed for warming chilly toes. There was a deer head mounted on the chimney.

In the dining room I saw that the Lions and the Rotary met here and that there were candles on the table, all of which contributed to a very homelike feeling.

The menu seemed to be a mixture of both French and Dutch dishes.

"We try to make everyone feel at home here," Ale went on. "Both Kees and I enjoy innkeeping very much and part of the fun is to meet new people from many lands."

HET WAPEN VAN ATHLONE, Hoofdstraat 19, De Steeg, Gelder-land, Holland. Telephone: 08309-1343. A village inn with 15 beds, serving breakfast (houseguests only), luncheon and dinner daily except Wednesday from September 1 to May 1. Rates: Dfl 50 (includes breakfast).

Arnhem

Arnhem was one of Holland's unexpected experiences. I knew that it had been a battleground in World War II and that a motion picture entitled "A Bridge Too Far" had been filmed in the vicinity, but I had no idea of the tremendous extent of its natural and cultural appeal. The staff of the VVV office in Arnhem was most generous and helpful (as they are with every-one) in apprising me of all the possibilities offered to visitors;

first and foremost of which is the great Zuid-Veluwe Nature Reserve—240 square miles of undisturbed natural beauty—merging with the city's beautiful parks and near the scenic Rhine and Ijssel Rivers.

The greatest Van Gogh collection in the world—272 of his works—is housed in the Rijksmuseum Kroller-Muller, and there are many other fine galleries along with castles and museums to be visited in Arnhem.

The Netherlands Open Air Museum is a valley at the northern edge of Arnhem featuring a fascinating collection of authentic architecture from all corners of the country.

I visited several small towns in the Arnhem area and found country inn accommodations in a few of them which I am happy to share.

DE KROMME DISSEL, Heelsum

I was having dinner in a restaurant which is located in the Hotel Klein Zwitserland in the Arnhem suburb of Heelsum. My companion was Hans Withagen of the Arnhem VVV office.

It was a most enjoyable evening. The service and the food were excellent and there was the added touch of soft piano music with selections ranging from Strauss to Burt Bacharach. The interior has been quite elegantly designed to represent a traditional Dutch farmhouse. There were old farm tools hung along the brick walls and the beamed ceilings and stone floors completed the rustic chic atmosphere. A rather small fire, more for atmosphere than warmth, burned in a handsome fireplace.

Heavy wooden tables set with snow white napery and gleaming silverware were further emphasized by silver candlesticks.

The atmosphere may have been bucolic Dutch but the menu and service were sophisticated French and featured much preparation at the table. My dinner was crab cocktail, steak au poivre and fresh strawberries.

The atmosphere, food, service and music in this restaurant all combined to encourage good conversation, and Hans Withagen and I talked away the whole evening mostly about the many attractive aspects of Arnhem, natural and cultural. The Hotel Klein Zwitserland was a large four-star hotel. I had very comfortable lodgings there for one night.

DE KROMME DISSEL (Hotel Klein Zwitserland), Heelsum, Holland. Telephone: 08373-3118. A lavish country restaurant about 30 minutes from downtown Arnhem. Open daily except Monday. Lodgings in Hotel Klein Zwitserland.

HOTEL KELTENWOUD, Bennekom

Bennekom is one of the many resort areas just outside of Arnhem. It is surrounded by miles of country roads and forests, and has quite a few beautiful homes.

Following some strategically placed signposts, I sighted Het Keltenwoud through the trees with many guests enjoying breakfast on the outside terrace. It looked like a very comfortable place.

I introduced myself to Fred, the son of the owners, and he showed me through many bedrooms, the dining room and the parlors, which were all pleasantly furnished.

In this type of hotel, there are frequently quite a few photographs of the various members of the innkeeper's family on display including grandchildren. This, of course, contributes to a feeling of being in a home.

This inn had a unique bit of history which Fred explained to me this way:

"During the war there were some Jewish families in this area. There was a secret room in the stable where some of those families were kept. It was common for the Dutch people in this area to hide their friends this way."

In America I have found quite a few inns that were stops in the Underground Railroad, the system that passed escaped Negro slaves from house to house until they were safe and free. Here in the forests outside of Arnhem was another example of man's humanity to man.

HOTEL KELTENWOUD, Dikkenbergweg 28, Bennekom. Telephone: 00309-5406-4219. A forest-side family inn a few miles outside of Arnhem. Many sports nearby. Rates: Dfl 60-65 (includes breakfast).

DE LUNTERSE BOER, Lunteren

I found this inn to be most interesting for a number of reasons. First, it is adjacent to a beautiful public swimming pool which looked very enticing to me during the warm midday hours of my visit. There are also quite a few tennis courts nearby. Like the Hotel Keltenwoud, the De Lunterse Boer is on the edge of the Zuid-Veluwe, the great Arnhem Nature Preserve, so there are many outdoor activities available.

The second thing of interest is the fact that this inn has been operated by two women for the past twenty-five years and they are both highly involved, articulate individuals.

After I had introduced myself and explained that I was writing a book about European inns, they requested to see my American book and asked me about its distribution, readership and so forth. They wanted to make sure *Country Inns and Back Roads, European Edition* was the right kind of a book to represent them. I appreciated their attitude.

I also appreciated the De Lunterse Boer. The main dining room and parlors are in a building similar to the Restaurant Nynke Pleats in Piaam. It has a thatched roof and country furniture. There is a view of the forest in all directions. The housekeeping is meticulous.

Lodging rooms are in another building a short distance

away. They are extremely comfortable and homelike. All have a shower and w.c. and a balcony overlooking the woods.

The average European traveler is a little different from the average American. When I asked my hostess what single factor found the most favor with their guests she unhesitantly replied: "They all love walking in the silent woods."

DE LUNTERSE BOER, Lunteren. Telephone: 08388-3657. A country inn in beautiful natural surroundings near Arnhem. Rates: Dfl 80 (includes breakfast).

HOTEL DE EEKHOORN, Rhenen

I left Lunteren and drove south for my first glimpse of the Rhine River. In many ways this was the essence of Europe—a majestic waterway that rises in the Alps and flows to the sea. It is a source of legend and history that is unique. Here in this part of the world it is in the final stage of its journey. In this small Dutch village on the banks of the Rhine I found the Hotel de Eekhoorn, a restaurant specializing in pancakes that has a few modest rooms.

The terrace, riverside bedrooms and dining room all enjoy a pleasant view of some meadows overlooking the Rhine which is about 300 yards away.

The atmosphere is pleasant and informal and I was introduced to everyone from the cook to the owner. The lodging rooms were casual but clean. The specialty of the house was pancakes, and the restaurant catered mainly to the many people driving along the highway next to the Rhine.

The longer I remained, the more this place grew on me.

HOTEL DE EEKHOORN, Utrechsestraatweg 3, Rhenen, Holland. Telephone: 08376-2276. A modest restaurant and pension overlooking the Rhine River. Rates: Dfl 45-75.

RESTAURANT 'T KALKOENTJE, Rhenen

If this place had rooms it would be a total country inn. As it is, it is a tiny and beautiful restaurant just a few feet from the shores of the Rhine with its own grove of fruit trees and a resident tethered goat.

The building is a thatched-roof white farmhouse which looks as if it has been unchanged for at least 100 years. The interior has the unmistakable patina of graceful old age. The

furniture has mellowed to that wonderful deep brown which comes from years of dusting and waxing. The parlors and inside dining room have beautiful antiques.

There are shelves of books on every available square foot of wall space. These are interspersed with dozens of delicately handpainted Dutch tiles.

Although I was five hours behind schedule and not the least bit hungry, I stayed an extra hour sitting on the sunny terrace with all of the rambler roses and flowers. I ordered and ate every bite of a delicious mushroom omelet. Even the goat looked on approvingly.

Meanwhile, the Rhine traffic was just a few yards away and occasionally the crew of a barge or boat would wave merrily at me.

There is one word to describe this tiny restaurant on the Rhine—exquisite.

RESTAURANT 'T KALKOENTJE, Remmerden 143, Rhenen, Holland. Telephone: 08376-2344. Open Wednesday through Saturday, serving midday and evening meals. No lodgings.

Maastricht and the Province of Limburg

Holland was a land of surprises. One of the principal delights that unfolded like a tulip bulb in bloom was Maastricht and Limburg.

The road south from Arnhem, instead of affording the usual vistas of endless grazing lands intersected with canals and dikes, was bordered by fertile fields on sloping hills with swift-running brooks and many open woods. Along the banks of the Maas River with its famous bridges were many castles, churches, and ruins with a rich history. Surprisingly, the province of Limburg has many rather high hills, some with pleasant views.

Upon my arrival in Maastricht, the provincial capital of Limburg, I went to the VVV office, where I met Mr. Nicholas de Korte, who was to accompany me on a "Merry-go-round" tour of the area. This would include a small country inn, a famous castle-hotel, a stop for dinner at a chateau, and on to another castle for an overnight stay.

HOTEL MOOI LIMBURG, Bemelen, South Limberg
Bemelen, South Limberg

This was the Dutch country inn that Nicholas said was first on the list. It is located on a hill with a view that includes rolling hills and sloping meadows. The owner was very proud of a brand new swimming pool which would certainly be most appreciated by guests of the inn during the warm weather. This is really a very small inn where guests become almost one of the family.

373

I saw all of the lodging rooms including those on the top floor underneath the thatched roof. The thatching keeps out the heat of the sun, I was told. There was one corner room with a balcony that I liked very much.

We sat for awhile on the terrace and I learned that it was a very short distance to the American cemetery in Limburg. The Dutch people in this section feel very close to the Americans because it was an American division that liberated this part of Holland in World War II.

This little country inn seemed like a very nice place in which to stay for a number of days to explore not only Maastricht but the entire province of Limburg.

HOTEL MOOI LIMBURG, Bemelen, South Limburg. Telephone: 04407-1212. A family hotel 5 kilometers from Maastricht. Swimming pool. Rates: Dfl 48 (includes breakfast).

KASTEEL NEUBOURG, Gulpen, South Limburg

We turned off the main road and drove down a long tree-lined dirt road over a moat and through a gate to reach the

main entrance of this castle hotel. An impressive placard indicated that it has been designated as an "official monument" which means that no alterations can be made in its basic structure without going through channels.

We walked into the main reception room which had white walls and several magnificent crystal chandeliers. I was in awe already. It was really a fantastic castle, even more impressive than a film set.

The main lounge was decorated in various tones of green and with chairs of a rich green fabric. There was a large beautiful fireplace at one end and several marvelous examples of framed Dutch needlework to be seen.

I strolled through one parlor after another. Each one seemed more ornate and impressive than the previous one. The ceilings, walls and floors all had decorations that reminded me of the Schonbrunn Palace in Vienna.

The dining room was already lavishly set for the evening meal and there were beautiful fresh daisies everywhere, quite a contrast to the formal atmosphere.

The director of the castle, Mr. Reuwer, escorted me on a tour including a few of the 26 lodging rooms. Most of them can best be described as mammoth. After all, what did I expect in a castle? They all have impressive views of the Limburg countryside including the moat. From the third floor I could see the pattern formed by the 2000 rose bushes that were recently planted in the formal rose garden.

One of the rooms had a double bed with a marvelous inlaid wooden headboard. The bathroom and w.c. were six steps up at another level.

Returning to the first floor the director showed me the menu which for the most part had French cuisine and French style service.

HOTEL-RESTAURANT KASTEEL NEUBOURG, Gulpen, Limburg, Holland. Telephone: 0 4450—1222. A castle-hotel in the south Limburg hills. Rates: Dfl 70-86 (includes breakfast).

CHATEAU DE NEERCANNE, Maastricht

Nicholas and I were seated on the terrace of this beautiful chateau, reviewing our excursion and mentally preparing for

what I felt would be an exceptional dinner.

We had followed the "Merry-Go-Round" route through a series of back roads and over the most beautiful parts of this entire area. He explained that it is very popular because it reminds Hollanders of Switzerland.

At one point we were headed down a beautiful valley, the trees and the sun making long shadows over the road, when I noticed a building sitting near the top of some cliffs. "That's the Chateau de Neercanne," he remarked. "That's where we are going for dinner."

We passed through the gate and walked through the main entrance into a reception area that had lavish displays of fruits and cheeses on a large table. We were escorted to the garden and the terrace, and were now contemplating this rural scene which almost seemed like a Renaissance painting.

Other guests were arriving, and soon the wrought-iron chairs and tables were filled with attractively dressed people, chatting amiably and placing their orders for dinner which would be served in the main dining room.

This is the only restored terraced castle in Holland and dates back to 1611. Everything about it adds up to the word "elegance."

One of the most interesting features is the fact that there are caves carved out of the side of the cliffs where the wine for the chateau is kept and these may be visited by guests. There is an impressive herb garden and almost twenty-five acres of woods which have many paths. I was told that 80,000 trees have recently been planted on the property.

The head waiter informed us that our table was ready and we joined others in the candlelit dining room.

Here at Chateau de Neercanne with all of the beautiful surroundings—the flowers, the attention and service and the ambiance—there were a few moments I felt like I was visiting royalty 400 years ago.

CHATEAU DE NEERCANNE, Cannerweg 800, Maastricht, Holland. Telephone: 043-13406. A most elegant restaurant a few miles from the center of Maastricht. Serving lunch and dinner everyday except Sunday evening and all day Monday. No lodgings.

CASTLE WITTEM, Wittem, South Limburg

The bells were tolling 8 A.M. at Wittem Castle. I had been awakened earlier by the sound of many birds in the tall trees surrounding the castle and I leaned out of the windows to watch some of them dive and catch an elusive fish or two from the moat for breakfast. Swans were just making their appearance, their white feathers glistening in the morning sunlight.

The previous night I had the privilege of meeting the owner of this castle, Mr. Ritzen. Although I have visited other castle-inns, this was the first time that I had talked to a man who actually owned a castle! This man, with a delightful sense of humor, explained that the earliest parts of the castle dated back to an 11th century tower and that over the years it has been built to its present size. "We have done everything we can to modernize, but we believe we have still kept the real feeling of the castle," he said. "We have furnished it with antiques and at the same time have made improvements that mean our guests can be comfortable—even in a castle."

Comfort in my particular case involved a handsome tower room with very attractive furniture and an adjoining bath and w.c. which was the last word in contemporary fixtures.

Even as I was gazing out of my high window, the modern-day housekeepers in attendance at the castle began to appear, armed with scrubbing brushes, dust cloths and vacuum cleaners. The gardener was already at work. The cooks were bustling around in the kitchen and the waiters were beginning to arrive. Perhaps this scene was not so far removed from the activity in this castle 200 or more years ago.

Breakfast consisted of a basket of assorted breads, a plate of cheese, ham and liverwurst, jam and a 3-minute egg. "I'm certain that the food is much better than it was in 1611," he remarked.

The Wittem Castle is also a member of the prestigious Alliance Gastronomique Netherlands.

Besides all of the scenic attractions in South Limburg, there is a golf course, swimming pool and tennis in the immediate vicinity.

The surprising thing is that there is also a ski area here as well.

HOTEL RESTAURANT, CASTLE WITTEM, South Limburg, Holland. Telephone: 04450-1208. A luxurious castle with modern accommodations a few miles from the center of Maastricht. Breakfast, lunch and dinner served everyday. Rates: Dfl 40 (includes breakfast).

Netherlands in Retrospect

My entire experience in the Netherlands was delightful and unique. I loved the canals, flowers, wonderful farms, lakes, the continual parade of boats, smoked eels, great salads, and the narrow little roads that seemed to go nowhere but everywhere. I found a complete change of pace in the hilly southern part of the country which seems quite like the northeast U.S.

I think I expected the Netherlands to be entirely composed of canals, bridges, and people wearing wooden shoes. However, it is much, much more including one of the most impressive collections of ancient and historical buildings in Europe. There are historical and art museums in almost every town and it is a country with a rich cultural heritage.

I enjoyed the jolly smiles and attitudes of the Dutch people.

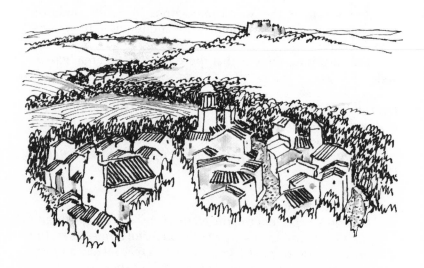

MAPS and GUIDES

Having road maps and guides in advance makes planning a European trip much more enjoyable and helps reduce the inevitable confusion of driving in a strange place. Many of the following guides and maps are available at your local bookstore; if not, you may order directly from us. The address: The Berkshire Traveller Press, Box 50, Stockbridge, Massachusetts 01262. All prices include postage and handling.

Michelin Green Guides contain over-all sightseeing maps covering the principal attractions or areas of the country, along with detailed descriptions of the country's culture, cuisine, economy, geography, and life styles. Suggested touring intineraries provide added interest. Villages, towns, cities, and points of interest are listed alphabetically. The descriptions are concise and star-rated for interest. The educational value of these guides makes them of considerable interest to the armchair traveler and the student.

Michelin Red Guides list every suitable hotel, motel, resort, and restaurant by cost and quality. They also list the principal attractions rated according to interest. For every town of any size the guide contains detailed town or city maps with emphasis on locating hotels, restaurants, and tourist attractions.

Austria
Road Maps: Michelin 987: Germany-Austria   3.00
Guides: Michelin Green Guide 512: Austria   6.50

Belgium
Road Maps: Michelin 409: Belgium   3.00
Guides: Michelin Red Guide 608: Benelux   10.50

England, Ireland, Scotland
Road Maps: Michelin 986: Great Britain and Ireland   3.00
Guides: Michelin Green Guide 543: London   6.50
Michelin Red Guide 658: Great Britain and Ireland   10.50
Michelin Red Guide 668: Greater London   2.50

France
Road Maps: Michelin 989: France   3.00
Michelin 998: Northern France (1/1,000,000)   2.00
Michelin 999: Southern France (1/1,000,000)   2.00
Michelin Sectional Maps of France:
061: Paris Chaumont   2.00
065: Auxerre-Dijon   2.00
069: Bourges-Macon   2.00
081: Avignon-Digne   2.00
084: Marseille-Menton   2.00
091: Clermont-Ferrand-Lyon-Chambery   2.00
093: Lyon-Marseille   3.00
010: Paris (1/10,000)   3.00
101: Outskirts of Paris (1/50,000)   3.00
Guides: Michelin Green Guide 354: Paris   6.50
Michelin Green Guide 321: Chateaux of the Loire   6.50
Michelin Green Guide 348: Normandy   6.50
Michelin Green Guide 312: Brittany   6.50
Michelin Green Guide 361: Dordogne   6.50
Michelin Green Guide 330: French Riviera   6.50

Michelin Red Guide 648: France   12.50
Michelin Red Guide 698: Paris   2.75

Germany

Road Maps:	Special Road Map Shows all Romantik Hotels in Germany, Austria, and Switzerland	5.00
Guides:	Michelin Green Guide 503: Germany	6.50
	Michelin Red Guide 628: Germany	12.50

Italy

Road Maps:	Michelin 988: Italy-Switzerland	3.00
Guides:	Michelin Green Guide 533: Italy	6.50
	Michelin Red Guide 678: Italy	11.50

Netherlands

Road Maps:	Michelin 408: Netherlands	3.00
Guides:	Michelin Red Guide 608: Benelux	10.50

Norway, Sweden, Denmark

Road Maps:	Map of Scandinavia (includes Finland and Iceland)	Free: handling & postage .75
Guides:	"Scandinavia Travel Facts" 36 pages of useful information.	Free: handling & postage .50

Spain

Road Maps:	Michelin 990: Spain & Portugal	3.00
Guides:	Michelin Green Guide 521: Spain	6.50
	Michelin Red Guide 638: Spain & Portugal	10.50

Switzerland

Road Maps:	Michelin 427: Switzerland	3.00
Guides:	Michelin Green Guide 563: Switzerland	6.50
	"The Inn Way . . . Switzerland"	5.50

Only book on the subject today: authorative guide to over 100 inns in one of the most beautiful vacation spots. Packed with information by experienced traveler, writer and editor. Maps and descriptions of eleven districts, also knowledgeable advice on transportation, money, clothing, dining and reading menus.

Miscellaneous
"How to Convert the Metric System into the U.S. System and
Vice Versa" $5.50
Designed as a concise and handy guide and reference book, with
index, the rapid conversion between the two systems of weights
and measures. Most of the 170 pages are devoted to conversion
tables that show the exact metric and U.S. values (with decimals
and fractions) for: time, temperatures, lengths, speed, clothes
sizes, electric current, tire pressure, household measures, etc.
Additional information of a more technical nature, also.

*Remember, if your local bookstore can not supply you with
any of the maps and guides listed, you may order from the
Berkshire Traveller Press, Box 50, Stockbridge, Massachusetts
01262. Prices include postage and handling.*